LEGAL ANECDOTES, WIT, AND REJOINDER

LEGAL ANECDOTES, WIT, AND REJOINDER

COMPILED BY

EDWARD J. BANDER

VANDEPLAS PUBLISHING
UNITED STATES OF AMERICA

LEGAL ANECDOTES, WIT, AND REJOINDER

Compiled by Edward J. Bander.

Published by:

Vandeplas Publishing
April 2007

801 International Parkway
5th Floor
Lake Mary, FL. 32746
USA

www.vandeplaspublishing.com

ISBN: 978-1-60042-017-7
Library of Congress Control Number: 2007924980
Copyright Edward J. Bander

Printed in the United States of America

"A collection of anecdotes and maxims is the greatest treasure for a man of the world."
Goethe, See Times Literary Supplement, Sept. 11, 2005, p. 8

"… he liked wit and anecdote."
The Education of Henry Adams: An Autobiography. Boston: Houghton-Mifflin, 1918, 1946.

"As with bricks and tiles, so with those little shards of information we call anecdotes: at their best, they link us with the past in a very direct way, and they acquire additional lustre by association."
Review by Peter Parker of The New Oxford Book of Literary Anecdotes, Times Literary Supplement, August 4, 2006, p. 32

TABLE OF MAJOR TOPICS

Key: (1) = anecdote (1f) footnote to anecdote – for page references, see Quick Index

Abolition
Abortion
Abraham's bosom
Abstractions
Achilles' heel
Adams, Henry
Ade, George
Administrative law
Adultery,
Advertising
Advisory opinion
Advocate
Affirmative action
Afflatus
After-dinner speaker
Age
Alcoholic beverages
Ambition
American Law Institute
Ames, Professor
Analogy
Anecdotes
Antitrust cases
Appeal at once
Appellate court
Approval, need for
Arlington National Cemetery
Arnold, Thurman
Assignees
Association ... N.Y.C.
Attorney fees
Attorney General
Automobiles
Axis, The
Baker, Russell
Bankers
Baseball

Bawdy tinge
Beale, Joseph A.
Beck, James M.
Biography
Bishop
Black, Hugo
Blackman, Harry A.
Blackstone's Commentary
Bostonians
Brandeis, Louis
Brennan, William Joseph Jr.
Brevity
Brewer, David
Briefs
Brown, Henry Billings
Burger, Warren
Burke, Edmund
Burlesque houses
Burton, Harold H.
Butler, Charles Henry
Butler, Pierce
Candor
Capital punishment
Cardozo, Benjamin Nathan
Carson, Edward
Carter, Jimmy
Casanova
Case
Casebooks
Catholic Claims
Certiorari
Chapman, John Jay
Child, education of
Choate, Rufus
Christ, what dignity
Christian religion
Citation

Civil War
Civilization
Client
Closing argument
Cohen, Morris
Coleman, William
Collisions at sea
Collusions
Columbia Law School
Comma is there
Conscious as we are
Constitutional law
Constitutional lawyer
Continuance
Contract
Corporation as a client
Court of Appeal
Criminal law
Cross-examination
Cujos est solum
Davis, John W.
Day, William R.
De minimis
Deans
Death and dying
Defects of his qualities
Definitions
Deliberate speed
Diplomatic immunity
Doctor
Donahue, Frank J.
Douglas, William O.
Eisenhower, Dwight D.
Electric chair
Emerson, Ralph Waldo
Enthusiasm
Estate taxes
Facts
Fair trial
Final examination
Footnotes
Four horsemen

Frank, Jerome N.
Frankfurter, Felix
French novels
Fuller, Melville Weston
Gallows humor
Generalization
Gift in contemplation
God and court
Cossip and philosophy
Gray, Horace
Grier, Robert C.
Guests that overstay
Hall, Marshall
Hand, Learned
Harding, Warren
Harlan, John Marshall
Harvard Law School
Harvard University
Heart transplant
Height
Hell, Holmes, Fanny
Holmes, Oliver Wendell
Horse cause
Hughes, Charles Evans
Humbug
Humor
Innuendo
Insurance
Intellect
Jackson, Robert H.
Jesus Christ is my advocate
Jobbists
Judges
Jury
Justice
Kaufman, Irving R.
Kennedy, John F.
Knapp, Whitman
Knox, Philander
Labor leaders
Lamb, Charles
Lang, Andrew

Laski, Harold
Law
Law books
Law classroom
Law clerks
Law dean
Law firms
Law library
Law office
Law Partner
Lar professors
Law reviews
Law school
Law students
Law suit
Laws
Lawyers
Learning
Legal mind
Legislative history
Lincoln, Abraham
Litigation
Malthus
Marshall, John
Marshall, Thurgood
Massachusetts Bar
Massachusetts S.J.C.
McReynolds, James C.
Memorial addresses
Mencken, H.L.
Mendoza line
Menuhin, Yehudi
Miller, Samuel
Motions
Murphy, Frank
Naivity
Noonan, Gregory
North
Novelists
O'Connor, Sandra Day
Objections
Obscenity

Opinions
Oral argument
Oratory
Oyster
Panaceas and sudden ruin
Paternity
Pitney, Mrs. Malcolm
Points of law
Precedent
Prisoners
Professors
Question of fact
Realtor
Rehnquist, William Hubbs
Retirement
Rickles, Don
Rodell, Fred
Rogers, Will
Roosevelt, F. D.
Rule in Shelley's Case
Sacco-Vanzetti case
Satan
Self-made man
Shall and will
Shiras, George Jr.
Sit down, you damned fool
Smith, F.E.
Solicitor General
Stare decisis
Stone, Harlan Fiske
Story, Joseph
Strut
Suffolk University Law School
Symbols
Tact
Taft, Howard William
Taxes
Ten Commandments
Thomas, Clarence
Thoreau, Henry David
Torts
Trial judge

4

Trial practice
Truman, Harry
Unite States Constitution
United States Government
United States Sup. Court
Virtue
Vomit
Vulgar herd
Ward, Lester
Warren, Earl
Warren, Edward Henry
White, Edward Douglas
White, Byron
Wills
Witnesses
Women
Yale Law School
Young lawyer

TABLE OF CONTENTS

Anecdotes
     by the number, 1 - 176

Footnotes, 177 - 245

Bibliography, 247 - 257

Quick Index
     by page, 259 - 262

Afterwords, 263

6

ALPHABETICAL ARRANGEMENT OF ANECDOTES
-a-
Abolition
(1)
    I can remember the time before the Civil War when I was moved by the abolition cause so deeply that a Negro minstrel show shocked me and the morality of Pickwick seemed to me painfully blunt. I have no right to an opinion as to public conditions for I am a recluse and don't even read the papers. Moreover, at times I have felt as you do. Nevertheless, I rather more than hope that there is more intelligent and high minded thinking of public matters than ever before. One has to remember that when one's interest is keenly excited, evidence gathers from all sides around the magnetic point, and that one must mistrust the suggested conclusion. Just after the Civil War there appeared on the fences and elsewhere S T 1560 X. I believe it was an advertisement, perhaps of bitters, which then had a locus standi. I said and proved to myself that if one should accept that as a revelation of the secret of the universe one would be astonished by the corroboration that a fortnight would furnish. I think that a type of the way our minds act. I venture this word of caution from the experience of an old man.

                        Very sincerely yours,
                        O.W. Holmes

Abortion
(2)
    A Massachusetts doctor charged with procuring an abortion argued to the Supreme Judicial Court of Massachusetts that he was protected by the Statute of Frauds – no one should be held for the debt, default or "miscarriage of another" unless evidenced by some memorandum in writing.

Abraham's bosom
(3)
    I am on most friendly terms with all the judges, but I suspect that if I should be gathered to Abraham's bosom some of them would think it an advantage to the law, even if they missed a friend.

Abstractions
(4)
    Holmes, the philosopher, could do that [deal with abstractions] because he got his directions out of thought, but a man like Al Smith particularly, but even TR and most people, haven't got the capacity of imagination and insight that justifiably led Holmes to say, "I don't know facts. I merely know their

significance."

Acheson, Dean, (119f), (159f), (223f), (281f), (313f), (334f), (422f), (449f), (585f), (620f), (656f), (694f), (720f), (757f)

Accounting for lawyers
　　See Law students

Achilles' heel
(5)
　　"I early realized the illusion of personality in the really mechanical action of the mind. When I was wounded in the heel, I would see man after man approach with self-gratulatory smile as he made a reference to Achilles. Each had the feeling of personal achievement while he really was moving along the path of least resistance. ..."

Adams, Henry
(6)
　　Holmes would walk home – in all sorts of weather. He did this until he was well into his eighties. He used to stop and pay a short call every evening on Henry Adams, who lived on the site of the present Hay-Adams Hotel. Holmes recalled that as time went by he found himself stopping in only every other day, then only once a week, then once a month, until he stopped going entirely. He explained why. "I find that my energies are too depleted by Henry Adams' sterile skepticism."

Adams, Joey, (662f)

Adams, John Quincy, (757f)

Ade, George
(7)
　　George Ade (a well-known humorist in the early part of the century) had finished his speech at a recent dinner party, and on seating himself a well known lawyer rose, shoved his hands deep into his trouser pockets, as was his habit, and laughingly inquired of those present:
　　"Doesn't it strike anyone as a little unusual that a professional humorist should be funny?"
　　"Doesn't it strike the company as a little unusual that a lawyer should have his hands in his pocket?"

Administrative law
(8)
    I remember an incident that occurred in his seminar on administrative law in 1939. I was welcomed as an old alumnus who wanted to learn something. One of the youngest members of the group was the ebullient Edward F. Prichard, a third-year man whose mind and wit endeared him to everyone – especially to his "Perfessor." It was the session immediately following President Roosevelt's nomination of Felix to be a Justice of the Supreme Court. Felix had suggested an original approach to a problem in administrative law and asked "Prich" what he thought of it.
    "That," ejaculated Prich, "is the most tenuous legal proposition I have ever heard!" We waited for the cutting rejoinder. None came. Instead, Felix merely admonished mildly:
    "I hope, Mr. Prichard, that your capacity for surprise has not been exhausted."
    "No, it has not," snapped Prich, "an I'll tell you why. You can never tell what one of these new judges may decide!"

(9)
    My field is administrative law and as you know it is sometimes said that this is the only area of law in which the questions and problems remain the same, but the answers are constantly changed.

Adultery
(10)
    Holmes liked Stone and enjoyed their occasional interchanges of wit. Stone had drafted an opinion in a conspiracy case under the Prohibition Act, involving only a buyer and seller of liquor, and had had trouble explaining why two such parties should not be held guilty of a conspiracy to make the sale. Holmes wrote him a note to the following effect: "Why don't you point out that a purchase and sale, like adultery, requires mutually consenting parties performing correlative functions?" Stone got the point, and Holmes' thought, minus the unconventional analogy, went into his opinion.

Advertising
(11)
    "Now if you had this copy in front of you at the FTC, how would you react? …Here is the advertising copy:
    "We hold these truths to be self-evident, that all men are created equal, they are endowed by their Creator with certain inalienable rights…"
    Now I would have to say that advertisement would create some very serious problems at the FTC. Permit me to break the copy down; that should

give you some sense of how we operate:

"We hold these truths to be self-evident."

Well, it is obvious that there are no self-evident truths anymore as far as the FTC is concerned. Under the Pfizer decision, all affirmative claims in advertising must be substantiated prior to the making of the claim. Three copies on Xerox paper, suitable for review by our lawyers. Next, we have:

"All men are created equal."

That claim raises a problem that we see constantly at the FTC. As I am sure all of you appreciate, that is a minority opinion in this country. We have nothing against the assertion of a minority opinion in advertising, but we think it must be qualified; thus, there is nothing wrong with the claim so long as all of the qualifications are stated in the ad itself. Finally we have:

"They are endowed by their Creator with certain inalienable rights."

We would view that as a kind of testimonial, and, first of all, would inquire whether the Creator is sufficiently qualified by training and experience to do that kind of "endowing." And then we would insist upon a written release from the Creator.

Advisory opinion
(12)

Perhaps the most successful advisory opinion over rendered was that given by Chief Justice Taft to Calvin Coolidge just after Harding had died. Coolidge, somewhat awed by his new responsibilities, asked Taft what he should do. "I told him," the Chief Justice recounted a short time later, "to do nothing. I told him that I thought the public were glad have him in the White House doing nothing...."

Advocacy
    See Litigation

Advocate
(13)

Edward Carson ... could reduce himself to tears at times, and on such occasion, Tim Healy, his opponent, himself exercising one of the weapons of the advocate, said to the jury, "When I see my learned friend in tears, I reflect that it is the greatest miracle that ever happened since Moses struck the rock in the wilderness."

Affirmative action
(14)

It is certainly true that [Sandra]O'Connor was picked because she was a woman. When Justice Antonin Scalia was railing against affirmative action in one of the justices' private conferences, O'Connor said, "Why Nino, how do you think I got my job.?"

Afflatus
(15)

The secretary thought the word "afflatus" [281 U.S. 389, 397 (1930)] might cause comment, and reminded the Justice that a good many people thought he rather delighted in using terms not commonly understood. "Yes," said Mr. Justice Holmes, "I felt myself that it was rather a cabriole word."

The same secretary once objected that the last paragraph of an opinion was not quite clear. "What the hell do you mean? Not clear! Give it to me. Well, if you don't understand it, there may be some other damn fool who won't. So I would better change it."

The former secretaries, who adore the Justice, delight in such stories. One of them objected to the phrasing of a certain opinion, maintaining that the shading given to one word meant that "there isn't more than one man in a thousand who will understand it."

"I write for that man," the Justice retorted.

After-dinner speaker
(16)

... the story of the after-dinner speaker who had been proceeding for about five minutes when suddenly there came a shout from the rear of the room. "Sit down! You're stupid!"

The speaker politely disregarded the interruption, when again came this cry, "Sit down! You're stupid!"

This time he determined that he ought to squelch this fellow if it happened again, and of course it did happen again with the cry "Sit down! You're stupid!"

So the speaker replied, "And you're drunk!"

"Yes," came the retort, "but tomorrow morning I'll be sober and you'll still be stupid."

(17)

That brings to mind a reference to a great after dinner speaker by the name of Chauncey DePugh, who was a State Senator from Peekskill, New York, who fancied himself a great after dinner speaker and he had the signal honor of introducing President William Howard Taft at a banquet, and he got up and said, "Ladies and gentlemen, I want to introduce a man to you who is pregnant with the highest ideals of citizenship, a man who is pregnant with all that made our country great, a man who is pregnant with those foremost concepts that put America ahead in national affairs. Ladies and gentlemen, President William

Howard Taft."

President Taft put his big belly on the speaker's stand and said, "Mr. DePugh has referred constantly to my pregnancy. It it's a boy, I'll call it William. If it's a girl, I'll call it Wilhelmina and it it's gas, and I think it is, I'll call it Chauncey DePugh."

Age
(18)

Holmes at the age of 90 to a girl of 16: "I won't refrain from talking about anything because you're too young, if you won't because I'm too old."

Air cushion
See Hall, Marshall

Alcoholic beverages
See also After-dinner speaker
(19)

… It occurred at the Washington Press Club's Salute to Congress dinner and involved Redskin running back, John Riggins, who apparently had had too much to drink. "Come on, Sandy baby, loosen up," the intoxicated Riggins told her as they were seated together at a table sponsored by People magazine. "You're too tight." ..Years later, when Riggins, who left professional football and tried an acting career, debuted in a Washington area community theater, O'Connor showed up with a dozen roses for his curtain call.

(20)

Sir Edward Carson was one of the most lethal cross-examiners. In one of the classic stories about him, he pointed his long index finger at a red-nosed witness.

"I believe you're a heavy drinker?" he asked in his brogue.
"That's my business!"
"And have you any other business?" Carson asked and sat down.

(21)

"Is it possible that the Court smells liquor on counsel?"
Mr. Fallon bowed. "If your Honor's sense of justice is as keen as your sense of smell," said he, "then my client need have no fear in this court."

(25)

I made a little jest yesterday that pleased me. By brother Clarke was saying that knocking off wine and spirits had made it necessary for the clubs to raise their annual charges. I said they used to raise the Devil and now they raise the dues.

(26)
A secretary of Justice Holmes told me that once when he arrived at the Justice's office rather late he made excuse for his tardiness; and also explained to Justice Holmes that his breath might indicate he had not come directly from the breakfast table. In fact the secretary admitted, he had stopped on his way to the Justice's office, as some friends were leaving Washington that morning and there had been a little celebration. On hearing this Justice Holmes observed:

"Yes, I can visualize a rather long mahogany counter, on which one's arm can rest while holding a goblet with something in it, and below is a brass rail on which one foot is resting. Thinking of this makes me regret some of the limitations imposed on one who occupies my position."

(27)
There were, in fact, three untasted bottles [of champagne] that Henry White had sent him, not so long ago, that had perplexed his conscience. And he had said to himself, and later to others, more than once: "The Eighteenth Amendment forbids manufacture, transportation and importation. It does not forbid possession or use. If I send it back I shall be guilty of transportation. On the whole I think I shall apply the maxim de minimis, and drink it. ..."

(28)
Follett could not help expressing to his opponent his astonishment of seeing him indulging in so solid and carnal a diet by way of preparation for the task he was about to enter upon, and for which a clear unclouded brain was so essential.

"As to clearness of brain, "said Maule, "I find that mine is too clear already. The truth is, I am striving to bring my intellect down to a level with the capacity of those idiotic judges."

(29)
This was the judge who, when he was a lawyer at the bar, had by no means achieved the reputation of being a teetotaler. And then suddenly the announcement was made that he was being elevated to the bench. A newspaper of that time, feeling perhaps that this was the worst appointment since the Emperor Caligula made his horse a consul, commented on the appointment and questioned whether the new judge would be happy seeing he had been compelled to desert the bar. A friend of the new judge asked him whether he would sue for libel on account of the innuendo. And the judge, said, no, he would just sit tight.

(30)

... In a little cabinet in the Robing Room was kept some material by which the Justices might be refreshed after an arduous session on the Bench. It seems, however, that a rule had been made that the contents of the cabinet should be opened only in case it was raining.

On one occasion, the story continues, upon retiring from the Bench, a certain Justice remarked that as it had been a hard day it might be well to resort to the cabinet.

"But it is not raining," said another Justice.

Thereupon Chief Justice Marshall looked out the window and then observed: "No, it is not raining here, but it is probably raining somewhere in the jurisdiction."

(35)

We'd have all sorts of people come there [The House of Truth] for dinner. We'd take turns at the various duties. On one occasion it was my job to shake cocktails. In those days we shook cocktails in a shaker. During one month that was my task. In connection with that I remember how heart-searing – how a complement can have, what shall I say, unwarming ambiguity. I was shaking my cocktails one night when our guest was Mr. Justice Lurtin, he said to me, "I hope you mix drinks as well as you argue cases."

Well, to be praised by a Justice of the Supreme Court, for a kid like me, that was something. Wasn't I proud and happy? He sipped his cocktail and said, "You mix drinks even better than you argue cases."

If ever one complement displaced the pleasure of another, that was it.

(36)

Holmes saw in amazement that it was his secretaries, at least a dozen of them. Fanny had got them here from all over the country ... He moved forward, greeted the company, then walked over and picked up a long-stemmed glass at his place. "What are these for?"

"Champagne," Fanny said.

"Close the shutters." Holmes grinned. "I wish my daddy could see me now. He always said I'd die a drunkard."

(37)

I used to say it is vain to say that this is the best of possible worlds – when it could be so improved if we could go to bed drunk and wake fitter than ever for achievement.

All men are created equal
See Advertising

Allen, Robert S., (117f), (150f), (153f), (159f), (378f), (424f), (559f), (596f), (635f), (740f)

Alumni
See Columbia Law School

Alverstone, Lord, (691f)

Ambition, 691
(38)
In the first [a barrister's life] he is ambitious and cares only for work; in the second he is mercenary and cares only for fees; in the third, a stage reached only by a few, he cares neither for the work nor the fees.

American Law Institute
(39)
If I ever get to Congress I am going to pass a law to the effect that law professors are fungible. In the event that any dean makes an offer to a professor in any other school the opposing dean may, at his option, substitute any other professor for the one selected, upon giving five days notice by registered mail and defraying all crating and shipping charges. In the even that the offering dean does not accept the professor tendered by the opposing dean the man shall be automatically transferred to the staff of the American Law Institute to work with Mr. Boston in attempting to restate the law of proximate cause. No human device has ever been discovered better adapted to keep a man out of mischief than the task of annotating the Restatement of Laws.

Ames, James Barr
(40)
See also Law classroom
"If you wanted to know what the law used to be, ask Langdell; if you want to know what it is going to, ask [Joseph A.]Beale, if you want to know what it ought to be, ask Ames; but if you want to know what the law is, ask Gray."

Analogy
(45f)
Holmes liked Stone and enjoyed their occasional interchanges of wit. Stone had drafted an opinion in a conspiracy case under the Prohibition Act, involving only a buyer and seller of liquor, and had had trouble explaining

why two such parties should not be held guilty of a conspiracy to make the sale. Holmes wrote him a note to the following effect: "Why don't you point out that a purchase and sale, like adultery, requires mutually consenting parties performing correlative functions?" Stone got the point, and Holmes' thought, minus the unconventional analogy, went into his opinion.

Andrews, William, (130f)

Anecdotes
(46)
[Editor's note: It is not the truthfulness or documentation of an anecdote that makes it admirable as much as the anecdote pointing out what otherwise might take a scholarly and penetrating study (which all too few will take the time to read) to illustrate. The skill is thus much dependent on the teller's choice of anecdote rather than the ability to ferret out the truth.]

Antitrust cases
(47)
According to John W. Davis, Solicitor General of the United States (1913-1918), Justice Holmes did not have to believe personally in a law to uphold it. Following one of Davis's arguments in an antitrust case, Holmes asked him:
"How many more of these economic policy cases have you got?"
"Quite a basketful," David replied.
"Well bring 'em on and we'll decide them. Of course I know, and every other sensible man knows, that the Sherman [antitrust] law is damned nonsense, but if my country wants to go to hell, I am here to help it."
Echoing Justice Holmes' sentiments, his younger colleague, Harlan Fiske Stone said about the New Dealers: "If the damn fools want to go to hell, it's not our duty to stop them if that's what they want to do."

Appeal at once, (48f)
(48)
Then there is the story of the counselor who called his corporate client and told him that justice had prevailed. The client answered, "Well, order a transcript and appeal at once."

Appellate court, see also (540)
(49)
For some time [an English judge] sat on the trial court, but now serves with a panel of three. He said as a judge of the trial court he could and did do justice but on the appellate court of three the chances were two to one against

it.

Approval, need for
(50)
As one observer put it [Hamilton, On Dating Mr. Justice Holmes, 9 U. of Chic. L. Rev. 1, 22 n. 30 (1941)]: "Van Wyck Brooks reports that when Holmes was a small boy his father rewarded every bright saying with a spoonful of jam. In later life the jam had been replaced by his secretary's shout of approval." This is an unfair cut if it means he sought praise for praise's sake. The jam proved the saying had indeed been bright and was incentive to think up another. Holmes put a great deal of stock in this kind of incentive. No hypocrite, he valued it for others as well as for himself, and nothing better shows the stark contrast between his attitude and [Judge] Doe's than their remarks on posthumous praise. Doe thought the only decent time for praise was after death. Holmes thought that would be too late.

Aristotle
See Footnotes

Arlington National Cemetery
(55)
Perdurable – a neighbor of ours who is an admirer of the late Justice Oliver Wendell Holmes decided, on a recent visit to Washington, to pay the Great Dissenter a moment of graveside homage in Arlington National Cemetery. Not knowing where Holmes was buried in Arlington, he called the Interment Section. He was answered by a woman, who advised him to hold on awhile, and, after a considerable wait, informed him, "I'm sorry, but according to our records Oliver Wendell Holmes is still alive." When we were told about this, we thought we could hear the dissent from Arlington, but maybe this time Justice Holmes was wrong.

Arnold, Thurman, (39f), (57f), (58f), (59f), (70f), (171f), (190f), (195f), (334f), (393f), (532f), (552f), (590f), (720f)
See also Casebooks, Law reviews, (532f)
(56)
Thurman Arnold at Boston University Law School around 1950 and told of his first opening a law office. He prevailed upon the telephone company to give him a catchy number. It turned out a railroad company had recently released one of their numbers – something like 123 1234 - and Mr. Arnold gleefully comandeered it. The result were not as he expected for the office was soon getting calls from people wanting to buy tickets or time schedules. Arnold replied to each call and amused his audience with the misdirections he

gave to those seeking railroad information. He concluded by informing the law students that the number was still valid and he welcomed their business.

(57)
The Hunt Club. "A social (?) club formed by Mr. Justice Douglas, Thurman Arnold, and other assorted personages while Douglas and Arnold were at Yale together. The club's activities, membership and purposes are as hidden and mysterious today as they were in 1935."

(58)
"If you can think of a subject which is interrelated and inextricably combined with another subject, without knowing anything about or giving any consideration to the second subject, then you have a legal mind."

(59)
He [Attorney General Walls] asked me whether I had taken a course in legal ethics at Harvard. I replied I had not. ...He replied, "If in the course of your practice you become involved in difficult and protracted litigation, and if in the course of that litigation it becomes apparent that somebody has got to go to jail, be sure that it's your client."

(60)
And then there was the "publicity game," in which [Thurman] Arnold, [William O.] Douglas, and a third law school colleague, Wesley Sturges, gave one another points for any mention or picture in a newspaper – one point for a speech, five points in the New Haven Register, ten points for The New York Times, twenty-five points in a national magazine, fifty points for The New York Times Sunday Magazine, and one hundred points for a Times editorial. Once, when he was about to give a speech in New Haven, Arnold was puzzled to get a telegram from Sturges asking to be mentioned in his address, which would have meant another point for him. Upon returning to the office the next day, Arnold confronted his colleague about the breach of the game's rules of etiquette, only to find out that Sturges had gotten a similar telegram from "Arnold" asking for the same favor in his speech that same evening in Bridgeport. The grinning rail-thin imp [Douglas] with the uncontrollable shock of hair, they realized with a laugh, had struck again.

Assignees
(65)
Professor: Why is a covenant that runs with the land like a tight skirt.
Student: Because it binds the assignees

Association of the Bar of the City of New York, (199), (286)
(66)
        And Justice Hughes is alleged to have said in the men's room of the Association of the Bar of New York City that "Here, we are all peers."

(67)
        Mr. Wickersham once told me that a distinguished English judge to whom he was showing the building (Bar Association of the City of New York on 44th Street) was greatly impressed and remarked that it was a magnificent home for the American Bar. "Not the American Bar," said Mr. Wickersham, "only the New York Bar." "The Bar of the State of New York?" queried the visitor. "No," said Mr. Wickersham, "merely the lawyers practicing in the City of New York." "Dear, dear," exclaimed the visitor, "what a suggestion of comfortable emoluments!"

(68)
        The other evening, outside the New York Bar Association Building, hard by our own restless haunt, a threesome of unsightly adolescents – complete with Elvis Presley hairdos and a getup based on some blurred impressions of the Wild West – were being manacled together by a couple of detectives, on the ground that they had just stolen a rather sharp-looking green coupe from Virginia. The detectives, who were obviously fans of "Dragnet," the monosyllabic show on TV, wore slouch hats and tan topcoats, and carried flashlights. They said nothing, and their captives said nothing. In the middle of all this a pair of elderly gentlemen emerged from the Bar Association Building.

"In my day, in these circumstances," said one of them, "those youths would have had more representation than you could conceivably get in Congress."

"As a matter of act," said his companion, "I should like to take this on."

"With your arthritis?" said the first gentleman.

"A, there we are," said the second.

As they walked into the night, we thought we heard the rusty clangor of an ambulance bell long since stilled

Atlee, Clement R. (159f)

Attorney fees, (191)
        See also   Association of the Bar of the City of New York, Client, Prisoners
(69)
        Legend has it that Mr. Justice Holmes stated that the standard to be

applied by a court in allowing attorneys' fees was to be reasonably mean.

(70)
An anecdote is told about a lawyer who won a substantial verdict for his client. He gave his client twenty-five per cent of the amount won. The client protested, saying: "After all, it's my case that won; you only argued it." The lawyer replied: "The case you brought me wouldn't have won you a cent. The case that got the verdict was my case, not yours."

(71)
Client: What is this contingent fee business?
Lawyer: Well, to put it very simply, it means this: If you lose the case I don't get anything, but if you win, you don't get anything.

(72)
Recently, a corporate executive amused an audience of lawyers by describing his corporation's annual earnings as seven times legal fees.

(73)
The story is told in different ways, but it invariably concerns the English solicitor who is called on by his client to justify his bill for services. After compiling the various items of service and putting a value on each, the solicitor is short by one guinea from the amount he had billed. As the last line in the statement, he writes, "Lying in bed thinking … one guinea."

(74)
But we were asked to break up into groups, small groups of twelve or ten and discuss law and law practice and lawyers and their problems, then designate one member of our group to go to meet and discuss what their group discussed and hopefully they would end up at the end of these discussions by pronouncing some great principle that was common t to all lawyers all over the world. … finally the president of the Tokyo Bar arose and you can imagine how expectant we all were. He was going to announce this principle that had been the combined talents of all our minds for an hour and he got up and said something like this, "Lawyers of the world have reached great principle: our fees are too low."

(75)
In the first [a barrister's life] he is ambitious and cares only for work; in the second he is mercenary and cares only for fees; in the third, a stage reached only by a few, he cares neither for the work nor the fees.

(76)
[When a client was presented with a $25.00 fee and protested that all he could afford was $15.00, Mr. Choate's clerk accepted that amount and explained the situation to Mr. Choate.] "Oh," said Choate, with a rich smile mantling over the lower part of his face, "you took all he had, did you? Well, I've nothing to say to that – that's strictly professional."

(77)
When a nouveau riche guest aboard the yacht Corsair asked [J.P.Morgan] about the operating expenses of the boat, Morgan replied to the effect, "Anybody who even has to think about the costs can't afford it." The lawyer Fallon, when asked about his fee, answered, "Anybody who even has to think about my fee can't afford it."
[no source]

(78)
"I quite agree with you; my fee is exorbitant, " said [Lord] Carson. "But come over here." He led his client to the window and pointed to the network of the Temple lights. "In every one of those chambers is a man who will do your case, which is a comparatively simple one, just as well as I, and at a fraction of the cost."
"No, no, I must have you, " was the reply.

Attorney General, (476f)
(80)
This recalls the story of one of my predecessors who tried to get into the Department of Justice building on a holiday. He was stopped by a guard who wanted to see his building pass. Not having one with him he explained to the guard that he was the Attorney General, to which the guard replied: "I wouldn't care if you were J. Edgar Hoover, himself, you can't get into this building without a pass."

Automobiles
(81)
Fashion, as I long have said, is a law of life, and I suppose as soon as the odious automobiles get cheap the rich will give them to their servants, as Mr. Dooley said the other day.

Axis, The
(82)
Within a year, by the 1941-1942 Court term, the Court's "liberals" – Black, Douglas, and Murphy – were in increasing rebellion against Frankfurter's

leadership. By June 1942, the three – Frankfurter came to refer to them as "the Axis" ...

-b-
Bachelor
See McReynolds, James C.

Bacon, Francis
a much-talking judge is like an ill-tuned cymbal
See Smith, F. E.

Bacon, Vice-Chancellor
See God and Court

Bailey, Buck
See Law classroom

Baker, Liva, (116f), (208f), (311f), (312f), (541f), (617f), (655f), (716f)

Baker, Russell, (627f)
(83)
Russell Baker told this story (I believe I heard it at an Association of American Law Library banquet): Baker was leaving a press conference at the White House, when President Johnson motioned to him to come into the Oval Office. They had talked for some time, when Johnson pressed a button and an aide came in. Johnson wrote a note, which the aide read and dropped into a waste basket. Soon the phone rang, Johnson listened and hung up. Then Johnson had to excuse himself for some reason and when he left the room, Baker reached into the waste basket to read the note. It read, "Who the hell am I talking to?"]

Balfour-Brown, (786f)

Ballantine, Serjeant, (124f)
See Cross-examination

Balzac, Honore,
See Definitions

Bander, Edward J., (56f), (83f), (218f), (309f), (397f), (506f), (507f)

Bankers
(84)

"What happens to old deans? They never die, they just lose their faculties." ... "Old bankers never die, they just lose their interest," ... "What happens to old lawyers? They never die, they just lose their appeal."

Bar Association
See Association of the Bar of the City of New York, Gift in contemplation of death

Barrister
See Lawyers

Barry, Henry Harte
See Client

Baseball
(87)

Some of our agency administrators are like the three baseball umpires who were discussing their jobs and operating techniques. Said the first, "I calls 'em, as I sees 'em." Said the second, "I calls 'em as they are." But the third one learnedly stated, "They may all be balls or strikes, but they ain't nothin' until I calls 'em." 41 Title News No. 1 28 (1962).

Judge Roberts before the Senate Committee on judges are like umpires. "And I will remember that it's my job to call balls and strikes, and not to pitch or bat." NYTimes, p. 1 [check for date]. Bill Klem, a major league umpire from 1905-1941 is alleged to have said, "Fellas, it ain't nothin' till I call it!" (National Hall of Fame web site). See also NYTimes item by Scott Shane, Nov. 5, 2005, p. A11: "nine-judge court to the nine-team sport... Then there was Patrick J. Fitzgerald, the special prosecutor to the C.I.A. leak case, explaining last week's indictment of the vice president's chief of staff by asserting that the aide, I. Lewis Libby Jr. had, in baseball terms, thrown sand in the umpire's eyes." It should also be noted that there is "baseball truism that says you never notice the umpires when they're doing their job right." Paul F. Campos, Jurismania. Oxford University Press, 1998, p. 60.

(88)

C.J. Earl Warren was in New York this week for the Charles Evans Hughes centennial. He therefore missed the baseball opener. Warren's predecessor, Fred Vinson, always enjoyed watching baseball games on his TV set at home. The late Chief Justice confided: "This, for a change gives me a chance to yell at the umpire."

Basketball
>   See White, Byron "Whizzer"

Bastard, judge must be a little bit of a
>   See Trial judge

Bathtub mind, (388)

Battalions of lawyers
>   See Lawyers

Bawdy tinge
(91)
>   The two jurists [Stone and Holmes] had much in common – a passion for legal scholarship, a liking for humor with a bawdy tinge, a delight in the arts, and a profound interest in history.

Beale, Joseph A.
(92)
>   ... Professor Warren seldom closed a class without giving a definite answer to any pending problem. One day a student, troubled by a particularly knotty problem in a moot court case, applied to Professor Warren for assistance. Standing before the master, the student stated the issue and awaited the answer. The professor, leaning back in his chair, eyed the student quizzically and replied, "Well, if you want to know what the law was, see Dean Pound. If you want to know what the law ought to be see Professor Beale. But if you want to know what the law is, young man, sit down."
>   ... it was said that the first question [in his course on Legal Liability] could be answered by any student in the class, the second only by the best students, the third only by members of the faculty, the fourth only by God and Joey [Joseph A.] Beale, and the fifth only by Joey Beale..

(92a)
>   Student of Beale's inquisitorial method: He has a dampening effect on my conversational ability.

Beck, James M., (384f), (621f)
(93)
>   Mr. Beck was an industrious and doubtlessly a learned Philadelphia lawyer, but how long-winded, and how by the yard he loved to quote Shakespeare at them. ... Beck liked to end his arguments with a good solid quotation ("not

inappropriate," he would suggest) and then, without looking at his brief, he would recite: ... Holmes could stand it no longer, and leaning to the Chief, who sat next to him, whispered in his ear, not inaudibly: "I hope to God Mrs. Beck likes Shakespeare!"

Behrens, Leonard, (464f)

Benet, Stephen Vincent, 335f

Bent, Silas, (15f), (117f), (144f), (251f), (300f), (320f), (382f), (408f), (414f), (442f), (570f)

Bernstein, Harvard Law School Bulletin, Spring 1979 p. 36
    See Warren, Edward Henry

Better read them (law books), (500f)
    See Law books

Beveridge, Albert J., (30f)

Bickel, Alexander, (719f)

Biddle, Francis, (27f), (47f), (50f), (93f), (117f), (178f), (179f), (181f), (306f), (382f), (412f), (413f), (418f), (419f), (495f), (625f)

Biggs, John Jr., (119f), (422f)

Biography
(100)
    You speak of my biography [Bent, Justice Oliver Wendell Holmes]. I have not read it, but I should think it was harmless. I had nothing to do with it. Perhaps when I die my executor (John Palfrey and/or Felix Frankfurter) may do something, with more materials, but I have done my best to destroy illuminating documents.

Birkett, Norman, (13f), (20f), (385f), (464f), (494f), (650f)

Biskupic, Joan, (14f), (19f), (122f), (718f), (758f)

Bishop
(101)
    There is a famous English story of a country house party forty or fifty

years ago, where two of the guests (one was a judge, one was a bishop) were discussing the relative importance of their functions. The bishop said, "I am very superior to you, you can only say 'you be hanged,' and I can say 'you be damned!'." But the judge replied, "There is a very great difference, and it is on my side. When I say 'you be hanged,'' you are hanged.

Bishop, Joseph W. Jr., (102f), (275f)

Black, Hugo, (262f), (591f)
(102)
  Within a year, by the 1941-1942 Court term, the Court's "liberals" – Black, Douglas, and Murphy – were in increasing rebellion against Frankfurter's leadership. By June 1942, the three – Frankfurter came to refer to them as "the Axis" ...

(103)
  "Hugo thinks maybe we made a mistake in Gobitis," Douglas told Frankfurter.
  "Has Hugo been rereading the Constitution?" asked Frankfurter.
  "No, he's been reading the newspapers," Douglas replied.

(104)
  [Frankfurter diary entry] There I ran into Bob Jackson looking none too happy. He took me off into a corner and said "Do you feel as depressed as I do after these Saturday conferences?" I replied that I certainly do not come away normally happy and certainly did not do so today because every time we have that which should merely be an intellectual difference gets into a championship by Black of justice and right and decency and everything and those who take the other view are impliedly supporters of some exploiting interest.

(105)
  "Those Republicans will ruin us all," Black told a clerk. "John Harlan is one of the smartest, nicest guys who ever lived. I love him. But you know, he's a Republican. You know, that's Potter's problem too," Black said.

Blackman, Harry A, (142); (140f), (191f)
(107)
  If there is any truth to the old proverb that "one who is his own lawyer has a fool for a client," the Court by its opinion today now bestows a constitutional right on one to make a fool of himself.

Blackstone's Commentaries
(109)
"Mr. Jones," said Chief Justice Marshall on one occasion, to an attorney who was explaining to the court some elementary principle from Blackstone's Commentaries, "there are some things which the Supreme Court of the United States may be presumed to know."

Block off the old chip
    See Day, William R.

Boeckel, R. M., (115f), (158f)

Book
    See Law books

Book review
    Recusal and, (397f)
        Wyzanski, Charles F., (397f)

Bookmark
    See Young lawyer

Boston University, (56), (197), (654)

Bostonians, (56), (118), (197), (221), (270), (394), (409), (521a), (563), (594a), (654); (40f). (112f), (394f), (404f), (144f). (475f), (521af)
(112)
    I heard the other day that you can tell a Bostonian anywhere, but you can't tell him much – which I thought good.

(113)
    "When we were in Paris on the Champs-Elysees, he said, 'I just have no idea why people come here when they can go to Commonwealth Avenue [in Boston].'"

Botein, Bernard, (242f), (791f)

Bottom-up and top-down judges, (87f)

Bowen, Catherine Drinker, (36f), (123f), (178f), (405f), (406f), (420f), (426f)

Bowen, Lord, (217f)

Bowker, A. E., (124f), (455f)

Bradley, Joseph Philo, (137f)

Brain, clearness of
    See Alcoholic beverages

Brandeis, Louis, (115f), (119f), (120f), (158f), (306f), (378f), (422f), (424f), (465f)
(115)
    " How can you be so sure," a friend once asked, "that a particular line of action is the right one?" "When you are 51 percent sure that you are right," he replied, "then go ahead." (see also Cardozo, Benjamin Nathan)

(116)
    "At first, Frankfurter, recalling the legal giants on the Harvard Law School faculty during his student days, shrank back [at the possibility of being offered a job on the Harvard faculty]. Brandeis, asked for his advice, told Frankfurter he ought to let the people who invited him worry about his qualifications."

(117)
    For years Brandeis urged Holmes to read more along economic and social lines. Holmes is a prodigious reader, but his tastes run to the classics and general literature. One of his favorite diversions is paper-backed French novels which he reads by the score, heaping them in piles on the floor of his library as he consumes them. So, to counteract this "low" literary taste, Brandeis once informed Holmes that he would send some worthwhile material for summer reading.
    Several weeks later a large box sent by the Library of Congress reached Holmes at his Massachusetts home. He had his servant open the lid and scanned the upper layer of books. They dealt with workmen's compensation acts, insurance laws, labor codes, and similar subjects. Holmes read the title.
    "Bob, put this box down in the cellar," he ordered his servant, and returned to the paper-backed novels. In the fall the box of books was returned to the Library.

(118)
    Justice Felix Frankfurter tells this story about the late Justice Louis D. Brandeis, who was once counsel to Filene's in Boston. One day Lincoln Kirstein Sr., head of Filene's, called on Brandeis for advice. It was on a proposed

merger with another Boston department store. Kirstein seemed apprehensive and mentioned many stipulations he wanted in the contract, in case the merger proved unsatisfactory.

"Mr. Kirstein," was Brandeis' counsel, "the best way to get a divorce is not to marry the girl."

(119)

[Attributed to both Brandeis and Holmes] "a man could do twelve months' work in 11 months but couldn't do twelve months work in twelve months."

(120)

"I can see now," Edward F. McClennen recalls, "the expression of terror in his face when I told him that he would have to wear a silk hat. It lasted until inspiration brought him relief, and he said, "Holmes wears a soft one.'"

Brassiere
See United States Supreme Court

Brennan, William Joseph Jr.
See also (425)
(122)

Justice Brennan used to say that the crucial skill needed by a Supreme Court justice was the ability to count to five, and he was a master at it. So was O'Connor, beating Brennan at his own game as the Court became more conservative.

Brevity
(123)

Grandfather Jackson's high desk stood in a corner of the library. Wendell had always been proud of Judge Jackson, pleased when in court he had to refer to his rulings. Now he stood at the desk to write his opinions. "Doesn't it tire you?" Fanny asked, watching him write, one knee propped against the desk. "Yes," Wendell replied, "But it's salutary. Nothing conduces to brevity like a caving in of the knees."

(124)

„, not famed for his brevity, had been for some considerable time enforcing his arguments before a Kentish jury. Mr. Justice Wightman, interposing, said Mr. __ you have stated that before": and then, pausing for a moment, added, "but you may have forgotten it. It was a very long time ago."

(125)

For two hours a Judge had listened with deepening desperation to a barrister gnawing at a dry bone of law. Goaded beyond endurance, he burst out at last:

"Mr. so-and-so, you have said that before – many, many times before."'

"I'm very sorry, my Lord, I quite forgot."

"Don't apologize," said the Judge. "I forgive you, for it was a very long time ago."

Brewer, David, (390f)
(126)

Justice Brewer, who served from 1889 until 1910, was a very lovable character, and had a quiet, but often very humorous manner of expressing himself. One evening while I was walking home with him after a dinner we had attended, he said in reply to my inquiry as to how he had enjoyed the regular Saturday conference of the Court:

"It lasted a long time, and Butler, you don't know how tiresome it is to have to discuss legal problems with eight other men, none of whom knows any law."

(127)

Mr. Justice Brewer, who was the recognized authority on all Indian matters, interrupted the young Kansas lawyer to ask"

"Mr. Counselor, what do you think the status of an allottee is?"

The Kansas attorney stopped in front of Chief Justice Fuller and, spreading both his arms wide up in the air, exclaimed:

"If you fellows up there don't know, how do you think us fellows down here should know?"

The Court was stunned! Never before had it been described to its very face and in its own sacred precincts as – "You fellows up there." …

The shocked expression on the face of dear Chief Justice Fuller will never be forgotten. Justice Holmes, shaking with laughter, buried his face in his arms on the Bench to hide his amusement, and there was a sort of dazed expression on the features of the other members of the Court.

Brickbat
See Judges

Briefs
(128)

[Charles Warren] … It seems that Lydia B. Donley, when about eighteen years old, brought suit against the Secretary of the Interior, Mr. Ballinger, to enjoin him from desecrating the graves of her ancestors in violation of an Indian treaty, and she got some lawyer out of Kansas to prepare her brief for her and she came on and argued the case herself before the Supreme Court of the United States, and she started in her argument by reading from the brief, and she got along about five minutes, when Mr. Justice McKenna leaned forward and said, "Madam, I see that you are reading your brief," and she said, "Yes, sir," and went on reading. Again Mr. Justice McKenna leaned forward and said, "Madam, it is contrary to the practice of this court to have briefs read," and she said, "Yes, sir," and went on reading. A third time Mr. Justice McKenna leaned forward and he said, "Madam, you are reading your brief. The Court can read your brief as well as you can," and this young Indian woman looked up and she said, "Yes, I know the Court can read my brief. I am not sure the Court will read my brief. I feel safer reading it myself."

(129)
Justice Holmes learned about this prejudice in his first years on the Supreme Court. He was in the habit of studying the opposing briefs as soon as they were argued. He would brood on them for a day or two at most and write and deliver his opinion, This habit, which was natural to his temperament, alarmed his colleagues and spread the rumor that he was a glib and offhand fellow. He accordingly changed his routine while staying true to his bent. He wrote his opinion as before but aged it in a desk drawer for a month or two and then uncorked it for his brethren. Here thereby, he later disclosed, acquired that reputation for mellow judgment and judicial restraint which guaranteed his subsequent transfer to Olympus.

(130)
When Baron Martin was at the Bar and addressing the Court of Exchequer in an insurance case, he was interrupted by Baron Alderson, who observed, "Mr. Martin, do you think any office would insure your life? Remember, yours is a brief existence."

(131)
Holmes once tartly informed counsel that with a little history his brief would have been briefer.

(132)
I have adopted the plan of taking a volume, the last volume of Massachusetts Reports, and of making a full brief of an argument on every question in every case, examining all the authorities, finding others, and carefully composing an argument as well reasoned, as well expressed as if I

were going to submit it to a bench of the first of jurists.

(133)
[Judge Hand on going through a "mass of incoherent documents" and comparing them to a scene in Rabelais's Gargantua] [It] had been a great law suit between the Lords Suckfist and Kissbreach, it had gone on, as I remember, for twenty years, and all the jurists of France had delved into it and groped about ... Finally the exhibits and testimony had grown so great in bulk that it required twenty mules to carry them. The jurists having debated and debated, and quarreled and quarreled, finally declared that they were at an end. They were completely "philogrobolized," and so they asked Panurge to give judgment. That he did expeditiously and with a torrent of judicial wisdom which has never been equaled.

(134)
It is claimed that a lawyer submitted the following brief, quoted in its entirety:
I really don't see any grounds for reversing this case, but as in the last case I brought to this court, I did not see any grounds for reversing but the court found a good one, I hope it will do the same in this case.

Broad, Charles Lewis, (20f), (244f), (450f), (451f), (679f), (681f)

Brogan, Dennis W., (184f), (217f)

Brooks, Van Wyck, (50), (328f)

Brown, Henry Billings
(137)
The snug courtroom itself was so poorly ventilated as to be a source of friction. Within their own restricted circle the judges passed down a story of how Justice Gray, a large and full-blooded man, insisted on keeping a window open behind the screen. One day frail Justice Brown, feeling the draft asked a page to close the window. Justice Gray, overheated arose from the bench and went behind the screen to confirm his suspicions. "What damn'd fool told you to close that window?" he asked the frightened page. "Mr. Justice Brown," the page admitted. "I thought so," sputtered Gray as he stormed back to the bench.

Brown, Larry
    See Marshall, Thurgood

Buchwald, Art
    See Women

Bumble, Mr., (759f)

Burger, Warren,
(140)
    But it was not until he tried to change the justices' chairs that he provoked dissension. By tradition, each justice sat in his own chair behind the bench. Some preferred high-backed swivel rockers. Other chairs had lower backs or were big, upright, and square. Burger thought the chairs should all be the same, projecting and aesthetic uniformity. But the justices flatly refused to give up their chairs.

(141)
    [Chief Justice] Burger did not understand the difference and assigned the opinion to [Potter] Stewart. Stewart wrote back that he actually held the minority view and planned to dissent. He genially offered to write the majority opinion, too. After a moiety signed on to that opinion, Stewart just as genially circulated an opinion dissenting from the one he himself had written [Kentucky v. Wharton, 441 U.S. 786 (1979)].

(142)
    Commenting on the draft of a Burger opinion in a 1986 case, Cabana v. Bullock, Pamela S. Karlan told Blackman: "The Chief's opinion has come around. Like the Bourbons, he forgets nothing and learns nothing."

Burglary, (212), (257)
    See Pitney, Mrs. Malcolm

Burke, Edmund
(143)
"If laws seem to be man's enemies, men will," as Burke said, "be enemies to laws."

Burlesque houses
(144)
    [Holmes] used to attend a burlesque house in Washington; and one evening, when the show was a little rawer than usual, which is saying a great deal, he turned to the man on his right, a stranger and ejaculated: "I thank God I am a man of low tastes."

Burlingham, C.C.
> See Learning

Burton, Harold H.,
(145)
> Justice Harold H. Burton once gave one of the shortest oral opinions on record. A defendant who had been convicted of murder was before the court for sentencing. As usual, the judge asked if he had anything to say before the sentence was pronounced. The defendant said:
> "As God is my judge, I didn't do it. I'm not guilty." To which the judge replied:
> "He isn't, I am. You did. You are."

Butler, Charles Henry, (26f), (30f), (126f), (127f), (137f), (146f), (407f), (411f), (455f), (462f), (628f), (676f), (713f)
(146)
> On a certain afternoon at the Metropolitan Club, while I was speaking to a group of members in the lobby and claiming to have rendered a service to the country by safely escorting Justice Holmes, then well in his eighties, across several street crossings as he was returning alone to his home, one member exclaimed:
> "Butler, you think you have rendered the Country a service by saving the life of Justice Holmes. I don't. I think you ought to be indicted."

(147)
> Charles Henry Butler, the new Reporter of the Court, tells in his reminiscences how, just as Holmes went on the Bench to take the oath, he handed Butler a telegram, to be sent to the governor of Massachusetts containing his resignation as Chief Justice of the Supreme [Judicial] Court of Massachusetts. It was like Holmes to take no chances and to turn his corners squarely.

Butler, Pierce
(149)
> He was personally attracted to Holmes. He found the old man's robust wit and flashes of brilliance very stimulating. "Holmes and Butler had another spat today," he would say on returning from conference, and then he would tell the story, as of a case that the Court had debated at several sessions, Holmes and Butler carrying the opposing arguments, until finally Butler's position was accepted with only Holmes dissenting. Then Butler turned to Holmes and said with great solemnity, "I am glad we have finally arrived at a just decision. "Hell," snapped back Holmes, "Hell is paved with just decisions."

(150)
  Justice Pierce Butler was the lone dissenter from the Supreme Court's decision in the 1930s that upheld a Virginia statute providing for the sterilization of the mentally retarded [Buck v. Bell]. As a Catholic, Butler wrestled with his conscience. Justice Oliver Wendell Holmes, reading the majority decision which he had crafted, remarked: "Three generations of imbeciles are enough." Professor Powell read the opinion to his Harvard class, and added: "Mr. Justice Butler dissenting."

(151)
  Four horsemen (Butler, McReynolds, Sutherland, and Van Devanter)

By-laws
  See Choate, Rufus

-c-
Cabriole word
  See Afflatus

Camp, (681f)

Campbell, Lord, (795f)

Campos, Paul, (87f), (663f)

Candor as a form of deception
  See also Briefs
(153)
  Justice Holmes once told Solicitor General William D. Mitchell: "I have always appreciated your fairness to your opponents."
  Then as Mitchell's chest swelled, he added:
  "Candor I have always thought was the best form of deception."

Capital punishment
See also Kaufman, Irving I.
(154)
  As to capital punishment: if it was good enough for my father, it's good enough for me. (A line spoken by Victor Moore in Anything Goes.

(155)
  It is still the areas to allow a condemned man a final few words. A large crowd had gathered for the hanging and were disappointed when the convict waived his right. But from the audience, a gentleman strode forward and said,

"If the gentleman will yield his time, I am running for the Fifth District." The sheriff turned to the condemned man and said he would go along with it if it was OK with him. The answer: "I don't want to use it. If he wants to use it it is all right with me, but if it is all the same with you, I have heard the gentleman speak, and would appreciate it if you would hang me first.

(156)
A jury after being out thirty-three hours in a remote western town returned a verdict of not guilty. The judge thereupon directed an angry diatribe against the jury and ordered them back into the jury room with orders to return with a verdict more consistent with the facts. The jury found him guilty and the judge then advised them that the man already been hung.

Cardozo, Benjamin Nathan
(158)
Possibly it was Justice Cardozo who said that a judge convinces himself fifty one percent and then writes the decision as though he were one hundred percent satisfied. (See also Brandeis, Louis)

(159)
When he was appointed to the Supreme Court, Justice Cardozo missed the warm congenial atmosphere he left behind at the Court of Appeals in Albany. He found the Supreme Court stiff and remote and the only time he could establish real human contact with his colleagues was when they adjourned to the washroom next to the old Court chamber in the Capitol Building. But such opportunities for informal gossip came to an abrupt end with the new building in 1935. "Now that we have private washrooms," the mild-mannered Justice Cardozo complained, "there is no pleasure even in urination any more."

(160)
Asked to say who among his Supreme Court colleagues was the greatest living American jurist, Justice Benjamin Cardozo replied, "The greatest living American jurist isn't on the Supreme Court." Popular journals of Hand's day tried to remedy this oversight by referring to him as 'the Tenth Justice."

Carey, (661f)

Carson, Edward, (20f), (162f), (755f)
See also Advocate, Alcoholic beverages
(162)
During the early days in the Irish Courts, Carson once asked a witness what happened in his part of the country to people who told lies on oath. :"Their

side usually wins, Your Honour," was the answer.

Carter, Jimmy
(165)
Consent warrant: "That's when two policemen go into a house. One of them goes to the front door and knocks on it and the other one runs round to the back door and yells "come in."

Casanova
(166)
I once told the Justice that I was reading the Memoirs [Casanova's]. He turned abruptly on me. "A great mistake." Then a short and significant pause. "You should save them against the time when you are depressed and need them, as I did."

Case
    See also God and Court, Litigation
(170)
Edmund Plowden (1518-1585), great lawyer. He was asked what legal remedy there was against some hogs that had trespassed on complainant's ground. "There is very good remedy," began Plowden, but when told that they were his own hogs, said, "Nay, then, the case is altered."

Casebooks
(171)
… if ____ is writing a casebook not expecting to make a profit out of it "he ought to have his head examined." As a matter of fact, that's what these fool professors are doing all the time. With respect to my own casebook, which I wrote because I wanted to teach my own instead of someone else's materials, the royalties did not nearly cover my out-of-pocket expenses. If you succeed in inducing scholars not to write except for profit you will relieve this country of thousands of tons of very dull literature. It might well be that this would materially cut down the lists of practically all university presses. But that would be a bearable misfortune.

Catholic Claims
(172)
Law, Bishop of Elphin, when he was first in Ireland, had strong feelings in favour of the Roman Catholics. During his Residence in Ireland he became hostile to them. He came, and sat upon the Woolsack with me one day in the House of Lords, and began a Conversation respecting the Catholic Claims. He said he had told Ned that morning, so he styled his bother Edward, then Lord

Ellenborough, the long and the short of the Argument – all, that need be said about it – upon asking him what was his Argument he replied I can't see why we should allow those People any places upon Earth, who will not allow us to have any in Heaven.

Certiorari
(173)
      I must now tell you an amusing sequel. The case went to the court of appeals, where Judge Clark, already referred to by Professor Easley, wrote the opinion, and 98 percent of what I said was accepted; there was one very minor change. Mr. Davis petitioned for certiorari. The Court denied certiorari. Robert Jackson and I, who were associated partners in the Social Security cases, to which Professor Easley referred in the introduction, met each other shortly afterwards, and I said, "Bob, why didn't the Supreme Court grant a writ in that case? It involves hundreds of millions of dollars; it has great international ramifications; and it is a question in many respects of first impression." Bob looked me and said, "There are some of us who prefer the errors of a lower court to the errors of brethren"

(174)
      If you ask what a certiorari is I must answer with what Jeremiah Mason said to a client: "That is something that your Heavenly Father never meant you to know."

Chafee, Zechariah, (2f)

Chapman, John Jay
(175)
      As for Holmes, Chapman now imagined that the man had, parasite-like, fed upon his youthful emotions. In Holmes's efforts to help, Chapman could see nothing but a spiritual "detective" and puller of wires. When Minna wrote that he might rely upon Holmes and when, more particularly and most unfortunately, she called the Judge "the father of my inmost," Chapman grieved, despaired, and raged like a wild thing. He contemplated with pleasure how he was going to murder Holmes. And since his love was desecrated and his life over anyway, he wanted to commit suicide. For a year after he had learned of Holmes's mediation, Chapman held this murderous attitude toward him, obsessed by the phrase "father of my inmost." For the rest of his life he would have nothing to do with Holmes. For the rest of Holmes's life, so far as is known, he never suspected why Chapman disliked him.

Charm
>See, in general, Professors

Child, education of a
(176)
>Justice Holmes once said that the education of a child begins two hundred and fifty years before birth.

Chip off the old block
>See Day, William R.

Choate, Rufus, (132f), (177f), (629df)
>See also Attorney fees, Briefs

(177)
>One of [Choate's] friends, noticing the condition of his health, urged him to go away for a rest, saying, "If you continue your professional labors without a vacation, you will certainly undermine your constitution." "Sir," responded Choate gravely, "the constitution was destroyed long ago; I am now living under the by-laws."

Christ, what dignity
(178)
>The justices passed from the robing room across the Capitol corridor to the Court Room, led by the venerable Chief Justice Fuller, through the spectators held back by silk ropes between which the justices strode. And once, as he liked to remember, Holmes heard a countryman say to his wife, in awed tones: "Christ, what dignity"

Christian religion
(179)
>"No one has more respect for the Christian religion than I have; but really, when it comes to intruding it into private life …"

Churchill, Winston, (159f)

Citation, (476f)
>See also Closing argument

(180)
>It seemed that Professor Austin Scott had just finished presenting his deliberations to the Court
and had seated himself when opposing counsel stood up with Scott's work on Trusts in one hand said, "May it please the Court, Professor Scott has just argued

the last hour and it seems he is taking a contrary position to that which he takes in his works." Whereupon Professor Scott rose and said, "May it please the Court, I am in the process now of revising my editions, and I can assure you that when I come to this chapter I will conform it to the position I just argued.

> Publicity game
> See, in general, Arnold, Thurman

Civil War
> See also Abolition

(181)

Adds Louis Stark, who reported the case for the New York Times, "To Justice Holmes preservation of the fabric of federal-State relations was a principle higher than life. It was what he had fought for as a lad in the Civil War.."

(182)

This sharp skirmish was President Lincoln's only opportunity of seeing troops in action. He had no concern for his personal safety. Both on Monday and Tuesday, with nearly half of his tall form exposed above the parapet, he was under fire at Fort Stevens. During the charge of Bidwell's brigade, he clambered on top of the parapet, where General Wright and a few others were standing. A surgeon was killed by a sharpshooter's bullet within three feet of Lincoln. The President remained, after Wright had cleared the parapet of everyone else, and the general ordered him to withdraw. Wright's remonstrance was couched in dignified, if peremptory terms; and it was left for his exasperated young aide, Lieutenant-Colonel Oliver Wendell Holmes, to shout at the Chief Executive, "Get down, you fool!"

(183)

"I feel like Holmes when he was wounded at Antietam," Hughes whispered to Fletcher with a sigh that seemed to come from deep within him. "If I ever get out of this, I think I shall never love another country."

(184)

As he grew older Holmes grew even better looking and there remained to the end something pre-eminently military, something Gascon, in that moustache and that spare soldierly figure. "He may be a better lawyer than I am, but I was a d—d sight better soldier," so the legend runs, he commented on the criticisms of an eminent jurist who had attained Holmes's military rank behind a Washington desk in 1917-1918.

Civilization
(185)
> When a law clerk of Justice Holmes – fresh from the Harvard Law School – was helping the Justice to make out his income tax returns, the young man expressed sympathetic resentment at the burden the Justice had to bear. Holmes reproached his law clerk, observing that taxes are the price we pay for civilization. ... "The cure for most of our ills," he was fond of saying, "is more civilization."

Clancy, Paul R., (316f), (735f)

Clapper, Raymond, (378f)

Clare, Lord
See Law books

Clark, Hunter R., (140f), (575f), (577f)

Clark, Judge
See Certiorari

Clark, Tom C., (325f), (710f)

Clarke, Justice
See Alcoholic beverages (28)

Clarke, Sir Edward, (295)
See Tact

Classics
See Final Examination

Classroom
See Law classroom

Cliches
See Achilles' heel

Client, (235f)
(186)
"The first time I met [Arthur Garfield] Hays he represented a client who brought suit for the loss of a valuable fox terrier. The case was tried in the Supreme

Court. It appeared that the fox terrier – a female – was pursuing a peaceful course along the middle of a country road when a male, coming along, engaged her in a not unnatural function. My client's car upset the couple. Hays has been defending the underdog ever since."

(190)

An anecdote is told about a lawyer who won a substantial verdict for his client. He gave his client twenty-five per cent of the amount won. The client protested, saying: "After all, it's my case that won; you only argued it." The lawyer replied: "The case you brought me wouldn't have won you a cent. The case that got the verdict was my case, not yours."

(191)

If there is any truth to the old proverb that "one who is his own lawyer has a fool for a client," the Court by its opinion today now bestows a constitutional right on one to make a fool of himself.

(192)

An ambulance chasing lawyer found himself on the scene of an accident between two cars. Bodies were strewn all around. The lawyer saw one victim stirring, so bent over him with paper in hand as asked, "Are you a passenger, pedestrian, native, or transient?" The victim looked up with half-closed eyes and said, "My God, I am dying and he is starting a quiz program."

(193)

"Mr. Barry," he said on another occasion, "has your client never heard Sic utere tuo ut alienum non laedas?"

"Not a day passes, your Honour, on which he does not hear it. It is the sole topic of conversation where he lives at the top of Mushera Mountain," replied old Henry Harte Barry, the doyen of Kanturk.

(194)

The way Mr. Harriman spoke to his lawyers, and the boot-licking deference they paid to him! My observation of this interplay between the great man, the really powerful dominating tycoon, Harriman, and his servitors the lawyers, led me to say to myself, "If it means that you should be that kind of a subservient creature to have the most desirable clients, the biggest clients in the country, if that's what it means to be a leader of the Bar, I never want to be a leader of the Bar. The price of admission is too high."

(195)
> He [Attorney General Walls] asked me whether I had taken a course in legal ethics at Harvard. I replied I had not. ...He replied, "If in the course of your practice you become involved in difficult and protracted litigation, and if in the course of that litigation it becomes apparent that somebody has got to go to jail, be sure that it's your client."

(196)
> A young barrister began to recite a long speech before Lord Ellenborough, when his memory failed him, "My lord, the unfortunate client who appears by me – my lord, my unfortunate client ..." The Lord Chief Justice intervened gruffly: "You may go on, sir, so far the court is quite with you."

(197)
> Judge Dwight Foster, while teaching at Boston University Law School "once stated a proposition and cited a case, and ... said: 'I am sure that is good law. It cost a client of mine $2000.00 for me to learn it.'"

(198)
> Then there was the reassuring lawyer who advised his detained client, "Don't worry I will get you out if it takes ten years."

(199)
"I'm Sorry," Williams said [to Bernard Goldfine], "but you don't have a defense." ... Goldfine turned to Sam Sears and said, "Who does that young momzer from Washington think he is, telling me I have no defense? Defense? If I had a defense, I'd still have Slobodkin!" Ed.'s note: This was the mantra of Williams to those who questioned his value to their cause.

(200)
"The Ideal client," [Frank] Hogan liked to say, "is a rich man who is scared."

Clinton, Bill, (660)

Clocks
See Jackson, Robert H.

Closing argument
See also Oral argument
(205)
Fred Doyle ... had opposed to him a resourceful, able criminal lawyer by the name of Joe Walsh. They had had quite a lot of acrimonious interchanges

during the course of this trial, and at the close of the evidence Joe started to argue. He was a well-educated fellow, and he quoted some poetry – I don't know that it had much to do with the case – after he had recited a stanza from Milton's Paradise Lost he turned around to Doyle with considerable intellectual arrogance and said, "As you probably don't know, that is from Milton," and Doyle said, "Thanks for telling me; I thought it was from Mattapan!"

Club dues
    See Alcoholic beverages

Cohen, Felix S., (672f)

Cohen, L.C., (672f)

Cohen, Morris
(207)
    … having vainly expected my eminent friend, Morris Cohen, at luncheon. He had agreed to come, but being a philosopher did not turn up.

Cohn, (198f)

Coleman, William
(208)
    He never forgot a poignant conversation concerning that appointment which took place in his chambers. When his negro messenger heard about the appointment, he said, "Mr. Justice, that was a mighty fine thing you did, hiring one of our people to be your clerk."
    Frankfurter chided him gently. "Tom," he said, "I have heard that kind of remark from others, but I am surprised to hear it from you. Don't you know that I selected William Coleman because, on the basis of character and ability, I felt he deserved the position?"
    "Mr. Justice," replied the messenger, " do you think in this world our people get what they deserve?"

Collisions at sea
(210)
    In England a judge of probate, divorce, and admiralty, asked what he did, replied: "I deal with collisions at sea and collusions on land."

Collusions
(211)
    [A Lord Chief Justice] The greater part of my official time is spent on

investigating collisions between propelled vehicles, each on its own side of the road, each sounding its horn, and each stationary.

    Definition
        See Definitions
(212)
    In England a judge of probate, divorce, and admiralty, asked what he did, replied: "I deal with collisions at sea and collusions on land."

Columbia Law School
(214)
    George V. Kershway, one of the deans of the Columbia Law School, resigned to become the warden of Sing Sing Prison. ... Some people said he did it because it was the only place the alumni wouldn't come back and tell him how to run the institution. When he passed down the streets of New York, he would occasionally be greeted and not knowing which of the two institutions he had headed had spawned this particular individual and being a very good and very cautious lawyer, he used to say, "When did you get out?"

Comma is there
(216)
    One man complained that in the argument of an important case, the chief justice kept saying: "But, sir, the comma is there; the comma is there."

Commencement speakers, (629b)

Conboy, Martin
    See Obscenity

Conscious as we are of each other's unworthiness,
(217)
    ... remember the jest of Lord Bowen who amended the fulsome opening of an address by the judges to Queen Victoria into "Conscious as we are of each other's unworthiness."

Constitutional law
(218)
Grafitti appearing in the men's room hot air blower to dry hands in a leading law school, "PRESS HERE TO LISTEN TO PROFESSOR _____ ON CONSTITUTIONAL LAW"

(219)
> Powell loved two things in life: shredding the Supreme Court's latest decisions and doing the same to students in his constitutional law class.

Puking and
> See Vomit

Constitutional lawyer
(220)
> [said to the press at a Gridiron dinner]
> "Chief Justice Taft once said that a constitutional lawyer was one who had abandoned the practice of the law and had gone into politics. ...

Contingent fees
> See Attorney fees

Continuance, (701)
See also, in general, (544)
(221)
> Harrison Hale Schaff, an alumnus still living in Boston, recalls an interesting episode in which Professor Swasey was the hero. It was before the Supreme Court, in a session in which Oliver Wendell Holmes was the presiding Justice. At a certain point a murder case in which Mr. Swasey was the defending counsel was called, and Mr. Swasey arose, and in a low-pitched, agreeable voice, clearly presented his request for a continuance of the trial of his client. Mr. Holmes listened with the courteous attention that always characterized his attitude on the bench, and then said, in effect:
> "Mr. Swasey, the record shows that the trial of this case has at your request been continued once. Last summer when I was in England visiting the law courts, Mr. Justice Stephen invited me to sit with him on the bench in a criminal session during which he commented to me on the importance of speedy trials in the administration of criminal justice, particularly in capital cases while witnesses were available, evidence fresh in the mind, and before suggestions could create false psychological memories."
> Mr. Justice Stephen had for years been a terror to evil-doers in England. His name was one to conjure with in legal circles throughout the English-speaking world. The motion was obviously lost, though the judge paused before uttering the words of refusal silently to extend to the petitioner's counsel the courtesy of any further plea he might wish to advance. Swasey unmoved and motionless, looking Holmes full in the face with those brown eyes of his that shot golden gleams in his rare moments of suppressed emotion, had listened to the unfavorable trend of the Court's opinion. When the pause came to allow

him a final word he said, "Has your Honor read the morning papers?" Even the Court officers came to life, and Holmes inquired what press report might have a bearing on the case at bar.

"None," replied Swasey, "but they do report that yesterday Mr. Justice Stephen was judicially committed to an institution for the feeble-minded."

The bombshell was too much for the gasping attorneys and officials. Holmes and Swasey alone of those in the precincts of the Court retaining their equanimity. Following a brief colloquy at the bench the continuance was allowed and Swasey set out for his office.

Contract, (118), (505), (594), (794); (534f)
    Intention of the parties:
(222)
    However, as we have seen, the courts, before they enforce contracts must interpret them. In so doing, the courts frequently say they are carrying out the "intention of the parties." Holmes called that statement a "humbug."

(223)
    Justice Holmes used to say, "When my brethren talk of liberty of contract, I compose my mind by thinking of all the beautiful women I have known."

Cooke, Alistair, (129f)

Coolidge, Calvin
    See Advisory opinion, Retirement

Copley, John S., (466f)

Corax vs. Tisias
    See Young lawyers

Corporation as a client
(226)
    … the young graduate of a law school who went to one of the more prominent lawyers in town who had a fine corporate practice. He said, "Mr. Smith, how does one become a corporation lawyer?" Mr. Smith replied: "That is the easiest question to answer I have had today. Just get yourself a corporation for a client."

Corwin, Edward S., (50f)
Cost a client of mine $2000 for me to learn it
    See Client

Court of Appeal
(227)
    [Lord Pollock] Sitting in a court on circuit, he was disturbed by the bells of a nearby church:
"I was not aware that this was a Court of Appeal."

(228)
    You see a Court of Appeals judge has a sort of intermediate status. It is the duty of a Judge of a District Court to be quick, courteous, and wrong, but it must not be supposed from that that the Court of Appeals should be slow, crapulous and right, for that would be to usurp the functions of the Supreme Court.
[Yearbook of the Canadian Bar Association 151 (1963).] See also: You are really at the bottom rung of the Federal Judicial ladder, which is far beneath the State Judicial ladder. Your only function as a Federal District Judge is always to be quick, courteous, and wrong and he hastened to say that I was not to understand by that that the Court of Appeals was always slow, rude and right. He [Judge Magruder] said that was the function of the United States Supreme Court in Washington.

(229)
    One theory [as to why Puerto Rico is in the First Circuit] presented to me was that Mr. Justice Holmes arranged it. He was Circuit Justice for the First Circuit and I was told very seriously once that Mr. Justice Holmes organized the attachment of Puerto Rico to the First Circuit so he would have a place to spend a winter vacation. It is a very interesting theory except for two things: That sort of thing was entirely out of character for Mr. Justice Holmes and he never went to Puerto Rico as far as I have been able to determine.

(230)
    Counsel: Mr. Gardiner says that to err is only human ...
    Mr. Justice Hilbery: Having regard to the existence of the Court of Appeal, I should think to err is also judicial.

Courtroom
    Width of
        See Noonan, Gregory

Covenant that runs with the land
> See Assignees

Cox, Archibald
> See Oral argument, (627)

Cox, Professor, (476f)

Criminal law
(235)
> Criminal law is the only profession in which the better you get, the worse the class of people you represent.

Crook
> Double meaning of, (518)
>> See Smith, F.E.

Cropley, Charles Elmore
> See Holmes, Oliver Wendell, (413)

Crosby, Harley N.
> See Objections

Cross-examination
See also Hall, Marshall; Witnesses
(240)
An entertainer was being severely interrogated by a lawyer when under examination as a witness.
> Lawyer: You are in the entertaining business, I believe?
> Witness: Yes, sir.
> Lawyer: Is not that rather a low calling?
> Witness: I don't know but what it is sir, but it is so much better than my father's that I am rather proud of it.
> Lawyer: And what was your father's calling?
> Witness: He was a lawyer

(241)
> Plaintiff attorney questions prospective juror:: Do you know the attorney representing the other side?
> Juror: Yes, he's a crook.
> Plaintiff attorney: Do you know me?
> Juror: Yes, you're a crook.

Judge: If you ask her if she knows me, I'll hold you in contempt.

(242)

Sometimes special circumstances, in addition to special knowledge, impel a judge to intervene. At other times experienced and well-controlled lawyers are fearful of a judge's intervention in a lawsuit.

Serjeant Ballantine, a great English barrister of the nineteenth century, told of the time when a judge interrupted him while he was cross-examining a witness, saying, "Really, this is a long way from the point."

"I am aware of that," said Ballantine. "If I were to begin any nearer the witness would discover my object."

(243)

Sir Patrick Hastings cross-examining a witness with great severity: I advise you to answer the questions.

The dramatic answer rang out: The last time I took your advice I did twelve months.

(244)

The great F.E. Smith, later Lord Birkenhead, was once cross-examining a boy whose right arm, the prosecution alleged, had been crippled through the negligence of the defendant, a bus company.

"Will you show me," F.E. asked with great sympathy toward the boy, "just how high you can lift your arm?"

His face exhibiting great pain, the boy could barely bring his arm in line with his shoulder.

"Thank you," said F.E., "and now will you show me how high you could lift it before the accident?"

The boy's arm immediately shot up in the air, and the defense had no further questions.

(245)

Witness: Well, I spent a good bit of money in taking a year's study at Johns Hopkins, after I obtained my M.D., and thereafter spent two years at Vienna, Austria.

Cross-Examiner: (sarcastically) Well, doctor, I believe you know everything.

Witness: No, sir, I'm not fortunate enough to be a lawyer.

(246)

Lawyer cross-examining witness on a crucial point. Looks with satisfaction at the judge for his approval after each question.

"Haven't you been convicted of arson?" No answer.

"Haven't you been convicted of wife-beating?" No answer.

The lawyer appeals to the judge. "Your honor, we have a recalcitrant witness. Can't we have an answer to these questions.?"

With that the witness spoke up and said, "Were you asking me those questions? I thought you were asking that of the judge."

Cruz, R. Ted, (660)

Cujos est solum ejus est ad inferos et usque ad coelum
See also (252)
(247)

A story is told of the famous Serjeant Sullivan – the last of the serjeants at law. While arguing a case concerning the invasion of aerial rights over land he was interrupted by the judge who asked: "Serjeant Sullivan, have your clients never heard of the maxim cujos est solum ejus est ad inferos et usque ad coelum?" "M'Lord," replied Serjeant Sullivan, "M'Lord, the peasants of Northern Oirland talk of little else."

Cunningham, (217f)

Curran, John, (500)

Curtis, Charles P., (166f), (378f), (475f)
-d-
Darrow, Clarence, (471f)

Daumier
    See Satan

Davenport, William H., (325f)

Davis, John W., (622f), (740f)
(250)

Justice Oliver Wendell Holmes, commenting admiringly on the skill with which John W. Davis presented his arguments to the court, remarked that Davis "skated so rapidly over the thin ice of his cases," it was necessary to stay wide awake throughout the presentation.

Davis, Michael D., (140f), (575f), (577f)

Davy, Serjeant, (500f)

Day of Judgment, (300f)

Day, William R.
(251)
     When Mr. Justice Shiras resigned, Roosevelt appointed in his place William R. Day of Ohio, a wisp of a man. His son, a former football player and a six-footer, once argued a case before his father and others of the Court. Mr. Justice Holmes surveyed the upstanding dimensions of this offshoot of his associate and passed a pencilled note along the bench: "He is a block of[f] the old chip."

De minimis non curat lex
See also, (247)
(252)
     One hot afternoon, in the old days when Ireland was ruled from Westminster, the last of the Serjeants-at-Law, the great A.M. Sullivan, KL was arguing a case at the Law Courts in The Strand. It was a tiresome point about an Irish family dispute and a judge tried to cut short the flow of that millifluous brogue, with "Brother, have your clients not heard of the maxim, De Minimis Non Curat Lex?"
     "My Lord," retorted the Serjeant, "in the bogs of Connemara, they speak of little else."

Dean of Ely
    See Death and Dying

Deans
    See also Columbia Law School, Law dean
    Lose their faculties
        See Lawyers, (545)
    Raiding other law schools for professors
        See American Law Institute

Death and dying
(254)
     Judge Hand said that he'd heard Justice Oliver Wendell Holmes say, "I'm ready to go," on his 95th [sic] birthday. And when Hand had said, "Take me with you." Holmes replied, "You don't know what you're saying. No man really feels he's ready to go. I'm sure when my time comes and I'm beckoned, I'll say, 'Couldn't you make that a couple of weeks from now?'"

(255)
A good story, but one rather hard upon the profession, is told of a certain Dean of Ely. At a dinner, just as the cloth was being removed, the subject of discourse happened to be the extra-ordinary mortality among lawyers.

"We have lost," said a gentleman, "no less than seven eminent barristers in as many months."

The Dean, who was very deaf, rose just at the conclusion of these remarks, and gave the company grace; "For this and every other mercy, make us devoutly thankful."

Death sentence
    See Electric Chair

Declaration of Independence
    See Advertising

Defects of his qualities; qualities of his defects
(256)
One recalls the epigram of Justice Holmes: "We can forgive a man the defects of his qualities, if only he has the qualities of his defects."

Definitions
(257)
    Professor: What constitutes burglary?
    Student: There must be a breaking.
    Professor: Then if a man enters a door and takes a sovereign from your waistcoat pocket in the hall, would that be burglary?
    Student: Yes, sir; because that would break me.(257f)

(258)
Fee simple: a small retainer
Eiusdem generis: he treated them nicely
Voir dire: don't forget to send me a telegram, honey
Collusion: when a moveable body meets a resistible force
Obiter dictum: ouch
Ibid: what you do on ebay
Res judicata: Jewish religion
Summary proceedings: picnics, golf, etc.
Supra: the person you tip on Christmas
Loco parentis: poor pa is off his rocker
Honore Balzac: don't hit below the belt

(259)
Consent warrant: "That's when two policemen go into a house. One of them goes to the front door and knocks on it and the other one runs round to the back door and yells "come in."

(260)
    Definition of a lawyer: A legal gentleman who rescues your estate from your enemies, and keeps it himself.

(261)
    Jury: Twelve men who are chosen to decide which of the parties has the better barrister
    Lawyer: shrewdest distance between two points; a person who helps you get what's coming to him; he who is summoned when the felon needs a friend; old lawyers never die. They just lose their appeal.
    The court in charge: If ever there was a case of clearer evidence than this of persons acting together, this case is that case.
    Forger: a fellow who gives a cheque a bad name
    Lawsuit: a machine which you go into as a pig and come out of as a sausage (261f)

Delaney, V.T.H., (648f)

Deliberate speed
(262)
Dear Sir:
    In recent letters to the New York Times, an attempt was made to determine the origin of the term "deliberate speed," which appeared in Brown v. Board of Education (349 U.S. 294, 301 (1955). The opinion was by Justice Warren but the phrase has been said to be contributed by the late Justice Frankfurter.
    In the letter of March 3, 1965, it was written that the phrase was suggested by Francis Thompson's poem, "The Hound of Heaven." In a subsequent letter, it was suggested that Sir Walter Scott's Rob Roy was a more likely source.
    I would like to offer a statement by Justice Holmes in Virginia v. West Virginia (222 U.S. 17, 19-20 (1911) as my candidate for the source: "But a state cannot be expected to move with the celerity of a private business man; it is enough if it proceeds, in the language of the English Chancery, with all deliberate speed."
                                        Sincerely,
                                        Edward J. Bander.

Delusion of adequacy
>See Hughes, Charles Evans, (433)

DePugh, Chauncey
>See After-dinner speaker

Derby, Augustin, (501f), (533f)

Dershowitz, Alan
>See Law students, (538)

Devil, (25); (335f)
>See also God and Court

Devlin, Patrick, (228f), (641f)

Dickens, Charles, (759f)

Diplomatic immunity
(265)
>Diplomatic problems in Washington are not confined to appointments of envoys, as a recent exchange of letters has revealed.
>
>The issue involved a yellow Labrador retriever named Jason in a Washington area favored by diplomats. The dog was described by his owner as humiliated because he must promenade on a leash, while a dog from a Latin-American embassy was free to run about unhampered, enjoying the diplomatic immunity of his owner.
>
>Though Jason's master presumably can accept the fact that he may get a parking ticket while a foreign diplomat does not, he felt impelled to inquire whether ambassadorial immunities really applied to the diplomat's dog
>
>Following legal research that was described as "formidable.," Walter N. Tobriner, president of the District Board of Commissioners, ruled that, indeed, "there is no enforceable remedy against a diplomatic dog-at-large unless an independent criminal intent can be attributed to man's best friend."

Divorce
>See Brandeis, Louis (118), Holmes, Oliver Wendell (417), Law (499)

Doctor, (2), (245), (586); (410f)
(266)
>Dr. A. Dickson Wright: When I finish one of my cases I am always

puzzled whether I have left anything in or not; the lawyer is always puzzled whether he left anything out.

(267)
    Doctors bury their mistakes while lawyers write theirs down and follow them as precedent.

Dodson, Sir Gerald, (458)

Doe, Judge
    See Approval, need for

Dogs
    See Client (186), Diplomatic immunity

Donahue, Frank J., (48f), (173f)
(270)
    We have a judge in Boston who is indeed brilliant, but a character. A jury case was being tried before him, a personal injury case, and the jury sent a note to him with a question asking if, even if there was not any liability, they could still give the plaintiff some money.
    Donahue sent for the jury. He said to them, "I have your written question, and I assume from the question that you have found there is no liability."
    The foreman said, "That is so, Your Honour." He said, "All right, sign this slip then."
    After they had signed the slip, which directed a verdict for the defendant, he said, "I will now answer your question. You may retire to the jury room and pass around the hat."

Donnellan, Mary
    See Holmes, Fanny

Dooley, Mr. (81), (103f), (549af)

Douglas, William O., (698); (60f), (103f), (273f), (274f), (397f), (465f), (503f), (513f), (719f)
(273)
    The feelings were mutual, as Douglas on various occasions referred to his diminutive colleague [Frankfurter], as "the little Giant," the "little bastard," or simply "Der Fuehrer."

(274)
To environmentalist, "Wild Bill" Douglas was the highest legal advocate for the wilderness regions in the government. To the press, "Wild Bill" Douglas was the Justice who liked to wear a Stetson and a western-style coat with no tie, walking around Capitol Hill and conducting life in his own fashion. To the general public, "Wild Bill" Douglas was the only Justice from the far west and the last one from the old American frontier, whose background now led him to reach out on the Court to vote for the downtrodden, the poor, and the oppressed.

But of all these characters, it was the "Wild Bill" Douglas who inhabited and terrorized the Court building who was always one revelation away from bringing the institution into disrepute.

(274a)
[Justice] Douglas would express the opposite opinion [after Chief Justice Burger indicated how he would vote] in as dismissive a way as possible. If Burger had voted to affirm, for example, Douglas would say when his turn came: "Chief, for the excellent reasons that you have spelled forth, I vote to reverse."

>   Buzzer
>   See Law clerks

Doyle, Fred
>   See Closing Argument

Dress code
>   See Lawyers (540), United States Supreme Court (714)

Due process
>   See Vomit

Duff, James C., (660)

-e-
Easley, Professor
>   See Certiorari

Eastman, Max, (154f), (759f)

Einstein, Lewis, (37f), (100f), (174f), (207f), (281f), (415f), (416f), (417f), (490f), (494f), (618f), (675f), (734f)

Eisenhower, Dwight D., (13)
(275)
    President Eisenhower is reported to have called Warren's appointment "the biggest damfool mistake I ever made," ...

Eiusdem generis
    See Definitions

Eldon, Lord, (172f), (430f)

Electric chair
(280)
    Martin Stone, an early television personality, also enjoyed a successful career as a lawyer. An example of his quick-wittedness circulating in New York had one of his clients phoning Stone from the death house at Sing Sing with the desperate news that he was about to be taken to the electric chair in a few minutes.
    "You're my lawyer. Tell me what to do." In a flash, his attorney replied: "Don't sit down."
See also:
    You know about the lawyer whose client said "They are going to electrocute me tomorrow morning, what shall I do?" the lawyer counseled: "Don't sit down."

Ellenborough, Lord, (640f)
    See Catholic Claims, Client, (196)

Emerson, Ralph Waldo
    See also Taxes
(281)
    Once he quoted Emerson at his own expense. This happened when, still an undergraduate at Harvard, he had written an essay criticizing Plato as being a superficial thinker. With youthful conceit he had shown this to [Ralph Waldo] Emerson who promptly rebuked him in one short sentence that he had never forgotten: "When you strike at a King you must kill him."

Emoluments
    See Association of the Bar of the City of New York

Entertainers
    See Cross-examination

Enthusiasm but not enthusiism,
(282)
I value enthusiasm but not enthusiism.

Error
> To err is human
> > See Court of Appeal

Ervin, Sam, (735f)

Estate taxes
(283)
The explanation of the month came from the president of the Bank of Las Vegas – a man who was asked why it was that Howard Hughes was buying up so much of the inheritance-taxless Nevada. "There are very few places in America," the banker said, "he could afford to get caught dead in."

Estes, Joe E., (444f)

Evarts, William M., (71f)

Evidence
> See Hall, Marshall; Professors

-f-
Facts
> See also Abstractions, God and Court (379); Questions of fact, Stone, Harlan Fiske (688), Taft, William Howard

(284)
There was once a professor of law who said to his students: "When you're fighting a case, and if you have the law on your side hammer it into the judge." "But if you have neither the facts nor the law" asked one of his listeners. "Then hammer hell into the table," answered the professor.

(289)
Frankfurter: "You remember Holmes' remark: 'I don't know facts, I merely know their significance.' Jerry [Judge Frank] knows a helluvah lot of books, but not their significance."

Fadiman, Clifton, (424f)

Fair trial
(292)

[On granting a stay of execution in the Sacco-Vanzetti case] "You don't have to convince me that the atmosphere in which these men were tried precluded a fair trial," said Justice Holmes. "But that is not enough to give me, as a federal judge, jurisdiction. If I listened to you any more I would do it. I must not do it."

He turned on his heel and went into the house.

Fallon, William
    See Alcoholic beverages (21), Attorney fees (77)

Fashion
    See Automobiles

Federal District Judge
    Appointment method
        See Truman, Harry
    Quick, courteous and wrong
        See Court of Appeal

Federal penitentiary
    See Harvard Law School

Federal system
    Umpire of the Federal system
        See United States Supreme Court, (722)

Federal Trade Commission
    See Advertising

Federal-state relations
    See Civil War

Fee simple
    See Definitions

Feeble-minded
    See Continuance

Fees
    See Attorney fees

Field, Stephen, (383f)

Fields, W.C., (16f)

Final examination
(300)
 Supreme Court Justice Oliver Wendell Holmes was an avid scholar who never lost his zest for learning.
  One day, when Holmes was 90, a friend found him reading Plato.
  "Still studying at your age?" asked the friend.
  "I'm preparing for the final examination," explained the jurist.

First Circuit, (229f), (581f)
 See also Height

Fitzgerald, F. Scott, (552f)

Fitzgerald, Patrick J.
 See Baseball

Flattery
 See Laski, Harold

Follansbee, (216f)

Follett
 See Alcoholic beverages, (28)

Fontenelle, (424f)

Footnotes,
See also Law reviews, (532)
(305)
 "I have agreed to the foot-note by Aristotle, as amplified, to which Jerry [Justice Jerome Frank] attached his opinion," he noted once to Hand. ... Hand had once written to a state judge that "[p]ersonally, I ... abhor footnotes. ... But the practice has become so general that I fear I am enlisted in a lost cause."

(306)
 Even when Holmes concurred in Brandeis's weighty opinions, he sometimes grew weary reading them. On one occasion Holmes "knit" his

brow" over a long opinion, profusely decorated with the usual footnotes as to economic data, trade journals, and committee reports. Beautifully clear and no doubt true, Holmes thought, as he leaned back in his chair; then he wrote on the margin: "This afternoon I was walking on the towpath and saw a cardinal. It seemed to me to be the first sign of spring. By the way, I concur."

(307)
    Herbert Wechsler, Stone's clerk from 1932, likened Stone's penchant for footnotes to "a squirrel storing nuts to be pulled out at some later time.

Forger
    See Definitions

Foster, Judge Dwight
    See Client, (197)

Fountain, Richard, (38f), (75f), (145f), (227f), (230f), (243f), (260f), (261f), (451f), (491f), (500f), (564f), (612f), (652f), (679f), (697f), (793f)

Four horsemen
(308)
    Four horsemen (Butler, McReynolds, Sutherland, and Van Devanter)

Franco, (629c)

Frank, Jerome N., (289), (305); (222f), (289f)
(309)
    One of Judge Jerome Frank's law clerks objected to the length of one of his opinions. He spent all of a week and finally cut it down from sixty-five pages to one-half page. He left both on Judge Frank's desk without comment. The following morning Judge Frank rushed into his clerk's office and shouted, "Bully for you," displaying the clerk's work, "we'll add it to the end."

Frank, John Paul, (159f)

Frankfurter, Felix, (4f), (6f), (8f), (35f), (36f), (116f), (118f), (194f), (208f), (312f), (314f), (315f), (316f), (325f), (329f), (397f), (438f), (442f), (449f), (467b), (541f), (591f), (617f), (618f), (623f), (667f), (673f), (690f), (716f), (720f), (734a)
    See also Administrative law, Coleman, William; Douglas, William O.
    Der Fuehrer, See Douglas, William O.
    Hypothetical

See McReynolds, James C., (591)
Little bastard, See Douglas, William O.
Little Giant, See Douglas, William O

(311)
Court observers have often said that Frankfurter's impromptu explanations from the bench on opinion days of what his opinion said were much more persuasive than what he wrote.

(312)
'The climax came when Senator Patrick A. McCarran, who had been trying throughout the hearings to draw Frankfurter as a dangerous radical at best, held up a book called Communism by Frankfurter's friend Harold Laski and asked, 'If it advocates the doctrine of Marxism, would you agree with it?'
Frankfurter answered: 'Senator, I do not believe you have ever taken an oath to support the Constitution of the United States with fewer reservations than I have or would now, nor do I believe you are more attached to the theories and practices of Americanism than I am. I rest my answer on that statement.'...
Frankfurter always savored as one of the more delicious moments of his life when, in 1945, the same Senator McCarran asked him to to recommend two Nevada boys for study at Harvard Law School. Frankfurter obliged, but not without just a little teasing. Didn't the Senator, Frankfurter asked, want to save them from that 'horrendous fate?'

(313)
Your note on The Crillon pad reminds me of a long game between Felix and Lefty Lewis. On a visit to FF's chambers Lefty purloined a Supreme Court memo pad and thereafter wrote FF notes on its paper. FF told me about it and said he would test Lefty's self-restraint by making no reference to the paper in answering the notes. Lefty saw the challenge and continued blandly using the pad. Of course, in time it was used up. When this became clear FF and I conferred with the result that FF sent without note or comment another pad in a Supreme Court envelope. This broke Lefty. Thus do great jurists and scholars amuse themselves.

(314)
... Chief Justice Hughes, on more than one occasion when at Conference he and I found ourselves in disagreement, would in a playfully mischievous way begin with "Professor Frankfurter" and quickly correct himself to "Justice Frankfurter." He indulged in this bit of whimsy just once too often when I remarked, I hope with equal good humor, "Chief Justice, please don't apologize. I know of no title that I deem more honorable than that of Professor of the

Harvard Law School."

(315)
    We are given, incidentally, the astonishing information that in the Holmes-Frankfurter conversations Holmes "did practically all the talking."

(316)
    Now about Felix Frankfurter, who, according to Ervin, taught everything but public utilities in his course on public utilities.

Frankfurter, Mrs.
    See Symbols

Franklin, Benjamin
    See (707f)

Freedman, (29f), (463f), (546f)

French novels, (117), (412), (442), (442f)
(320)
    His fondness for French fiction is such, that once, when he told a portrait painter that he could have but an hour for a sitting, Mrs. Holmes interrupted with: "Take as much time as you need; he only wants to get away to one of those naughty French novels."

Freund, Paul, (185f), (467af), (727f)
    See also Memorial addresses

Friendship
    Appointment because of
        See Truman, Harry

Fuess, Clause Moore, (132f), (177f)

Fuller, Melville Weston, (127), (147f), (178f), (325f), (326f), (421f)
(325)
    Justice Holmes was fond of telling a story. In his early days, he said, "I'm afraid my temper was a little short." And there could hardly be two men more different than Mr. Justice Holmes, who wielded a rapier, and Mr. Justice Harlan, who wielded a battle-axe. A rapier and a battle-axe locked in combat are likely to beget difficulties for innocent bystanders. Justice Harlan, who was oratorical while Justice Holmes was pithy, said something that seemed not

ultimate wisdom to Holmes. Justice Holmes said he then did something that isn't done in the conference room of the Supreme Court. Each man speaks in order and there are no interruptions, no cut-ins – of cuts-in, whichever the plural is – because if you had that you would soon have a Donnybrook Fair instead or orderly proceedings. But Holmes said, "I did lose my temper at something that Harlan said and sharply remarked, "That won't wash! That won't wash!" Tempers flared and something might have happened. But when Holmes said, "That won't wash," the silvery-haired, gentle, small, Chief Justice [Fuller] said, "Well, I'm scrubbing away. I'm scrubbing away."

(326)
    The scene as he delivered it was described by the Chief Justice in a letter to Mrs. Fuller. "When his voice, refined and clear, rose in the Court Room you could have heard a pin drop and his sentences were as incisive as the edge of a knife." It was many years before the world discovered the immense power of Holmes's opinions, but Fuller early came to know it. One of his secretaries tells how, whenever a new opinion by Holmes was brought to the Chief Justice, he would stop whatever he was doing and read it aloud with such exclamations of pleasure and admiration as, "Isn't that marvelous? Doesn't he write superbly?"

Funerals, (3), (513)
    Attending, (419)
    Vacancies on the court and, (723)

-g-
Galbraith, John K.
    See Kennedy, John F.

Galanter, Marc, (7f), (48f), (58f), (71f), (73f), (101f), (284f), (335f), (448f), (475f), (552f), (672f), (700f), (752f), (785f), (789f)

Gallows humor
(327)
    Gallows humor: Another prisoner waived aside a proffered glass of rum with the comment, "I lose all my sense of direction when I'm drunk." ... Commonly quoted comments are, "This will teach me a lesson I'll never forget" and the response to an impatient warder, "What's the hurry, they can't start without us." ... A man, who had murdered his parents complained, "What would you execute an orphan? ... Christie, the multiple murderer, was opposed in principle to capital punishment.

Game laws,
>See Young Lawyer, (785)

Generalization
See also (688a)
(328)
>No generalization is wholly true, not even this one.

(329)
>Most lawyers hand out these generalities which nobody disputes. Holmes said, "But the point that matters is whether the boy got his finger pinched."

Geniality
>See Warren, Edward Henry

Gentlemen, (300f)
>See Law classroom (506), Mencken, H. L.

Gerhart, Eugene C., (442f), (446f), (464f), (586f), (610f), (624f), (735f)

Ghostwriting
>See Kennedy, John F.

Gibson, Ernest W. Jr.
>See Truman, Harry

Gift in contemplation of death
>See also McReynolds, James C.

(332)
>A ninety year old lawyer appeared a Bar Association meeting in a magnificent new tuxedo with wine-colored lapels. I said: "Old boy, you must have gotten a ten-dollar fee or something," and he said: "Hush, don't tell anybody, but I ordered this to show my gifts are not in contemplation of death."

Gignoux, Edward T., (228f)

Gilbert and Sullivan, (660)

Gilbert, Michael, (28f), (35f), (76f), (124f), (162f), (194f), (196f), (217f), (242f), (270f), (385f), (451f), (466f), (471f), (679f), (680f), (691f), (755f), (786f), (791f)

God and Court, (145f), (334f), (378)
See also Bishop, Insurance; Kaufman, Irving; Ten Commandments, United States Supreme Court, (715)

(334)
[Professor Corwin] says that they ought to change the invocation from "God save the Government of the United States and this Honorable Court," to "God save the Government of the United States or this Honorable Court." He insists that God can't possible do both, and he should not be asked even to try. He should be given his choice and let it go at that..

(335)
God and devil are having a boundary dispute. Can't reach an agreement so God says he will bring the case to court.
Devil: where are you going to get a lawyer.

(336)
Like any other members of their society, lawyers could claim no more than that to a degree they had channeled or harnessed forces which they had not created. "Sonny," Holmes in legend replied to his inquiring law clerk, "I just remember, I'm not Lord God Almighty."

(337)
Holmes's distinction of himself from God cannot be traced to a document; the story so fits the character of speaker and situation that it demands acceptance for its validity in spirit if not in letter.

(338)-(377) Reserved for future use

(378)
About seventy-five years ago I learnt that I was not God. And so, when the people ... want to do something I can't find anything in the Constitution expressly forbidding them to do, I say, whether I like it or not, "Goddamit, let 'em do it!"

(379)
It was all very well for Vice-Chancellor Bacon to say at the end of a case (as Lord Simon once assured me that he did): "This case bristles with simplicity. The facts are admitted. The law is plain. And yet it has taken seven days to try – one day more than God Almighty took to create the world." Page 145
"If laws seem to be man's enemies, men will," as Burke said, "be enemies to

laws." Page 416

(380)
>Making innumerable Statutes, men
>Merely confuse what God achieved in ten

(380a)
Golfer, the
>John Marshall Harlan

Gossip and philosophy
(381)
>The difference, as Mr. Justice Holmes once observed, between gossip and philosophy is merely background.

Goulden, Joseph C., (595f), (788f)

Governor, (421), (435), (436), (454)
>See also Judge (454)

Gray, Horace, (137f)
(382)
>Holmes used to say of [Justice Horace] Gray that the premise of his opinion and the conclusion stood forth like precipices, with a roaring torrent of precedents between, but he never quite understood how Gray got across. ...

Gray, John Chipman
>See Law firms; see also (521af), (688af)

Greenman, Russell L., (647f)

Gressley, Gene M., (39f), (57f), (334f), (532f)

Grey, Thomas, (660)

Grier, Robert C.
(383)
>After the first argument of the legal-tender case following the Civil War, the court had been afraid that Justice Grier would cast the deciding vote at a time when he was no longer able to address himself to the issues involved. A committee of judges, including Justice Field, had waited on Grier and urged his resignation. Years later, Field himself, had tarried on the bench after he was

too old to meet the responsibilities of a judge, and his brethren had deputed Justice Harlan to remind the old man of what his committee had said to Grier. Harlan had aroused the venerable Justice as he was vegetating on a settee in the robing room. Did not Justice Field remember that he was one of the committee which had waited on Justice Grier? Did he not recall what the committee had said on that occasion? Suddenly alert, his eyes once more blazing with the fire of youth, the old man had retorted, "Yes! And a dirtier day's work I never did in my life."

Grozier, J.F., (640f)

Guests that overstay
(384)
      I must not detain you longer lest you convey to me as broad a hint as that of the clergyman of which Justice Holmes once told me. It seems that there was a clergyman in some New England village, who always welcomed guests within his house with lavish hospitality, but, if the guest lingered too long, the clergyman, when morning prayers were held, would, in the course of the prayer, say: "O Lord, bless thy servant who is a guest within this home, and give him a safe and pleasant journey, when he leaves tomorrow, on the eleven-ten train."

Guilt
    Not guilty
        See Burton, Harold H.; Capital punishment

Gunther, Gerald, (102f), (133f), (160f), (289f), (305f), (386f), (387f), (449f), (514f), (550f), (593f), (614f), (626f), (715f)

-h-
Hagedorn, (144f), (410f)

Hall, Marshall
(385)
      My father remembered Marshall Hall and it was not his classic profile that he described to me, nor his flamboyant oratory. ("Look at her," Sir Edward once said to a jury, pointing to his trembling client in the dock, a young prostitute accused of murder, "God never gave her a chance, will you?") It was Marshall's dramatic entry into a courtroom that impressed my father. His head clerk would come in, carrying the brief and a pile of white linen handkerchiefs, then came a second clerk with the water carafe and an air cushion (lawyers and pilots, as a result of sitting for long hours, are martyrs to piles.) Sir Edward himself would then burst through the swing-doors, to be installed in his place

by flurry of solicitors and learned juniors. He would subside on to the inflated rubber circle, and listen to the case for the prosecution. If the evidence against Marshall Hall's client looked black he would, so my father assured me, slowly unfold the top handkerchief and blow a clarion call to battle. When the situation became really desperate he would remove the air-cushion and re-inflate it, a process which always commanded the Jury's undivided attention.

Hallett, Moses, (640f)

Hamburger, Philip
    See Hand, Learned

Hamilton, Walton H.
    See Approval, need for

Hand, Learned, (726a); (102f), (133f), (160f), (256f), (289f), (305f), (386f), (387f), (475f), (514f), (550f), (715f)

    Craved appointment to Supreme Court
        See United States Supreme Court, (715)

(386)
    Justice Robert Jackson once related that as a young country lawyer in upstate New York, he had been taught "to quote Learned, but cite Gus."

(387)
    Hamburger also reported that he was astonished to hear that Hand wrote out all his decisions and speeches in longhand, 'frequently after hours of intensive struggle." The judge could not bear dictating, and so he agonized over his long yellow pads with pen in hand. "For me, writing anything is like having a baby," … .

(388)
    Learned Hand once said that a good lawyer had what he called "a bathtub mind." He filled it with one case, became a master of the subject matter in that case, then pulled the plug and refilled the tub with the next case.

Handler, Milton, (180f)

Hanging
    See Bishop, Capital punishment

Harding, Warren, (340)
(389)
[President] Harding had been an admirable chief and had many fine qualities, but he could never deny a request from a friend. Hughes repeated the story that Harding himself had told in a flash of candor during an off-the-record talk to the National Press Club.

"Warren," his father had said to him, "it's a good thing you wasn't born a gal."

"Why?" Warren had asked.

"Because you'd be in the family way all the time. You can't say No."

Harlan, John M., (391); (718f)
Harlan, John Marshall, (104); (611f), (791f)
(390)
I used to say that he [Harlan] had a powerful vise the jaws of which couldn't be got nearer than two inches to each other.

(391)
It was one of John Harlan's favorite stories. A large photograph of his grandfather, the first Justice John Marshall Harlan, adorned a wall of his chambers. One day he identified the photograph to a visiting Japanese dignitary. "I did not realize, Justice Harlan," the visitor replied, respectfully, "that the post was hereditary."

Harper, Fowler V., (617f), (658f)

Harriman, Mr.
See Client, (194)

Hart, H.L.A.
See footnote, (274af)

Harvard Law School, (394f), (734a)
See also Arnold, Thurman (59), Brandeis, Louis (116), Frankfurter, Felix (312), Height
(392)
"Forty-four months in the federal penitentiary," he used to say, "was a good corrective to three years at Harvard Law School."

(393)
A complete law library is a fearsome thing. Harvard possesses the largest collection in this country. Professor Thomas Reed Powell, when asked

whether Harvard was the largest law library in the world, replied, "I am sure it must be, because it is the only library where three hundred thousand books can be lost at the same time."

(394)
[on recommending Harvard Law graduates to FDR] "It was the most natural thing in the world," said Frankfurter. "If you want to get good groceries in Washington, you go to Magruder's, or in New York to Park and Tilford, or in Boston to S.S. Pierce. If you wanted to get a lot of first-class lawyers, you went to the Harvard Law School."

(394a)
I suppose you know that Washington is full of impractical lawyers, and I must say that many of them seem to have come from Harvard. You might as well realize right now that I think the Harvard Law School is highly overrated! ... I also hope that you did not come under the influence of Frankfurter when you were in law school. ... He is dangerous to the welfare of this country.

Harvard University
    See also Stone, Harlan Fiske
(395)
On a Harvard man in Washington: "I cannot tell you how utterly refreshing it is to come from the harsh realities of Harvard to the ivy towerism of Washington."

(395a)
The status of Harvard in American elite culture at the time far exceeded any comparable university in Britain. It is summed up by a story of a late nineteenth-century president of Harvard, who asked his secretary to place a telephone call to the then US President, Teddy Roosevelt. When the President picked up the phone, the secretary said, 'I have the President for you, Mr. Roosevelt.'

(395b)
Someone said of Richard Whitney, "I have known graduates of Groton or of Harvard, or members of the New York Stock Exchange, to go to jail, but I never knew this to happen to anyone who was of Groton and Harvard and the Exchange."

Hastings, Sir Patrick
    See Cross-examination

Hay, Peter, (7f), (20f), (47f), (58f), (127f), (145f), (150f), (159f), (181f), (196f), (244f), (280f), (284f), (292f), (450f), (454f), (455f), (475f), (480f), (500f), (536f), (537f), (552f), (679f)

Hayes, Eddie, (235f)

Hays, Arthur Garfield, (186); (1f)

He isn't, I am. You did. You are.
    See Burton, Harold F.

Healy, (162f), (755f)

Health
    See Choate, Rufus

Heart transplant
(396)
    [attorney for the defendant after imposition of a fine] "Your Honor, I would just like to make one additional statement." The court gave him permission. Allan started, "Your Honor, I just want you to know that if I ever need a heart transplant," and then with a pause and a nod over towards the state's attorney, he continued, "I hope I can have the state's attorney's, because it's never been used."

Heaven
    See Satan

Height, (273), (629b)
    See also United States Supreme Court, (716)
(397)
    "The late Charles E. Wyzanski, Jr. [a Federal Judge who sat in the First Circuit] once told me a story. Felix Frankfurter had remarked to Holmes that he, Holmes, always looked so tall. Holmes had replied "That is because, Felix, you always approach me on your knees.."

(398)
    Frankfurter took considerable satisfaction in his academic triumphs over his taller, seemingly more formidable colleagues [Frankfurter was 5'5" short]. He remembered one tall handsome fellow… and a second strapping student who was a great football hero. "Those two fellows seemed to know everything," said Frankfurter, but then reported that both had flunked out at the

end of the first year. The problem, Frankfurter archly observed, was that the football player considered the classroom to be like the football field. "You take the ball and run with it," he said, "but he didn't have the ball."

Hell
>See also Satan
>"Go to hell," the student replied
>>See Warren Edward Henry

(399)

When Butler's position finally triumphed with only Holmes dissenting, the victor turned to Holmes and said with utter gravity: I am glad we have finally arrived at a just decision," "Hell," Holmes snapped, "Hell is paved with just decisions."

>Precedent and
>>See Antitrust cases

Herbert, A.P. (235f)

Herz, (475f)

Hiss, Alger, (757f)

Holmes, Fanny
(403)

I have been much bothered with coughing at night – and on her insistence that smoking was at least part of the trouble, have without admitting it to her – stopped all except the morning cigar, and to my infinite chagrin the cough seems to be stopping.

(404)

Mrs. Holmes mounted guard over the justice, making things pleasant and congenial so he could work better, and passing muster of the many people who wanted to see him. He never read the newspapers, but she did, keeping him posted on what was going on in the world.

(405)

Quite a number of Congressmen's wives had called on her, Fanny replied politely. There was a veiled note in her voice that caused the President [Theodore Roosevelt] to look up, sharply. "You found the ladies pleasant?"

"Washington," Mrs. Holmes replied blandly, "is full of famous men and the women they married when they were young."

(406)
> The stories were endless. Mary Donnellan said the Judge was very fussy about his books. One time in Washington some old volume was lost and the Judge made an uproar, cussing at his secretary and everybody that came near. All through it Mrs. Holmes hadn't said a word, just looked at him in that sharp way she had.
>
> But when the Judge came back from Court the book was in its place on the shelf. An American flag stuck out above it and underneath Mrs. Holmes had hung a sign, neatly printed: "I am a very old man. I have had many troubles, most of which never happened." Mary said the Judge laughed until he cried.

Holmes, Oliver Wendell, (727); (3f), (5f), (15f), (25f), (27f), (37f), (47f), (50f), (57f), (81f), (93f), (100f), (112f), (117f), (144f), (150f), (159f), (174f), (178f), (207f), (251f), (256f), (281f), (282f), (300f), (328f), (378f), (382f), (384f), (390f), (397f), (403f), (415f), (416f), (417f), (418f), (419f), (420f), (422f), (423f), (424f), (426f), (440f), (442f), (449f), (465f), (475f), (482f), (490f), (494f), (512f), (533f), (563f), (570f), (608f), (616f), (618f), (621f), (630f), (675f), (719f), (733f), (734f), (757f), (792f)
    Abstractions
        See Abstractions
    Advantage to law if he passed away
        See Abraham's bosom

(407)
> ...Mrs. Butler requested me to purchase one of a display of magnificent American Beauty roses in the window. ...
>
> On arriving there, she wrote on her card: "An American Beauty for an American beauty."
>
> She put the card in an envelope and directed the chauffeur to deliver it and the rose to Justice Holmes. Later during the day there came an acknowledgment from Justice Holmes in which he wrote that the world "for" should have been "from."

    Approval, need for
        See Approval, need for
    Asleep on bench
        See McReynolds, James C., (588)
    At 90
        See Age, Final examination

Automobiles
> See Automobiles

Best of all possible worlds
> See Alcoholic beverages, (37)

(408)

Mr. Justice Holmes once said, when questioned about certain details of his life: "Since 1865 there hasn't been any biographical detail."

Destroy illuminating documents
> See Biography

Block off the old chip
> See Day, William R.

Bostonians
> See Bostonians

Brevity like a caving in of the knees
> See Brevity

Briefs being briefer
> See Briefs, (131)

By the way, I concur
> See Footnotes, (306)

Candor
> See Candor as a form of deception

Cavalier attitude
> See Stone, Harlan Fiske

Champagne
> See Alcoholic beverages

Christian religion
> See Christian religion

(409)

Some thirty years ago, I purchased a first edition of the The Autocrat of the Breakfast Table, and on the fly-leaf of which there was inscribed: "Dr. William Hunt, with the grateful acknowledgment of Oliver Wendell Holmes."

This Dr. Hunt was the Philadelphia physician-surgeon who had attended the younger Holmes after he had been seriously wounded at Antietam. Tipped into the volume there is a letter from the elder Holmes dated Boston, Nov. 17th, 1875, and reading as follows:

"... My son, who with myself will always recall your kind attention with gratitude, is now married and a lawyer no doubt known to many of the profession in Philadelphia by his edition of Kent's Commentaries. I think they will tell you that he has proved himself worth the trouble you took to save him. The five bullet marks left by three balls, remain as honorable trophies but give no other token of themselves in the way of pain or inconvenience."

Wen I found this letter, I sent the volume with my compliments to Justice Holmes who had been hospitable to me in 1917-18 when I lived in Washington as a young man. He returned it to me with the letter in which he said that he preferred for me to keep it and that the question of whether he was "worth the trouble that Dr. Hunt had taken to save him was still moot."

 Classics
  See Final Examination
 Cliches
  See Achilles' heel
 Constitutional law and puking
  See Vomit
 De minimis
  See Alcoholic beverages

(410f)

The old man lived two years more, and on his deathbed thumbed his nose at the doctor.

 Depression
  See Casanova
 Dissenter, Great
  See Arlington National Cemetery
 Do not brutalize my book
  See Law books
 Education of a child
  See Child, education of
 Enthusiism
  See Enthusiasm but not enthusiism
 Facts
  See Abstractions, Facts, Questions of fact, Stone, Harlan Fiske; Taft, William Howard
 Father of my inmost
  See Chapman, John Jay

(411)

He told me that whenever there was a fire in any direction he would be glad to go to it with me even if he had to be routed out of bed. In fact it would not have surprised me had he left the Bench to witness a fire while the Court was in session.

 First Circuit and
  See Court of Appeals, (229), (229f)

French novels
> See French novels

(412)

He liked to talk with a flourish about wicked French novels – "now for some French indecency to restore the tone of my mind" he confided to Einstein – and to suggest if only he had time to indulge in capers there was nothing would please him more.

Generalities
> See Generalization

Get down, you fool
> See Civil War

God sees through all this modesty
> See Menuhin, Yehudi

God, I was not
> (378f)

Gold medal
> See Roosevelt, Franklin Delano

Good for you
> See McReynolds, James C., (591)

Gossip and philosophy
> See Gossip and philosophy

Hats
> See Brandeis, Louis

He was my father
> See Lang, Andrew

Height
> See Height

Hell is paved with just decisions
> See Butler, Pierce

Humbug
> See Contract, Humbug

I am a very old man
> See Holmes, Fanny

(413)

When Chief Justice Taft was sick for a few weeks, Holmes had to act as Chief, and take over the detail administration of the Court, which he thoroughly disliked. Mr. Charles Elmore Cropley, the clerk of the Court, bringing some orders for him to sign at his house at 1720 I Street, waited for an hour before the Justice came down to his library. "Your eminence," he said to the young man, "I am not an early bird – and besides, I don't give a damn for worms."

(414)
During the first term of Chief Justice White this tendency appeared to be checked. Teeth were put into the Sherman Act by the decisions dissolving the oil and tobacco trusts. In the second of these cases a lawyer, hopeful of demonstrating the minuteness of foreign competition, asserted before the Court that 'nobody but dudes and fools smoke foreign cigarettes." Mr. Justice Holmes interrupted gently from the bench. "Are you sure?" he inquired. "I have smoked them, and I am sure I am not a dude."

>I didn't read that far in the record
>>See Taft, William Howard
>I shall never love another country
>>See Civil War
>I write for that man
>>See Afflatus

(415)
However, this last year has brought in my share of superlatives. If I were naïve I should be intolerable.

>I'll put it in a letter to a friend
>>See Opinions, (617)
>I'm not Lord God Almighty
>>See God and Court, (336)
>Innuendo
>>See Innuendo

(416)
Reporters have been about seeking interviews which I have declined, but I yielded to the request for a chance to take a snapshot this morning from a young fellow who was punctual for the five minutes plus that I allowed him, did his job, and cleared out. I was glad afterwards for he told my driver that this was his first chance for some newspaper and that he felt that it had started him on his career. Poor little devil, had I known that, I would have been more considerate.

>Jobbists
>>See Jobbists, (449f)

(417)
If one can keep the pace, do one's job in the superlative degree, and keep out of the Insolvency, Divorce, and Criminal Courts until one retires on a pension I call it a success.

80

    Justice, to do
        See Justice
        Favor not justice
            See Labor leaders
    Labor leader
        See Labor leaders
    Lavatory facilities
        See Cardozo, Benjamin
    Law reviews
        See Law reviews, (533)
    Letter writing during oral argument
        See Oral argument, (620)
    Limitations on being a Justice
        See Alcoholic beverages (26), Fuller, Melville Weston, (326)
    Lucid and persuasive
        See Fuller, Melville Westin (326); Stone, Harlan Fiske, (688)
    Man of low tastes
        See Burlesque houses
    Metaphysical Club, (57f)
    Mrs. Beck likes Shakespeare
        See Beck, James M.
    Newspapers
        See Abolition, Holmes, Fanny
    Ninety-two has outlived duty, (420)
    Nothing you have said leads me to hope
        See Oral argument, (625)
    One club to which we all belong
        See United States Government

(418)
    Holmes used to tell his secretaries that the only "prime" authority was found first in his opinions in the Supreme Court of the United States; second, in his opinions on the Massachusetts Court; and, of much less importance, in the opinions of his brethren on the United States Court.

    Oral argument
        See Oral argument, (621)
    Panaceas and sudden ruin
        See Panaceas and sudden ruin
    Plato, (281f), (300)
    Plums
        See Opinions, (618)
    Poor man, poor man

> See Pitney, Mrs. Malcolm
Population and
> See Malthus
Prize fights
> See Roosevelt, Franklin Delano
Public matters
> See Abolition
Qualities of defects
> See Defects of his qualities
Right to die or resign
> See Death and dying, Law clerks, (512)
Robe, buying new
> See Retirement
Secret of the universe
> See Abolition
Skepticism, (512f)

(419)
When I was his secretary in Washington in 1911, he had to attend the obsequies of a Massachusetts dignitary for whom he had no particular esteem, and with a play of seriousness asked me whether I thought it all right if he wore his second-best overcoat to the funeral of a second-rate man.

(420)
After breakfast the Judge announced he was going to loaf all day. "Ninety-two has outlived duty," he said with what seemed a vast satisfaction. Half an hour later he was calling for secretary to read to him. "Let's have a little self- improvement, Sonny."

> Self-made men
> > See Self-made man

(421)
Lodge had once suggested to [Holmes] that he run for governor of Massachusetts, and when Holmes asked "Why?" Lodge had answered, "Because from there you could go directly to the United States Senate." "But I wouldn't give a damn to be a Senator," Holmes responded.

> Shall and will
> > See Shall and will
> Smoking
> > See Holmes, Fanny

Socialized property
: See Humbug

Soldierly figure
: See Civil War

Spat with Butler
: See Hell

Sterile skepticism
: See Adams, Henry

Stone and Holmes
: See Bawdy tinge

Success and early poverty
: See Poor

Symbols, we live by
: See Symbols

Taxes
: See Civilization

That won't wash
: See Fuller, Melville Weston

Three generations of imbeciles
: See Butler, Pierce, (150f)

Truth by the scruff of the neck
: See Yale Law School

(422)

[Attributed to Brandeis and Holmes] "a man could do twelve months' work in 11 months but couldn't do twelve months work in twelve months."

Undeserved reputation for attention and industry
: See Oral argument, (620)

Upward and onwarders
: See Laski, Harold

Voice was refined and clear
: See Fuller, Melville Weston

Vulgar herd
: See Vulgar herd

What we can do for our country
: See Kennedy, John F.

(423)

Justice Holmes had no heirs when he died on March 6, 1935, at the age of 93. He willed his estate, then amounting to something more than $300,000, to the nation.

(424)
Mr. Justice Holmes (age about 90) was walking through the park with Mr. Justice Brandeis (age about 85). They passed a rather nice-looking woman.

Holmes: "Brandeis, wouldn't it be wonderful just to be 75 again?"

(425)
See also (122)

Justice Holmes, at one time, was desirous of having a writ drawn to release a person incarcerated in an insane asylum. The asylum was in Vermont and Holmes wanted the writ granted in Massachusetts. When a timorous clerk suggested that a jurisdictional problem presented itself, Holmes scowled and said, "There are only eight people that can tell me I cannot do it, five of them must be in agreement at the same time, and you are not one of them."

(426)
One day when Holmes was eighty-seven a newspaperman, seeking copy, decided to walk round Capitol Square and ask passers-by if they had heard of Justice Holmes.

A mechanic in overalls was sitting on a bench reading the sports page. The reporter strolled up. "Holmes!" the mechanic said. "Oh, sire! He's the young judge on the Supreme Court that's always disagreeing with the old guys."

Zest for learning
    See Final Examination

Honesty
    See Judges, (461)

Honorable Court, God save
    See God and Court

Hoover, Herbert
    See Taft, William Howard

Hoover, J. Edgar
    See Attorney General

Horse Cause
(430)
Upon a trial of a Horse Cause before Lord Mansfield, a Witness was examined, who stated that the Horse was returned to his Master after the

Gentleman, who had bought it, had kept it nearly three Months – and, what said Lord Mansfield, was your Master willing at the End of three Months to take it back again – how could he be such a Fool? Who advised him to do that? My Lord, said the Witness, I advised him to take the Horse again – How could you be such a Fool, said the Chief Justice –What was your Reason for giving that Advice? Please you, my Lord, said the Witness, I told my Master, What all the World knows, that Your Lordship was always against a Horse dealer, right or wrong, and therefore he had better take it back.

House of Truth
    See Alcoholic beverages, (35)

Hovey, Richard B., (175f)

Howe & Hummel, (13f), (471f)

Howe, Mark DeWolfe, (3f), (5f), (25f), (81f), (112f), (256f), (282f), (390f), (403f), (494f), (563f), (608f), (630f), (733f), (792f)

Hoyt, Solicitor General
    See Oral argument, (628)

Hughes, Charles Evans, (137f), (159f), (183f), (220f), (383f), (389f), (431f), (432f), (434f), (435f), (436f), (437f), (438f), (588f), (622f), (683f)
    Court all Hughes now
        See United States Supreme Court, (713)

(431)
When an attorney argued a tax case which turned on whether a jig-saw picture was a game or a puzzle, Hughes asked with a twinkle in his eye, "Would the Court in that case be a game?"
    "No, your Honor, " the attorney drawled. "The court is a puzzle."

(432)
    As he took Mrs. Hughes for a walk in the sunshine, an old friend crossed the street to wish him
many happy returns. Hughes replied, with a good-natured smile, that he had similarly greeted [Elihu] Root on his eightieth birthday, and Root had expressed precisely what he (Hughes) now felt: "I'm as good as I ever was one hour a day."

(433)
With Hughes retirement, for the first time in history no member of the Supreme Court had a beard or mustache. "But," said Hughes, "Justice Frank Murphy's huge eyebrows take up the slack." ... It was to the barber, who brushed the Chief Justice's beard every morning, that Hughes first told the news of his impending retirement. Later that day, when the court session was over, he told his colleagues he was leaving. "I can go on for a few more years yet," said Hughes, "but I have a fear of continuing under the delusion of adequacy."

(434)
May we ask you to mail soon a shirt from your wardrobe to the Auction Editor, the Des Moines News, accompanying the same with an identification mark, and if possible, a short biography of the garment, as to what important events it has shared in your life?
Whatever your decision, please do not make this letter public.
Hughes framed the letter, and it became a prized possession...

(435)
One afternoon as [Hughes] was relaxing on the promenade deck a rather breezy young woman came up to him.
"Mr. Hughes," she said, "I don't know how we should address you. My father used to speak of you as "Governor Hughes." Afterwards I heard people saying "Justice Hughes.' Now here on the boat I hear them say 'Mr. Secretary.' I don't know how you should be addressed."
A quizzical expression Hughes' face gave way to a bland smile.
"Those who love me," he said, "call me Charlie!"

(436)
[Governor Charles Evans Hughes] was accosted by a friend who told him that he wanted to become Commissioner of Insurance. The Governor pointed out that he had no experience in the field and that if he received the appointment people would know that he got merely on the ground of friendship. "Well," he said, "Governor, do you mean that you refuse to appoint me to this job because I am a friend of yours?" Governor Hughes replied, "Yes, Jim, that is right.:" He looked the Governor straight in the eye and said, "From now on, Governor, that shouldn't bother you one damn bit."

(437)
At one of the gatherings of the State Department club, composed of officers and personnel of the department, he gaily announced that he and Undersecretary Phillips were prepared "to dine for our country."

(438)
        Frankfurter on C.E. Hughes: He did not exert authority, he radiated it.

Hughes, Howard
        See Estate taxes

Hugo, Victor
        See Law, (497)

Hull, George C., (781f)

Human Race Luncheon Club, (57f)

Humbug
See also (222)
(440)
        The notion that with socialized property we should have women free and a piano for everybody seems to me an empty humbug.

Humor
        Lack of sense of:
(441)
        Under a brusque exterior, which totally ignored the small graces of life, he was at heart as kindly a gentleman as ever breathed. His brusqueness was not due to disregard of other people's feelings, but to a pervading and controlling intellectual sincerity which saw no reason why the plain truth should not be even bluntly spoken at all times.
        Perhaps it was due partly to one deficiency in the make-up of so accomplished a lawyer – he had small sense of humor. His mind was of a serious and earnest cast. He had no patience with folly of any kind and he was apt to look at any attempt at fun in the business of life as inexcusable frivolity. The late Charles E. Lex, an excellent lawyer with an irrepressible humor ... used to say that when he had a leisure quarter of an hour he knew no more entertaining way of spending it than to tell McMurtrie a joke, and have him analyze it and show him logically that there was no fun in it.

Hunt Club
        See Arnold, Thurman

Hurst, James W., (336f), (337f)

Huston, (423f)

Hutchins, Robert Maynard
    See McReynolds, James C., (590)

Hutchinson, Dennis J., (530f), (685f), (722f), (743f), (744f)

Hyde, (494f)

Hypotheticals
    See McReynolds, James C. (591), Warren, Edward Henry

-i-

Impeachment, (274f)

Impotency
    See Law (499)

Income tax
    See Civilization

Indigent
    See Jesus Christ is my advocate

Infallible, See (446f)

Innuendo
(442)
    While Judge on the [Massachusetts] Supreme Judicial Court, he [Judge Oliver Wendell Holmes] found a long-winded lawyer especially trying. He advised him gravely to take a course of reading risque books, that he might learn to say things by innuendo.

Inscrutable workings of Providence
    See Judges, (450)

Insurance
    God-fearing limited liability company:
(443)
    Of course, sometimes counsel are driven to measures of what I can only call slight desperation. There was one somewhat pompous counsel who thought that he could do good with a High Court Judge who was a High Church

man, and he began his submission as follows: 'My Lord, in this case I appear for the plaintiff – a God-fearing limited liability company.'

Intellect
(444)
      He has what Justice Holmes describes as a 'three-story intellect with a skylight, ..."

Intellectual arrogance
    See Closing argument

Ivory tower
    See Harvard University, (395)

-j-
Jackson, Andrew
    See Marshall, John

Jackson, Robert H., (386), (446f), (451f), (586f), (624f)
(446)
      Some years ago during the oral argument in the case of Southern Pacific RR v. Arizona, as the time for luncheon approached, counsel for the State of Arizona looked first at the clock in the front of the courtroom and then at the clock on the rear wall. "Your Honors, " he said, "I don't know whether the time has come to suspend or not. These clocks don't seem to be in agreement." Quick as a flash, Justice Jackson interjected from the bench: "That's the influence of the Court!"

Jail, (395b)
    See Arnold, Thurman (59), Pitney, Mrs. Mahlon

Jefferson, Thomas, (397f)

Jesus Christ is my advocate
(448)
      You know, we have had lots of conversation about the indigent prisoner, and many before the court that should be represented by counsel, and this indigent appeared before the court, and the clerk had told him that he needed a lawyer and should have one, and he told the clerk that it was none of his blankety-blank business, he didn't need a lawyer. So when he got before the court he announced, "The Clerk has told me that I need a lawyer, Jesus Christ is my advocate." And the Judge smiled, leaned down from the bench and said,

"I understand, Sir, but don't you think it would be a good idea to have local counsel?"

Jig-saw picture
See Hughes, Charles Evans, (431)

Jobbists, (449f)
(449)
And if at the end some friendly critic shall pass by and say: "My friend, how good a job do you really think you have made of it all?" we can answer: "I know as well as you that it is not of high quality; but I did put into it whatever I had, and that was the game I started out to play."

Johnson, John G.
See United States Supreme Court, (720)

Johnson, Lyndon B., (627f)

Joyce, James
Ulysses trial, reading of passages
See Obscenity

Judges, (87f)
See also Trial judge
(450)
More F.E. Smith: "What do you think I am on the bench for, Mr. Smith?"

"It is not for me," replied the barrister gravely, " to attempt to fathom the inscrutable workings of
Providence."

Asking too many questions
See Objections, (611)
Appointment of Federal District judge
See Truman, Harry
Better informed, (451f)

More it will grow on you:
(451)
Mr. Smith, I have read your pleadings, and I do not think much of your case.

I am sorry to hear that, my lord (Smith replied). But your lordship will find that the more you hear of it the more it will grow on you

    Bias of
        See Horse cause
    Bishop and judge
        Relative importance of
            See Bishop
    Case is altered
        See Case
    Charge to jury
        See Judges, (452)

(452)
    The Judge charged learnedly and long, in an accident case, on negligence and contributory negligence, proximate cause and the last clear chance, and as the jurors were being led out, one of them said to the bailiff: "What do we do now?"

    The bailiff replied: "The Judge wants you to find out who was at fault for the accident."

    "Oh," he said, "is that it? Why didn't he say so?"

    Confine your argument to the points in this case
        See Points of law

(453)
    The judge who dreamed he was trying a case, awoke, and found he was. This violates the rule that justice must not only be done, but must be seen as well.

    Erroneous impressions by
        See Lawyers, (546)

    Fellow who knew the governor:

(454)
    It was [Robert] Kenny who once defined a judge as "just a fellow who knew the governor."

    Hanging as opposed to damning
        See Bishop
    Harassing attorneys
        I think I know now
            See Lawyers, (544)
    Ill-tuned cymbal

See Smith, F.E.
Intelligence, (455f)
Intervening in cross-examination
    See Cross-examination, (242)
It was a very long time ago
    See Brevity, (124)

Elementary law, judges and:

(455)

A traditional story of Marshal Wright's was that when Jeremiah – otherwise 'Jerry Wilson began an elaborate opening by citing many of the fundamental authorities, he was interrupted by an Associate Justice who said that Mr. Wilson ought to take it for granted that the Court knew some elementary law. To this 'Jerry" Wilson replied: "Your Honors, that was the mistake I made in the Court below."

(456)

... The story of the English Judge who always decided his cases from the Bench, never reserved decision, and never wrote any opinions, and so this day just as the case ended he dictated his judgment right into the record and walked of the Bench, and as he got into the robing room he turned to his clerk, slapped his thigh, and said, "My God, I've done it again. I said plaintiff when I should have said defendant.

(457)

A young barrister was belaboring an obscure point of the law before a judge known as Lord Justice Montgomery, who was an irascible old character, and another much older barrister sitting in the bar enclosure wrote a note and sent it up to the young lawyer who was arguing. In the note it said, "Sit down. The old bastard is with you." Lord Justice Montgomery said, "Young man, I notice that your brother handed you a note. May I see it?" The young man was terribly embarrassed, and he said, "I am sorry, Your Honor, but this is a confidential matter between my brother and I." The Judge said, "I am sorry, too, but this happened in my court room Hand me the note.: So he handed up the note. The Judge glared at the young man and said, "Young man, have you read this message?" He said, "Yes, sir." The Judge said, "Then read it again."

(458)

"It is upon their seats, like most people who follow a sedentary occupation, that judges shine most." [Sir Gerald Dodson, Old Bailey Criminal Court]

One wall of courtroom to the other
    See Noonan, Gregory
Political ambitions and:

(459)

[on judges entertaining political ambitions] "When a priest enters a monastery, he must leave – or ought to leave – all sorts of worldly desires behind him. And this [Supreme] Court has no excuse for being unless it's a monastery. And this isn't idle, high-flown talk. We are all poor human creatures and it's difficult enough to be wholly intellectually and morally disinterested when one has no other motive except that of being a judge according to one's full conscience."

Presenting an argument and not hear a damn word:

(460)

A Judge is a man who can look a lawyer, who is presenting an argument, squarely in the eye for an hour or two, and not hear a damn word.

Rather be a judge or lawyer
    See Marshall, Thurgood
Selection of, (707f)
Seven ordinary men
    See Young lawyer, (787)
Show me the judge and I'll tell you the law
    See Points of law
Sit tight
    See Alcoholic beverages, (29)

Some knowledge of the law:

(461)

First, a good judge must be honest. Second he must possess a reasonable amount of industry. Third, he must be a gentleman. If the judge has some knowledge of law it will help.

That is not the law
    It was until your Honor spoke:

(462)

A still older story told about the Court and pinned on some particular attorney, on some particular occasion, before some particular Justice, is that when counsel stated a conclusion of law, one of the Justices said:
    "That is not the law."
    "It was until your Honor spoke," Counsel replied

Three solemn, elderly gentlemen and Ulysses trial
> See Obscenity

Three stages a judge goes through
> Convinced that he is right:

(463)

There is a saying that every judge goes through three stages during his career on the bench. During the first five years after his appointment, he delivers every judgment, every opinion, with a lurking suspicion in the back of his mind that he is wrong. During the next five years, he delivers each opinion absolutely convinced that he is right. Thereafter he delivers his opinions with a growing indifference as to whether he is right or wrong. And when the indifference becomes habitual, he should retire.

> Growing indifference (see 463 above)
> Lurking suspicion he is wrong (see 463 above)

Trial judge
> Little bit of a bastard
>> See Trial judge

Upright judge, (464f)

(464)

When a disappointed litigant threw a book at his [C.J.Rrichardson] head as he was bending low over his desk, he straightened himself and said: "Now, had I been an upright judge, I should have had it."

> Worldly desires left behind on appointment
>> Judges, (459)
> You never can tell what a judge may rule
>> See Points of law

(465)

The position of a judge has been likened to that of an oyster anchored in one place, unable to take the initiative, unable to go out after things, restricted to working on and digesting what the fortuitous eddies and currents of litigation may come his way.

> Egad, it is I that was the d___d fool:

(466)

(I.J.B. Atlay's Victorial Chancellor) (listening to oral argument) (to himself) "What a d___d fool the man is!" then after an interval, "Eh, not such a d___d fool as I thought," then another interval, "Egad, it is I that was the d___d fool!"

(467)
During the 1894 [New York] Constitutional Convention, one delegate proposed limiting the term [of New York Judges] to 10 years. He said: Mr. Chairman, years ago, when I practiced law, I made up my mind that 14 years was too long for any man to sit as a [Supreme Court] Judge. There is a natural stupidity that grows upon a man who sits upon the bench for so long a time.

(467a)
[I]t is appropriate and heartening that this school chooses to honor a judge at the height of his powers ... the custom that such a distinction should await extinction is surely honored in the breach. In England, until recently, it was a tradition that living authors were not to be cited as authority in judicial opinions. On one occasion, the Lord Chief Justice, despite the tradition, could not refrain from citing Professor Holdsworth but when he did so he was careful to refer to Professor Holdsworth as one "who is happily not an authority." The reporter of the decision, in puzzling over this passage, concluded that it must have been a slip of the pen, so when it was published it read, "Professor Holdsworth who is unhappily not an authority."

Jurisdiction, (425)
See Alcoholic beverages (30), Fair trial

(467b)
"Does a man [sic] become any different when he puts on a gown?" the late Justice Felix Frankfurter was often asked, and he like to reply, "If he's any good, he does."

(467c)
Judge Botein, on being late to his session, was considering apologizing to the jurors and counsel when his clerk said, "Judge, I hope you won't think I'm speaking out of turn. But when you've been here as long as I have, you'll know that no matter what time the judge enters the courtroom, it's ten o'clock."

Jury
(468)
Judge Haskell threw it out on the ground that in my opening I had made remarks calculated to prejudice the jury. I was too crushed to make the retort with which years later, in a similar situation, Clarence Darrow confounded a hectoring judge: 'What do you think I'm here for? It's my business as a lawyer to prejudice the jury.'

(470)
I am sure that all of you trial men have at one time or another discussed your jury panel with your clients, and I am reminded of the time sent one out to one of the gentleman defendants and I said, "Let me know if you have any objection, if there are any of them that you know we will have trouble with and I want that information in advance. And the trial date was coming on, and I didn't hear from him, and finally I got the list back. It was pretty shop-worn and showed it had considerable use, and it was written at the bottom: "I have seen them all but two and they are all for us but these two."

Definition
    See Definitions
Ordered back into the jury room
    See Capital punishment
Pass around the hat
    See Donahue, Frank J.

Selection of:
(471)
Darrow evolved a formula for jury picking that has served succeeding generations of lawyers. "Never take a German, they are bull-headed. Rarely take a Swede, they are stubborn. Always take an Irishman or a Jew; they are the easiest to move to emotional sympathy. Old men are generally more charitable and kindly disposed than young men, they have seen more of the world and understand it."

Submit the case without argument
    See Young Lawyer, (793)
(472)
You ask me, my sons, were I in your place,
Would I ask for a jury to try my first case?
I don't know what facts or what law are involved
But your problem, my lad, can be easily solved. ...
Be certain of heaven, be sure of hell's fury,
But never, son, never, be sure of a jury.
Most rules have exceptions – this one's always true,
You never can tell what a Jury will do.

Just decisions
    Hell is paved with
        See Butler, Pierce

Justice, (475f)
>See Holmes, Oliver Wendell and other topics

(475)
A judge of the Federal bench tells of driving with Justice Holmes to the Capitol one morning some years ago, in that neat brougham drawn by a fat cob, with a highly respectable coloured coachman on the box, in which Holmes used to be recognized on the Washington streets. The Justice had got out of the carriage and was striding off, vigorous and loose-limbed, toward the dome when the younger man called out humorously: "Do Justice, Sir!" Holmes wheeled: "Come here, young feller!" and then, "I am not here to do justice. I am here to play the game according to the rules."

>Trial court vs. appellate court
>>See Appellate court
>Justice has prevailed – appeal at once
>>See Appeal at once
>Old West justice
>>See Capital punishment

(476)
... the tradition established by a succession of admirable Solicitors General but best expressed by Frederick W. Lehmann of St. Louis who wrote in a government brief, "The United States wins its point whenever justice is done its citizens in the courts."

Justice, Department of, (80f)
>See Attorney General

-k-
Karslake, Sir John
>See Tact

Kaufman, Irving R., (397f), (588f)
(480)
Frankfurter particularly resented Kaufman's manner in sentencing the two atomic spies to death.
"I despise a judge who feels God told him to impose a death sentence," Frankfurter wrote to Judge Learned Hand, and he added his intention to block Kaufman's advancement to the Supreme Court by extreme measures if necessary. "I am mean enough to try to stay here long enough so that Kaufman will be too old to succeed me."

Kemp, QC
> See Litigation

Kenealy, Edward Vaughan, (466f)

Kennedy, John F.
(482)
> In the article on ghostwriters in the government, "Vast Ghostland of Wasington," (April 26) by Don Oberdorfer, you allow John K. Galbraith credit for a quotation uttered by the late President John Kennedy in his inaugural address, "Let us never negotiate out of fear; but let us never fear to negotiate."
> It is alo interesting to note how President Kennedy's (or his ghostwriter's) now immortal quotation, "Ask not what your country can do for you ... ask what you can do for your country," is merely a rephrasing of the renowned Justice Oliver W. Holmes statement, "We pause to become conscious of national life, to recall what our country has done for each of us, and to ask ourselves what we can do for our country in return," spoken at Keene, N.H. on May 30, 1884.

Kenison, C.J., (69f)

Kenny, Robert
> See Judges, (454))

Kens, Paul, 383f

Kershway, George V.
> See Columbia Law School

Keynes, John Maynard, (550f)

King, Willard L., (147f), (178f), (325f), (326f), (421f)

Kirstein, Lincoln
> See Brandeis, Louis

Kissing,
> See Solicitor General

Klem, Bill
> See Baseball

Knapp, Whitman
> Brevity is the soul of Whit:

(484)

Whitman "Whit" Knapp, a partner in the firm of Barrett Knapp Smith & Shapiro delivered the shortest argument ever delivered before the United States Supreme Court. A wag commented that "Brevity is the soul of Whit." Knapp worked in the D.A.'s office under Tom Dewey and Frank Hogan.

Knox, Philander
(485)

A more typical reaction at the time was that of Attorney General Philander Knox, who Roosevelt asked to defend the U.S. role [in creation of the Panama Canal]. "Oh, Mr. President," Knox reportedly replied, "Do not let so great an achievement suffer from any taint of legality."

Kohn, Harold
> See Young lawyer (788)

Kornstein, Daniel J., (451f), (579f)

Kramnick, Isaac, (312f), (496f)

Krislov, Samuel, (50f)

Krock, Arthur, (250f)

Kurland, Philip B., (118f), (314f), (720f)

-l-
Labor leaders
(490)

Long afterwards, at a dinner at the White House for some labor leaders, I said to one of them who had been spouting about the judges: What you want is favor not justice; but when I am on my job I don't care a damn what you want or what Roosevelt wants, and then repeated my remarks to him. You may think that a trifle crude, but I didn't like to say it behind his back and not to his face, and the fact had justified it I thought and think.

Ladd, Mason, (517f), (537f)

Ladies' Day
> See Women

Lady Chatterley's Lover
> See Obscenity

Lamb, Charles
> See Lawyers, (542)

(491)
> Just called to the bar [Crabb Robinson], he told Charles Lamb exultantly that he was retained in a cause in the King's Bench, to which Lamb remarked: Ah, the first great cause, least understood.

Lamb, Edward, (522f)

Lambert, Tom, (92af), (246f), (438f), (467af), (514f), (518f), (534af), (539af), (539cf), (549af), (629af), (629bf), (629cf), (657af), (657bf), (680f), (726f), (726af), (727), (782f)

Lang, Andrew
(494)
> On another occasion he himself subjected to a similar ordeal a talker far more vain of his prowess than Holmes. This was Andrew Lang, and it must be admitted that Lang deserved the treatment. He had been asked to meet Holmes, and on coming into the room went up to Holmes, looked him over with ineffable insolence, and said: "So you are the son of the celebrated Oliver Wendell Holmes." "No," replied Holmes promptly, "he was my father."

Langdell, Christopher Columbus
> See Ames, James Barr; Law classroom

Langrock, (396f), (707f)

Laski, Harold, (282f), (312f), (424f), (496f), (563f), (608f)
(495)
> In June, 1922, Holmes wrote to Harold Laski who had suggested some books for reading: "You mention for Beverly Farms, good God! Webb on this and that – and Clothing Workers of Chicago. My boy I mean to enjoy myself if I can – to get the unexpurgated Pepys – even read (going on) John Dewey's last in a philosophical way or Pound on Law but if you think that I am going to bother myself again before I die about social improvement, or read any of those stinking upward and onwarders – you err. I mean to have some good out of being old ... I mean to go my own way, read what gives me pleasure, and leave the 'undone vast' for others." His writing was hard to decipher, and he

added: "Those two words from Browning look a little like 'undone vest' ... to be buttoned up by others. ..."

(496)
    An episode in Laski's relationship with [Harlan Fiske] Stone reveals the danger of Laski's unfortunate capacity to alter the record of events. Laski told him that Holmes's letters to him included numerous flattering comments about Stone. Stone pestered Laski for examples and finally, in January 1938, Laski sent him a collection of 'extracts,' Stone was thrilled: 'I do not know when I have been so touched.' he wrote back to Laski. But when the Holmes-Laski correspondence was published after Stone and Laski were dead, not a single one of the excerpts appeared in the book. Laski, it turned out, had manufactured a string of compliments for Stone's satisfaction.

Lavatory, (159f)
    See also Cardozo, Benjamin

Lavery, Emmet, (109f), (455f)

Law
    See also God and Courts, Points of law
    Facts and
        See also Facts
    It was the law until your Honor spoke
        See Judges, (462)
    Knowledge of
        See Judges, (461)
    Law is an ass, (759f)

    Machine that cannot move without crushing someone:
(497)
    The law, as Victor Hugo observed, is a machine that cannot move without crushing someone.

(498)
    In law there is nothing certain but the expense.

    Peculiarities and inequities of the law:
(499)
    I am reminded of a young lawyer who graduated from Duke not many years ago. He went out and set up a practice for himself, hung out his own shingle, which not many lawyers do anymore, incidentally. He opened his office

next to an older lawyer so he could get some help, which was understandable. He got his first case and he went to the older lawyer and said, "What do you think of my case?"

The older lawyer listened to the facts and said, "Well, it sounds pretty good, but because of the peculiarities and inequities of the law you might lose this case."

The young lawyer went on back to his own office. He won that case. Later he went to the older lawyer with another case which he thought was open and shut. He thought he had a case that he couldn't lose. But again the older lawyers said, "Because of the peculiarities and inequities of the law you might lose."

The young lawyer said, "Why do you always tell me about the 'peculiarities and inequities of the law'?"

The older lawyers said, "Well, fifteen years ago I was right at the top of the profession. I had plenty of clients, they were paying good fees. I had a wonderful family. I had a beautiful blonde secretary who could take shorthand, and all of a sudden the whole thing crumbled around my ears. My wife brought a suit for divorce on the grounds that I was impotent. My secretary brought a paternity action claiming I was the father of her child. And because of the peculiarities and inequities of the law I lost both cases."

>Taint of legality, suffer from
>See Knox, Philander

Law books
(500)
When John Curran was pleading a case before Lord Clare, the latter exclaimed at one of Curran's legal explanations, "Oh, if that be law, Mr. Curran, I may burn my law books!" Better read them, my lord," was Curran's celebrated retort.

>Do not brutalize my book:

(501)
Once I had taken a book from the shelves, and to read it better, flattened it out on my desk. He happened to see. "Young man," he said, "do not brutalize my book." I have never forgotten that admonition.

>Lawyer: These are for the judge:

(502)
A lawyer walked down the street recently with his arms filled with a lot of books. A friend meeting him remarked, pointing to the books, "Why, I thought you carried all that stuff in your head."

"I do," quickly replied the lawyer, with a knowing wink; "these are for the judge."

 Misplaced
  See Holmes, Fanny
 Reading the law
  See Young lawyer, (790)
 Thrown at judge
  See Judges, (464)

 Writing in U.S. Reports:
(503)
 " Did you write in this volume?" asked a furious Douglas, his voice quivering with anger as he held up a United States Reports volume containing Supreme Court opinions.
 "No sir," responded the concerned young clerk.
"I'm relieved to hear that," said the still angry Justice. "Books are treasures. They are temples of the intellect. They must be cherished and protected. I couldn't imagine that you were the sort of person who would write in a book."

Law classroom, (180f) See also Warren, Edward Henry
(505)
 It was an unusually hot spring day in the large contracts class of a familiar law school. The mysteries of accord and satisfaction were being pried from an apparently drowsy and none to responsive young man. The professor, trying to make his point by drawing out a comparison of two cases was becoming more and more nettled at his failure to elicit the desired answers from his prey. Finally his patience snapped and he shouted: "Young man, you are wasting your time and someone else's money in law school. You will never make a lawyer. You might as well get out right now."
 The culprit mumbled something in response that was only audible to his fellow students close around him.
 "What did that young man say?" shouted the professor to the young man sitting on the student's left. No answer.
 "What did he say?" shouted the professor again, this time to the student sitting on the young man's right. The response was prompt this time: "He said he didn't give a damn what you thought."
 An electric shock went through the room as the professor paused and stared at the ceiling in the sudden hush. Then he said, "I take it back. He will too make a lawyer."

 Appalled at how little I know:

(506)
A teacher at an Introductory Law course addressed his class at the last session of the first semester. He looked over what had been only three months before a group of highly confused but self-assured students, smug in the assurance of their being accepted at a prestigious law school. "Ladies and gentlemen," he intoned, "three months ago, when this course began you students were appalled at how little you knew about the law. Now, you are appalled at how little I know about it." The laughter that followed hurt the way labor pains give way to birth.

Some damn fool latched the door:
(507)
The story is told that Professor Buck Bailey of Texas Law School was a stickler on time. All the students respected his idiosyncrasy but one, a Texas ranger type who persisted in being an even ten minutes late. On one memorable occasion Professor Bailey locked the door to his classroom as the hour struck. Ten minutes later there was an attempt to open the door, then a frantic turning of the door knob, then a thud that indicated an unsuccessful attempt to storm the classroom. Then quiet. Throughout all this, old Bailey lectured with a twinkle in his eye and continued to do so until he heard a scraping at the window, three stories above ground. Then he saw the window rise, then came one foot over the ledge, then the other, and finally there was old Tex sitting on the ledge staring eyeball to eyeball at a grimacing Buck Bailey. "Is this any way to enter a classroom?" Bailey shouted. "No," said Tex, matter-of-factly, "but some damn fool latched the door."

If you want to know what the law is:
(508)
… Professor Warren seldom closed a class without giving a definite answer to any pending problem. One day a student, troubled by a particularly knotty problem in a moot court case, applied to Professor Warren for assistance. Standing before the master, the student stated the issue and awaited the answer. The professor, leaning back in his chair, eyed the student quizzically and replied, "Well, if you want to know what the law was, see Dean Pound. If you want to know what the law ought to be see Professor Beale. But if you want to know what the law is, young man, sit down."

… it was said that the first question [in his course on Legal Liability] could be answered by any student in the class, the second only by the best students, the third only by members of the faculty, the fourth only by God and Joey [Joseph A.] Beale, and the fifth only by Joey Beale.. [Editor's note: This is probably an adaption of: "If you wanted to know what the law used to be, ask Langdell; if you want to know what it is going to be, ask Beale, if you want to know what it ought to be, ask Ames; but if you want to know what the law is, ask Gray."]

    One long bier:
(509)
    The class of 1915 at the Law School ... was attending the hour devoted to the study of Real Property, with Professor Pease in the chair. ... It was a large class.
    The sun was shining through the window, leaving student Shaw in a shadow. He was fast asleep and the professor did not notice the somnolent fact.
    "Mr. Shaw!" rang out the professorial voice intending he should take up the discussion
    Mr. Shaw awoke, and before he gathered where he was, said: "One short beer!"
    "It will be one long bier, Mr. Shaw, if you don't stay awake!" said Professor Pease.

Law clerks, (26), (36), (50), (185), (309), (419), (420), (425), (503), (523), (530)
(512)
    During his years as Byrne professor of law at Harvard, Frankfurter selected from the graduating class each year an outstanding member to serve as law clerk to Holmes.
    Upon learning of the selection, Holmes invariably replied to Mr. Frankfurter the same way: "So and so sounds all right to me. Please tell him to report to my office on such and such a day at 10:00 a.m., and tell him to be here not a minute before or a minute after that time."
    When he reached 75, Holmes started adding this sentence to his annual letter to Professor Frankfurter: "Please tell the lad that I reserve the right to die or resign."

    Black appointee
        See Coleman, William
    Editing judge's opinion
        See Frank, Jerome
    Questioning style of Justice Holmes
        See Afflatus

    Terrorizing by Douglas:
(513)
    Groups of his law clerks were asked to stand in an around-the-clock

vigil next to the [Douglas's] coffin, much like a military honor guard. "This often amused me," recalled former secretary Fay Aull Deusterman. "I often wondered after all the hell he had put them through what the law clerks talked about at three in the morning when nobody was there." Perhaps, she decided they considered opening up the coffin and peering inside just to make sure that Douglas was not being buried along with his buzzer.

(514)
[Judge Hand] asked them [his law clerks] to criticize his drafts mercilessly as his written opinions evolved, relishing and attending to their critical comments with extraordinary open-mindedness and forming a near collegial relationship with what he called his "puny" judges – a takeoff on "puisne" judges ("inferior" judges).

(515)
[callow youth of law school going to clerk in the U.S. Supreme Court] Of low vision and high visibility transformed into young men of low visibility and high vision, as they learn to work their way gradually downward in life..

Law Dean
Has to do the things the janitor will not do:
(516)
"After all, being Chief Justice of the Supreme Court is a good deal like being Dean of the Law School – he [sic] has to do the things that the janitor will not do."

Never die, just lose their faculties, (545)

No one lower than:
(517)
I recall the story of a superintendent of high schools who wrote to the president of the university and said, "We are going to have a very wonderful commencement at our school this spring, and we want you to select an outstanding speaker for us. We do not want anyone lower than a dean."
The president wrote back and said, "We have no one around here lower than a dean so you are perfectly safe."

(518)
President of a university is Shepard of the flock and the Dean is the crook.

Law firms
(520)
> ... a farmer ... came to New York to see an old boyhood friend who had become a lawyer. ... He finally located his friend's name on the bulletin board in the middle of the long firm name. ... Underneath the firm name was listed fifty-four other names.
> ... "Mac," the farmer said, "tell me one thing: what are all those names under the line on your door?"
> Mac's eyes twinkled: "Those are our witnesses! How do you think we win our cases?"

(521)
> A Columbia University Law School graduate was interviewed at a white-shoe firm in the late 1950s.
> "It wasn't possible to tell from the candidate's name whether he was Jewish or not, " said Mr. Levin. The interviewing partner led the candidate into a conference room festooned with the seals of Ivy League universities and pointed to Yale's insignia, which bears a Hebrew inscription.
> 'The partner wanted to know if he could read it,:" said Mr. Levin.

(521a)
> A Boston paper once printed a story ... about two men who scraped acquaintance on the Boston-New York train, and in the course of conversation it appeared that both were lawyers. One said to the other, "I am with Ropes-Gray." "Why," said the other on surprise, "so am I."

> Boot-licking deference to leaders of the Bar
> See Client, (194)

Law library, (393)
(522)
"Old Bull" Warren at Harvard was right when he said that one didn't need brains to be a lawyer, only a cast-iron bottom. Sitting in a library from breakfast to midnight, as I often did, one is bound to get a lot of reading done.

(523)
> A certain English Judge has as his associate a young man just commencing his legal studies. One day the Judge said to the associate, "Go and get me 20 Benson & Hedges." The associate, after a long absence, returned and said most apologetically: "I'm sorry, Sir, but we don't appear to have it in the library."

Law office
>   Names on door
>   >   See Law firms
>   Opening of, (56)

>   Young lawyers and:

(525)
>   Receiving his degree of bachelor of laws in 1866, he was admitted to the Massachusetts bar a year later and began his career by reading in the office of Robert M. Morse and later practicing with his brother.
>   He was doing what he later embodied in advice to young lawyers: "after the law school, spend six months in a good office, to see how things are done, and also perhaps to get a little of the usual law student's conceit rubbed off. ...."

Law partner
>   Partner made a judge:

(527)
>   A lawyer is made a judge. The partner is despondent.
>   Lawyer: Do not feel you have lost partner, feel that you have gained a judge.

Law professors
>   See Professors

Law reviews
(528)
>   Then to bed, where we read a few pages of an erudite article in a current law school review. As usual, this was an irresistible soporific, so I soon turned off the bed lamp and went to sleep.

(530)
>   Write a page a day for no more than twelve days. Do not create or apply any "tests" – simply resolve the case on the basis of precedent. Cite no law review articles.

>   >   Attorney finds his work being cited against him
>   >   >   See Citation

>   >   Danger of writing for:

(531)
>   Robert Patterson, in presenting his case before the United States Court

of Appeals for the Second Circuit quoted to his client's favor an article written by Louis Nizer, counsel for the appellee.

Judge Hand threw back his lionesque head, something like Franklin Roosevelt used to do, and roared with laughter. "This ought to be a lesson to the bar in general," he said teasingly, "not to write treatises in law journals. You never know what side you will be on the next day."

>Waste of time:

(532)
You [William McGovern] make a mistake going in for this law journal stuff; it will absolutely kill you: it's no damn good, it's an absolute waste of time; law journals are no use whatsoever. They are just a bunch of God damn pundits putting forth a lot of nonsense that no one ever reads; it's all footnotes anyway. Besides, you will ruin your eyes!"

(533)
>As Mr. Justice Holmes once said, "I don't object that the boys on the law review say I am wrong: what I object to is when they say I am right."

Law school
>Worst book written by professor at major law school
>>See Rodell, Fred

(534)
>The old adage about law school is that first year they scare you to death, second year they work you to death, and third year they bore you to death.

(534a)
>As I've sometimes told my academic friends who have taken an administrative position in the university: "It's all right for a professor to become an administrator so long as he doesn't enjoy it."

Law students, (312), (655)
>Advice to
>>See Law Office, (525)
>Argue either way
>>See Warren, Edward Henry, (736)
>Cast-iron bottom
>>See Law Library
>Conceit
>>See Law Office
>Didn't give a damn what you thought

      See Law classroom
  Hypotheticals
      See Warren, Edward Henry

  Motorcycle cop:

(535)
Dressed in cap and gown on graduation day, the young man handed his diploma to his father and announced, "Well, I finished law school to please you and Mom. Now I'm going to become a motorcycle cop like I've been saying since I was six."

  One long bier if you don't stay awake
      See Law classroom

  Pearls to cast:

(536)
The legendary Harvard law professor Edward "Bull" Warren was so enthusiastic about his subject that he always went on after the bell at the end of class. His students were continually late to their next class, so they decided to start shuffling their feet to let the prof know when to stop. The first time they tried it, Bull roared: "Quiet! I still have a few more pearls to cast!"

  Questions and answers
      See Administrative law

  Sleeping:

(537)
I recall I was teaching a class in evidence one time when I spotted a boy in the back seat who had become a little drowsy and was sort of bent over. I thought, "Well, I will just call on him." I did. No response whatsoever. I called on him again and said, "Can't you discuss this case?"

He made no utterance of any kind at all. Finally I said to the man who sat next to him, "Won't you shake him and wake him up."

He responded, "Wake him up yourself. You put him to sleep."

(538)
The old story about the Harvard Law School dean telling students on the first day of class, "Look to your left, look to your right, because one of you won't be here by the end of the year," has been replaced in recent years by Professor Alan Dershowitz's adage: "Look to your left and look to your right, because by the time you graduate, there'll be no Left left."

(539)

A law student inquired of the Registrar: "Do you have a course in accounting for lawyers?"

Registrar: There is no accounting for lawyers.

(539a)

The instructor emulated Demosthenes who practiced his speeches with pebbles in his mouth. At the beginning of the course, each student was given a mouthful of marbles. Each day the instructor reduced the number by one marble. The student became a public speaker when he lost all his marbles.

(539b)

Nearly a hundred years ago, Prince Bismarck said that one third of the students of German universities broke down from overwork, another third broke down from dissipation, and the other third ruled Germany. I don't know which third of the students we have today, but I am confident that...

(539c)

When Lincoln Barnett once described the excitement of a group of students emerging from a physics lecture at the Institute for Advanced Study at Princeton. "How did it go?" One of them said, "Wonderful, everything we knew last week isn't true."

    You are in very shallow water
       See Warren, Edward Henry

Law suit
    See Definition

Laws
    Ten Commandments and
       See Ten Commandments

Lawyers, (49)
    See also Ambition, Attorney fees, Massachusetts Bar, Young lawyer
    Ambulance chaser
       See Association of the Bar of the City of New York; Client

(192)

    Appeared in shirt sleeves with braces showing
       Is that the reason I lost the case? :

(540)
One remembers the lawyer who practiced informally. I think in Missouri. He always appeared in court in his shirt sleeves without a jacket. Then one day he had an appeal which had to go to Jefferson City. One of his friends said, "You mustn't appear in your shirt sleeves with your braces or galluses showing. Wear your jacket."

The Old Adam dies hard, you know, and this was a rugged individualist. He argued the case in the court of appeal precisely in the dress in which would have argued it back home – and he lost.

A short time later one of the judges of the appellate court came to his town and he saw this judge and said to him, "Tell me, Judge, did I lose that case before your court because I appeared in my shirt sleeves with my braces showing?"

The judge said, "No, no that wasn't the reason."

The lawyer said, "Well it was a darned sight better reason than the one you gave me."

Battalions of
(541)
As Robert Jackson wrote when he was Attorney General: "Struggles over power that in Europe call out regiments of troops, in this country call out battalions of lawyers."

Children once:
(542)
Charles Lamb, quoted in "The Fireside Calendar and Engagement Book 1962: Lawyers, I suppose, were children once.

Definition of
    See Definitions
Fool for a client
    See Blackman, Harry A.
Gnawing at a dry bone of law
    See Brevity
Hands in his own pocket
    See Ade, George

Harassed by judge
    I think I know now:
(544)
A judge with a reputation for harassing attorneys was confronted by a newly admitted member of the bar and a junior in a large law firm. Not getting

satisfactory answers nor sufficient signs of fear he hurled a series of invectives at the young lad and finally in exasperation shouted, "Why in the name of heaven, with all that talent there did they have to send you here."

The lad muttered, "I wondered myself why when they sent me, but I think I know now."

> He will too make a lawyer
> > See Law classroom
>
> Honest
> > See Young lawyer, (785)
>
> I will get you out if it takes ten years
> > See Client ((198)
>
> If you are asking question on my behalf…,
> > See Objections
>
> Left anything out
> > See Doctor
>
> Local counsel
> > See Jesus Christ is my advocate
>
> Lose their appeal:
> > See also Bankers

(545)

"What happens to old deans? They never die, they just lose their faculties." … "Old bankers never die, they just lose their interest," … "What happens to old lawyers? They never die, they just lose their appeal."

> Make sure it is your client
> > See Client, (195)
>
> Mendoza line
> > See Mendoza line
>
> Never die, lose their appeal
> > See Bankers
>
> New York lawyers
> > Prejudice against fine writers
> > > See Learning
>
> Not fortunate enough to be a lawyer
> > See Cross-examination, (245)
>
> One didn't need brains to be a lawyer
> > See Law library
>
> Pompous, 663f
> > See also Insurance
>
> Poverty, ambition, and in love

        See Poor
Proper dress
        See this topic: (540)
Rather be a judge or lawyer
        See Marshall, Thurgood

Repeat argument three times:

(546)

It has been said that every lawyer should repeat each argument three times, especially when addressing a tribunal consisting of more than one judge. You state the argument the first time in order that one of the judges may grasp your point. You repeat the argument the second time in order that, while you are repeating it, he may explain the point to his brethren. Then you repeat the argument the third time in order to correct the erroneous impression which that judge has unfortunately conveyed.

        Stages of (first: ambitious; second: fees)
            See Ambition

Stealing from by defendant, (795f)

Subservient creatures
        See Client, (194)
Success and poverty
        See poor

Supply of requires more than one:

(547)

There is an ancient story, which lawyers love to tell, of the small town lawyer who almost starved until another lawyer moved to town – at which point they both waxed prosperous. The story tells us a great deal; it is really about a variation of Say's law, which preceded Lord Keynes's emphasis on demand management: and increase in supply (in our case, the supply of lawyers) creates an increase in demand.

(548)

One story of [Mr. Justice] Maule, the advocate, is that before the hearing of an appeal in the House of Lords he had a heavy lunch of stout and steak; Follett, his leader, who had lunched off sherry and biscuits, asked why he was lunching so plentifully. "To reduce myself to the intellectual level of the Judges," said Maule.

(549)
LAWYERS' LAW
The law the lawyers know about is property and land;
But why the leaves are on the trees,
And why the waves disturb the seas,
Why hone is the food of bees,
Why horses have such tender knees,
Why winters come when rivers freeze,
Why Faith is more than what one sees,
And Hope survives the worst disease,
And Charity is more than these,
They do not understand

>
> Tact
>   See Tact
> Taking up a collection for, (255f)
> Three things necessary for success at the bar
>   See Tact
> Too learned to be informed
>   See Virtue
> Traffic ticket reduced to second-degree murder
>   See Rickles, Don

(549a)
    A smart lawyer is one who can take a law meant to be a stone wall, find a hold in it and convert it into a triumphal arch large enough for a team of horses to drive through with colors flying.

Leach, W. Barton, (760); (251f)

Learning
(550)
    [C.C. Burlingham] told Wickersham that Veeder, although not well known at the bar, had a reputation as a fine writer: "I admit that in a way creates a prejudice against him because ordinary New York lawyers, worshipping at the shrine of Efficiency and Dispatch, are rather shy of learning."

Lecture
    See Prisoners

Leech, Margaret, (182f)

Legal aid
>See Association of the Bar of the City of New York, (68)

Legal ethics
>See Arnold, Thurman, (59)

Legal machinery
>See Taft, William Howard

Legal mind
(552)
>Professor Thomas Reed Powell of Harvard offered this: "If you can think of something which is connected with something without thinking of the something it is connected to, you have a legal mind."

Legal research
>See Law Library

Legal writing
>See Rodell, Fred

Legalese
>See Advertising

Legislative history
(554)
>In Frankfurter's article he tells of the quip that only when the legislative history is doubtful to you go to the statute.

Lehmann, Frederick
>See Justice

Leibowitz, Samuel, (471f)

Leiding, Oscar, (404f), (525f), (659f)

Lerner, Max, (3f)

Levinson, Sanford, (141f)

Levy, Beryl, 520f

Lewis, Anthony, (14f), (122f), (153f), (315f)

Lewis, Lefty, (313)

Lewis, Sinclair, (689f)

Lex, Charles E.
    See Humor

Libby, I. Lewis Jr.
    See Baseball

Libel
    See Alcoholic beverages, (29)

Library of Congress,
    See Brandeis, Louis, (117)

Lincoln, A.L.J., (172f), (430f)

Lincoln, Abraham, (597); (397f)
    Wins two cases taking opposite sides:
(560)
    … Lincoln was pleading two cases the same day before the same Judge and both had the same principle of law involved. In the morning he was pleading for the plaintiff and won the case in an outstanding manner. In the afternoon he took the opposite side and was arguing just as fervently and just as forcefully as to the merits of the case. Then the Judge stopped and asked him. "Have you changed your
attitude?" "No," he said, "I may have been wrong this morning but I know that I'm right this afternoon.

Literary skill
    See Afflatus, Fuller, Melville Weston; Rodell, Fred
    Disadvantage
        See Learning

Litigation
    Case bristles with simplicity, yet…,
        See God and Court, (379)
    I may have been wrong this morning, but I am right this afternoon

See Lincoln, Abraham

Never took a case he didn't believe in:
(563)
Two generations ahead of me there was a well known lawyer in Boston, Charles G. Loring, whom my mother-in-law pronounced a really good man because he never took a case that he didn't believe in – perhaps a more sardonic way of putting it would be that he believed in every case that he took.

    Oyster analogy
        See Judges, (465)
    Protracted
        See Arnold, Thurman, (59)

Of every hundred cases ... seven are lost by advocacy:
(564)
Kemp, a QC, was fond of quoting: ... of every hundred cases, ninety win themselves, three are won by advocacy, and seven are lost by advocacy.

Llewellyn, Karl N., (693f)

Loco parentis
    See Definitions

Lodge, Henry Cabot, (421)

Lone Ranger, (660f)
See also Rehnquist, William H.

Loring, Charles G., (563)

Loughran, John T., (787f)

Love, (691)

Lovell, Colin R., (131f)

Lurtin, Horace H., (35)

Lying
    Flattery amounting to
        See Laski, Harold

> What happens to a witness who doesn't tell the truth
> See Witnesses

Lyndhurst, Lord, (466f)

Lyons, Leonard, (254f), (433f)

-m-

MacDonald, John M., (327f)

Magruder, Calvert, (228); (229f), (397f), (465f), (581f)

Malenkov
> See United States Supreme Court, (717)

Malthus
(570)
> The allusion to Malthus reminds me parenthetically that Holmes in his college days was so stricken with the Malthusian theory that he thought it should be written in letters of fire on the heavens. "This fellow," he said to himself, "has stuck a sword into the very bowels of the principle of population." But he told a visitor, nearly three-quarters of a century later, that he observed the principle of population still walking jauntily about, apparently not at all discommoded by a sword in its vitals.

Manisty, Mr. Justice, (677)

Manners, Lord, (648)

Mansfield, Lord, (500f)

Margolick, David, (235f), (715f)

Maris, Judge, (229f)

Marmalade
> See Approval, need for

Marsh, Daniel I., (221f), (462f)

Marshall, John, (30f), (460f)
(575)
"John Marshall has made his decision, now let him enforce it" President Andrew Jackson in disagreeing with a Supreme Court ruling that protected Cherokee Indian lands from encroachment by the state of Georgia. Reiterated by John W. Davis after losing the Brown decision.

    It is raining somewhere
        See Alcoholic beverages, (30)

Marshall, Thurgood, (140f), (141f), (575f), (577f)
    Elevator at the Supreme Court:
(577)
A favorite [anecdote of Thurgood Marshall] involved unsuspecting tourists who mistakenly entered the Justices' private elevator. Finding a lone black man standing there, they said, "First floor please." "Yowsa, yowsa," Marshall responded as he pretended to operate the automated elevator and held the door for the tourists as they left. Marshall regularly recounted the story, noting the tourists' puzzlement and then confusion as they watched him walk off, and later realized who he was.

(578)
As a young student studying history, Powell had learned that military men and lawyers ran the world. He had no desire to be a military man, so he became a lawyer. Once, Powell invited Washington Redskin football star Larry Brown to lunch at the Court.

Brown asked Powell if he preferred being a lawyer to being a judge. "Would you rather be a player or a referee?" Powell replied.

(579)
Every time Marshall misbehaved, the principal made him stay after school and memorize part of the Constitution. Some punishment! "Before I left that school," Marshall later said, "I knew the whole thing by heart."

Martin, Baron, (130)
Marx, Groucho, (57f)

Mason, Alpheus T., (30f), (91f), (115f), (120f), (151f), (158f), (176f), (180f), (306f), (308f), (378f), (399f), (516f), (530f), (596f), (643f)

Mason, Jeremiah, (174)

Massachusetts Bar
(580)

    Mr. Justice White "Mr. Attorney-General, what is there in this law to prevent free and unbridled collusion between the court and the lawyers and petitioners?

    Hosea Knowlton: "Absolutely nothing, Your Honor, except the traditional character of the Bench and Bar of Massachusetts."

Massachusetts Reports, (132), (418)

Massachusetts Supreme Judicial Court
(581)

    … but there is no doubt that from time to time Judges do feel that perhaps counsel are going on too long, and recently, when I sat in the Supreme Court in Massachusetts on a brief visit. I found there they had a remarkable technique of dealing with counsel whose argument had ceased to appeal. Not only are the seats supplied for the Judges there capable of turning round, they are also capable of tipping right back, and I gather that counsel when they have lost the Court, lose the ball behind the horizon! That must be a very disconcerting experience.

Mattapan
    See Closing argument

Maugham, W. Somerset, (284f)

Maule, (28)

Maxims
    See Cujos est solum

May, (424f)

Maycock, Welburn, (472f)

Mayer, Martin, (57f), (115f), (180f), (235f), (270f), (388f), (394f), (438f), (454f), (462f), (467cf), (475f), (516f), (549af), (552f), (575f), (597f), (622f), (640f), (688af), (707f), (718f), (736f), (791f)

McCarran, Patrick, (312)

McClemen, Edward F., (120)

McCormack, Alfred, (10f), (45f), (149f), (399f), (688f)

McElwain, E, (622f)

McEwen, R.L., (172f), (430f)

McGovern, William, (57f), (532f)

McKenna, Joseph,
    See Briefs

McMurtrie, Mr.
    See Humor

McPhaul, John, (689f)

McReynolds, James C., (394a)
See also Four horsemen
(585)
    Justice McReynolds' gallantry and his warmth of nature occasionally betrayed him. Of course, one always had to have a single lady to balance the Justice who was a bachelor, and on this particular evening we had a most delightful lady who was the aunt of a reigning Justice of the Supreme Court at the present time.
    She was an elderly lady, not too disparate in age from Justice McReynolds. When the time came for him to go home he went up to her his most gallant manner and said, "Miss Laura, may I escort you home?" In the rather fluttery sort of way of a spinster lady, she said to my wife, "Do you think I am safe with such a handsome gentleman?" to which the Justice, with another gallant bow, said, "Miss Laura, you would be safe anywhere!"
    And then he went out, rather conscious of the fact that it hadn't turned out just the way he meant it to turn out.

(586)
    The case involved the estate of a Dr. MacFarlan of Philadelphia. The government contended that Dr. MacFarlan's transfer, at age 78, of over $600,000 of his estate to his children was a gift in contemplation of death and therefore taxable as part of his estate. The doctor had died less than two years afterward.
    Jackson stated these facts and chose his words with care and caution because of the advanced age of the members of the Court he was addressing.

Justice McReynolds, of Scotch extraction, who had been thumbing the record, looked up, chuckled and said: "Didn't you read the record? Didn't the court below find that this was a hearty Scotchman?"

"Oh, yes, Your Honor," Jackson replied. "That is the reason that the Government is so sure that this gift would only have been made in preparation for death."

The whole Court enjoyed a hearty laugh.

You're there now

(587)

There is a famous story of that assiduous but not entirely lovable character, the late Mr. Justice McReynolds. One day counsel said, "I'm coming to that your Honor."

"You're there now."

(588)

The story is told of the great Justice Oliver Wendell Holmes, who, at the time, was still sitting on the Supreme Court at the age of eighty-nine. The Court had temporarily adjourned for lunch, and when argument resumed thereafter Justice Holmes dozed off after about ten minutes of oral argument. Chief Justice Hughes soon detected that his colleague had fallen asleep and cautiously poked him in the leg. Holmes sat up, startled and burst forth with an epithet that shook not only the courtroom but also the lawyer presenting his case.

At this moment Justice McReynolds interrupted the lawyer to ask a a question irritating to Justice Holmes. Holmes turned sharply to the Chief Justice and audibly mumbled something which those in the courtroom interpreted as berating the Chief Justice for awakening him out of a peaceful slumber to hear the annoying question.

(589)

... the lawyer opened his appeal to the Court with these words:

"I come to you as John the Baptist saying 'Repent ye, repent ye.'"

Whereupon Justice McReynolds, who was enjoying the performance almost as much as Justice Holmes, leaned forward and said:

"But are you not aware of what happened to John the Baptist?"

"Yes, I am quite aware," was the immediate response. "He lost his head through the influence of a harlot. But I know the Supreme Court would not be so influenced."

(590)

"... an alleged conversation between [Dean] Hutchins and Justice

James C. McReynolds of the Supreme Court of the United States. The Justice is said to have remarked to the Dean: "I understand that at Yale you are teaching your students that the decisions of the Supreme Court of the United States are all nonsense." Dean Hutchins replied, "Not at all, Mr. Justice. We simply give them the decisions to read and let them judge for themselves."

(591)
    Associate Justice James McReynolds, young, bright, deeply conservative and viciously anti-Semitic, was by far Frankfurter's most hostile interrogator. Repeatedly hectoring Frankfurter, McReynolds interrupted his argument that the ten-hour-maximum regulation was constitutional..
    "Ten hours! Ten hours! Ten! Why not four?" McReynolds snarled.
    Frankfurter paused dramatically, then calmly addressed McReynolds. "Your honor," Said Frankfurter, "if by chance I may make such a hypothesis: if your physician should find that you're eating too much meat, it isn't necessary for him to urge you to become a vegetarian."
    He savored the moment, delighting for years in the memory of Justice Holmes loudly exclaiming, "Good for you!"

Megarry, Robert E., (145f), (180f), (193f), (466f), (470f), (657f), (756f), (794f)

Memorial addresses
(593)
    [On Hand's memorializing Justice Stone]: As Professor Paul Freund once put it, "Memorial addresses often provide an even truer insight into the speaker than into the subject, and it is probably safer that the views so pointedly put by Judge Hand be ascribed to himself than to the late Chief Justice." [Note: this was as regards to standards for personal rights and property rights.]

Men's room
    See Lavatory

Mencken, H.L.
(594)
    When the Newspaper Guild first approached the Sun papers with a proposal for a contract, Henry Mencken was singled out to be the negotiator for the management. He drew up a tentative contract and at the first negotiating meeting he read it aloud. It was larded with references to "the gentlemen of the press," "the aforesaid gentlemen," "the gentlemen known as the parties of the first part," and so forth. When he had finished reading this tentative contract, one of the Guild negotiators cleared his throat and said: "Mr. Mencken, ah,

what is the reason for the repeated use of the word 'gentlemen'?" Mencken was quick on the reply. "I used the word," he said, "in order to have something to concede when the bargaining gets tough.

(594a)
Frank Chase, head of the Watch and Ward Society, was the custodian of Boston morals He declared the story obscene ["Hatrack" in The American Mercury] and banned the magazine in his bailiwick. [H.L.] Mencken went to Boston and dared Chase to have him arrested for selling the Mercury on Boston Common. Chase swallowed the bait. A cheering, hilarious, and boisterous crowd watched the transaction and followed Mencken to the hoosegow. Mencken was acquitted, an injunction was obtained against Chase, and his Watch and Ward Society was thoroughly discredited.

Mendelson, Wallace, (6f), (8f), (690f)

Mendoza line
(595)
    He would create a "Mendoza line" below which partners fell at their peril. (The reference was to Mario Mendoza, a shortstop for the Pittsburgh Pirates, Seattle Mariners, and Texas Rangers whose lifetime batting average was .215. In baseball, an infielder whose average falls "below the Mendoza line" begins to think seriously about another occupation.)

Mentally retarded
    See Butler, Pierce

Menuhin, Yehudi
(596)
    A few days later, Stone dropped in to see Justice Holmes – then ninety-two – and told him how this gangling youngster [Yehudi Menuhin] had spellbound an audience of three thousand.
    "Ah," Holmes sighed, "what a triumph! I sometimes think I would give twn years of my life to be able to play like that."
    "Yes," replied the younger jurist, "but some of us would give ten years of our lives to be able to write opinions like yours."
    Holmes perked up and said with a twinkle, "My boy" – Stone was then sixty-two – "God sees through all this modesty."

Metaphysical Club, (57f)

(597)
Miller, Samuel
"His biographer tells the story that when his friends came to the White House to urge his appointment on Lincoln, the president kept busy with other things on his desk until he finally heard the words 'Supreme Court," when he said, 'Oh, this is important. I thought you wanted me to appoint him a brigadier general.'

Milton's Paradise Lost
    See Closing argument

Miscarriage of another
    See Abortion

Mitchell, William D.
    See Candor

Modesty
    See Menuhin, Yehudi

Moore, Victor, (154)

Moot court, (508)

Morgan, J.P., (77)

Morse, Robert, (525)

Mortimer, (385f)

Moses
    See Advocate

Motions
(600)
    The story concerns a trial justice who was newly-appointed in a small community. He had no legal training whatsoever; he was simply a business man. He was conducting his first case in the town hall and it was a case where the public were more or less stirred up and there was quite a crowd in the town hall. It was a criminal case involving a complaint by one farmer against another for malicious mischief. The State was represented by the County Attorney and the respondent also had an attorney. After the State's case was in counsel for

the respondent reviewed the evidence in argument and stated to the court that he felt the evidence was not sufficient to support the warrant, and then he said: "If Your Honor please, I move that the warrant be quashed." Somebody in the back of the room immediately said, "Second the Motion." With great dignity, the trial justice then arose and said, "Ladies and gentlemen, you have heard the motion made and seconded. All those in favor say aye." Everybody said "aye," and he said, "The ayes have it, the motion is carried, the warrant is quashed and respondent is discharged."

Mountains out of molehills, (717)

Mr. Dooley, (81); (103f), (549af)

Mumford, Lewis, (675)

Murphy, Frank, (433)
    The Saint:
(602)
    Justice Roberts "considered Justice Murphy insufferably self-righteous, labeling him "The Saint."

Murphy, Walter F., (12f), (60f), (103f), (153f), (273f), (274f), (465f), (503f), (513f), (719f)

Murane, Edward E., (448f), (470f), (789f)

-n-
Naivity
(604)
    When [Alexander] Bickel cited an opinion by Justice Douglas as an example of shallow judicial thinking, Rodell's riposte was that while those were Justice Doublas's words, what he "really meant" was much more radical.
    Bickel: I may be naïve, Fred [Rodell], but when a Justice of the United States Supreme Court says x, I believe he means x.
    Rodell: You're right, Alex, you are naïve.

Nasby, Petroleum, (759)

Navasky, Victor S., (392f), (604f)

Negotiable instruments
    See Paternity

Nepotism, (436)

Neutral
> Prisoner on being asked to take the stand, (651)

Newspapers
> Gobitis case and, (103)

Nicholson, Anthony, (193f), (252f)

Nizer, Louis, (531f)

No worse than others which have been made
> See Objections

Noonan, Gregory
> Took 20 years to get from where you are to where I am: (606)
>
> Federal Judge Gregory Noonan, who died of a heart attack last Saturday, was an Assistant U.S. Attorney here. While Noonan presided at the treason trial of Sgt. Provoo, a witness, describing the tunnel at Corregidor, said it was about the same width as the courtroom. The lawyer asked the judge if knew how far it was from one wall of the courtroom to the other.
>
> "No," said Judge Noonan. "All I know is it took me 20 years to get from where you're standing to where I'm sitting."

North
> There is no North and South. They are all one
> > See Rogers, Will

Novelists
(608)
> The new generation [of novelists] had discovered the act by which it came into being and is happy in the discovery.

-o-

O'Brien, Daniel J., (627f)

O'Connor, Sandra Day, (660); (14f), (19f), (122f), (718f), (758f)

O'Hara, (18f)

Oberdorfer, Don, (482)

Objections
(610)
　　… Judge Harley N. Crosby, recounts an incident that happened in a jury trial over which Judge Crosby presided in the New York Supreme Court. … Bob objected to one of his opponent's questions and I overruled the objection. Some more objections were overruled. … Finally, I made a ruling which quite exhausted Bob's patience, and he said, "Your Honor, I am at a loss to understand that ruling unless (and then in an undertone) it is on the theory that it is no worse than some others which have been made.

(611)
　　The examination of a seasoned barrister was interrupted at a sensitive point by a question which the lawyer did not care for. "Have you an objection, counselor?" said the court as the lawyer put on a remonstrative look. "Perhaps, your Honor," replied the lawyer, "but I would first like to inquire on whose behalf your Honor put that question." "What difference would that make, counselor?" asked the court. "All the difference in the world," said the lawyer, "For if your Honor is asking the question on behalf of my opponent, then of course I must object to it, but if your Honor asks the question on my behalf, then I simply withdraw it.

(612)
　　'Judge,' said the prisoner, 'I don't know what to do.'
　　'Why, what is the matter,' asked the judge.
　　'I swore to tell the truth, but every time I try some lawyer objects.'

Obscenity
　　See also Mencken, H.L.
(614)
　　[Martin Conboy, U.S. attorney in Ulysses obscenity case] insisted on spending hours reading lengthy passages aloud, with emphasis on Joyce's concluding forty-six pages, "the stream-of-thought soliloquizing of Mrs. Molly Bloom at the end of a hard day," a soliloquy that is widely considered to be one of the finest, as well as most erotic, passages in modern literature. The newspapers had a field day describing the "Three solemn, elderly gentlemen" on the bench 'staring self-consciously" at the book while the U.S. attorney, "flushed and determined," voiced Molly Bloom's reverie.

(615f)
At the time of the recent trial for obscenity of Lady Chatterley's Lover in England, a Member of Parliament gave the books some qualified support.

"I have read this book," he announced. "I would not object to my wife reading it. I would not object to my daughter reading it. But I'm not so sure I'd want my gamekeeper to read it."

Old Howard, (144f)

Oliver Twist, (759f)

Opinion days
    See Frankfurter, Felix, (311)

Opinions, (141f)
    Brevity
        See Brevity
    Conclusions, and
        See Gray, Horace
    Dissenting from own opinion
        See Burger, Warren, (141)

    Draw the line:
(616)
"I have just sent back an opinion of one of our JJ. with a criticism of an argument in it of the 'where are you going to draw the line' type – as if all decisions were not a series of points tending to fix a point in a line."

    Egad, it is I that was the d___d fool
        See Judges, (466)
    Fifty one percent sure
        See Cardozo, Benjamin Nathan
    Hell is paved with just decisions
        See Hell

    I'll put it in a letter to a friend:
(617)
He was fond of citing the example of Holmes who, when asked by his brethren to cut out some gem from an opinion, replied, "Very well, I'll put it in a letter to a friend."

    Less publicized Supreme Court opinions, (660)

Law clerks work on
> See Law Clerks, (514)

My God I said plaintiff when I meant defendant
> See Judges, (456)

Plum here and a plum there:

(618)
Well, that is the background of this episode of [Thomas R.] Powell – his room was next to mine in the old Langdell Hall at Cambridge – bursting into my room with his books, saying, "I showed up your hero! Showed them what a question-begger Holmes was in the Pipeline cases!" ... Well, time passes. After Holmes's death there became available to me the volumes in which he year by year collected the opinions he wrote, his original circulation of printed opinions – he didn't keep any working papers. He wrote and then sent it to the printer, and that's all there was to it. But, in the cases in which he wrote, either for the Court, or in dissent or concurring, he did keep and had bound the opinions that he circulated and the returns he had, the comments from each of the Justices. ... And in his own annotation on his copy of the opinion that Powell dealt with in class as "Question-begging," Holmes wrote in his own handwriting, "This is a wholly unsatisfactory opinion," and then stated why it was unsatisfactory. ... and why he yielded to having his name put to such an opinion; namely, that if he hadn't done that the case would not have been decided that term with the risk of being adversely decided later.

After [the Pipeline opinion] came down, [John W. Davis] had occasion to visit Justice Holmes, and he made some comment to the effect that he was glad the government won, but that he was not entirely happy with the opinion. Mr. Davis reported that Holmes said, "Well, that's the trouble. I write out my opinions, and I send them around to my brethren. One of them picks out a plum here, and the other picks out a plum there, and they send it back to me with nothing but a shapeless mass of dough to father!"

Puny judges
> See Law Clerks, (514)

Shapeless mass of dough to father
> See Opinions, (618)

Shortest
> See Burton, Harold H.

Ten years of my life to write like that
> See Menuhin, Yehudi

We'll add it to the end
> See Frank, Jerome

>   Weighty opinions
>> See Footnotes, (306)
>   Write superbly
>> See Fuller, Melville Weston
>   Writing and delivering of
>> See Briefs, (129)
>   Writing them not dictating
>> See Hand, Learned, (387)

(619)

Justice Stanley Reed struggled with opinion writing and once said, "Wouldn't it be nice if we could write the way we think."

Oral argument

(620)

His letters, in his fine hand, fill volumes. Many of them were written on the bench while he was waiting for counsel to catch up with his understanding of their case. This gave him, he used to say, an undeserved reputation for attention and industry.

(621)

As a judge he followed the traditions of the English Bench, which decides nearly all cases upon an oral argument. I imagine he generally reached his own conclusion after the oral argument, and this is the more surprising, for Justice Holmes was never very tolerant of extended oral arguments. He believed that most cases could be argued, by any capable advocate, in a half hour and he generally was adverse to extensions of time beyond the one hour rule of the Court.

>   After going to bed at night
>> See Oral Argument, (624)
>   Basketball, dribbling during
>> See White, Byron, (745)
>   Boring advocates
>> See Oral Argument (626)
>   Brevity
>> See Knapp, Whitman
>   Collar Button Case
>> See Shiras, George, (676)
>   Dudes and fools smoke foreign cigarettes
>> See Holmes, Oliver Wendell, (414)

Exactly one minute and a half:
(622)
[The Chief Justice] held each speaker to exactly his allotted time. It is said, with some exaggeration, that one he called time on a leader of the New York bar in the middle of the word "if." When John W. Davis asked how much time remained and Hughes snapped, "Exactly one minute and a half," counsel suavely replied, "I present the court with one minute and a half."

Although the Chief presided graciously and with good manners, he was in no way lax in the way he guided argument. Consider, for example, his timekeeping activities. ... It has been reported that on one occasion he called time on a leader of the New York Bar in the middle of the word "if." And one on being asked by the same gentleman how much time remained, he replied, with beard bristling, "14 seconds."

How did you get here? :
(623)
The story every Frankfurter law clerk enjoys most telling quite naturally involved Justice Holmes. The first question Justice Holmes asked on his first day on the Supreme Court was the standard inquiry on the appeals procedure by which the pending case reached the high court.

"How did you get here?" Justice Holmes inquired timidly. And the attorney replied from the stand: "By the B. & O. Railroad, your Honor."

How do you think us fellows down here should know?
    See Brewer, David, (127)
Hypothetical
    See McReynolds, James C., (591)
I am none the wiser, (451f)
I want to hear the argument
    See White, Edward Douglas, (740)
I present the court with one minute and a half
    See Oral Argument, (622)
I'm coming to that your Honor
    See McReynolds, James C., (587)
In the middle of the word "if,"
    See Oral argument, (622)
Innuendo, say things by, (442f)
    See also Innuendo
Interrupted, incoherent, disjointed, disappointing
    See Oral argument, (624)
It was a very long time ago
    See Brevity, (124)

Judge disappears behind chair that tips back, (581f)
>See also Massachusetts Supreme Judicial Court

Judge doesn't hear a damn word
>See Judges, (460)

Logical, coherent:

(624)

I used to say that, as Solicitor General, I made three arguments of every case. First came the one that I planned – as I thought, logical, coherent, complete. Second was the one actually presented – interrupted, incoherent, disjointed, disappointing. The third was the utterly devastating argument that I thought of after going to bed that night.

Nothing leads me to hope:

(625)

The taxpayer had won below in the Second Circuit, which had held that income from a certain trust fund was a gift and therefore not taxable income under the terms of the Revenue Act of 1913. Holmes was interested. He himself enjoyed such an income, and said so during argument by the taxpayer's lawyer, who was too surprised to say anything until the end, when he ventured: "I hope, Mr. Justice Holmes, that the Statute of Limitations will not have run against you, so you will not be foreclosed from getting back the tax you have mistakenly paid out." The others looked at the Judge, who let a long enough moment slip by to allow the slightly self-conscious suspense to point up his reply. "Nothing," said the Justice, "nothing you have said leads me to hope. .."

Repeat argument three times
>See Lawyers, (546)

Scribbling notes during:

(626)

Listening to oral arguments in the Supreme Court a few days after Pearl Harbor, Justice Frankfurter turned to his favorite remedy against boring advocates: he busied himself by scribbling notes to his friends on small Supreme Court memorandum pads.

Submit the case without argument
>See Young lawyer, (793)

Teetered back and forth:

(627)

Former Solicitor General Archibald Cox, telling of his experiences in the U.S. Supreme Court, lightened his talk with some amusing incidents which pointed up the fact that the staid, dignified justices do enjoy a moment of fun from time to time. He told of the old school attorney, who in arguing a case teetered back and forth, and went from almost a whisper to a roar as he continued on and on. During the argument Justice Holmes wrote a note, called a page, and had it delivered to Justice Brandeis. Justice Brandeis read the note, crumpled it up,and tossed it in the direction of the waste basket. It missed the basket and rolled onto the floor near where the struggling attorney was standing. When court recessed, the lawyer insisted that his young assistant pick up the note and read it to him. "Do you think he argues best on his back or on his belly?" Justice Holmes had written.

>Three arguments
>>See Oral argument, (624)

>Time not used by counsel reverts to Court:

(628)
Frequently it was [Chief Justice Fuller's] lot, as befalls all presiding justices, to have to remind counsel that the allotted time had expired; and he always did so with firmness, but generally with a smile.

[When the Attorney General of Hawaii requested more time and] announced that Solicitor General Hoyt had told him he could have some of the Solicitor General's time ... The Chief Justice interposed: "Mr. Solicitor General, I understand your position, but Mr. Attorney General, the time not used by counsel does not belong to him to dispose of. It reverts to the Court."

(629)
Omitted from Webster's own account of the speech, Chauncey A. Goodrich wrote that Webster closed the speech [Dartmouth College case], telling the Court:

>... It is, sir, as I have said, a small college. And yet there are those who

love it!

>Uncorrupted by any merits
>>See Points of law, (641)

>Wrong this morning, but right this afternoon
>>See Lincoln, Abraham, (560)
>You mix drinks better than you argue cases
>>See Alcoholic beverages, (35)

Oratory, (155)
    See also After-dinner speaker
    Bag of wind, (17f)
    Flamboyant
        See Hall, Marshall, (385)
    Heard me before
        See Prisoners, (650)

(629a)
    Adlai Stevenson [after being introduced to a gathering]: After such an introduction I can hardly wait to hear what I have to say.

(629b)
    Commencement classic: At the University of Iowa, Secretary of Labor, W.W.W. remarked that 'commencement speakers have a good deal in common with grandfather clocks standing usually some six feet tall, typically ponderous in construction, more traditional than functional, their distinction is largely their noisy communication of essentially commonplace information.'

(629c)
    Attributed to Allen F. Smith: Mr. Chairman, I am reminded of the number of titles that Harry gave me. Professor, Dean, Vice President and that they are listed in descending order of capability of affecting anyone. The story is told of Eva Peron, at the height of the Peronist movement when she visited Franco in Spain. He had arranged a motorcade down the street but it didn't come off very well, for the assembled populace, instead of shouting, "Viva Eva" or whatever they were paid for, shouted "prostitute," "whore" and this was very upsetting to Eva. When they got back to the palace she was weeping and Franco, in an effort to pacify her said, "Do not worry, Madame. I haven't been in the army for thirty years and they still call me general, so I don't really object anymore almost any title that is given me."

(629d)
    When [Dean] Pound started to speak, he took out his pocket watch and placed it on the podium. Exactly 50 minutes later, he picked it up and put it back in his pocket, saying: "My father told me that if a man speaks for 50 minutes, it is because the spirit moves him. If he speaks for longer than that, it is because his ego moves him!"

Orren, Harding A., (73f)

Oyster
> Analogy of judge to
>> See Judges, (465)

-p-

Paine, Henry W., (462f)

Palfrey, John
> See Biography

Palles, Christopher, (648f)

Panaceas and sudden ruin
(630)
> I have no belief in panaceas and almost none in sudden ruin.

Panama Canal
> See Knox, Philander, (485)

Pannick, David, (13f), (451f), (564f), (795f)

Parker House, (424f)

Parker, Edward G., (76f)

Paternity
> See also Law, (499)

(631)
> Youth before court on a paternity case: Your Honor, I admit to having intercourse with this girl but I wasn't the first one.
> Judge: My son, in the field of negotiable instruments when a maker is unavailable, it is the last endorser who pays

Patterson, Robert, (531)

Peabody, James P., (37f), (100f), (207f), (281f), (415f), (416f), (417f), (490f), (494f), (675f), (734f)

Pearson, Drew, (117f), (150f), (153f), (159f), (383f), (424f), (589f), (596f), (635f), (740f)

Peasants of Northern Ireland talk of little else, (247)

Peck, David W., (40f), (92f), (508f)

Peers, (159f)
    See also Association of the Bar of the City of New York

Peete, Richard, (509f), (611f), (640f)

Peffley, Mr. Justice, (647)

Pepper, George Wharton, (67f)

Pepy's Diary, (464f)

Peron, Eva, (629c)

Personal injury
    See Torts

Persuasive authority, (647)

Phillips, Harlan B., (35f)

Philogrobolized, (133)

Pickpockets, (795f)

Pickwick, Mr., (1)

Pitney, Mrs. Mahlon
(635)
    ... They all come to see him, even Mrs. Mahlon Pitney, wife of the late Justice Pitney, who once told the aged friend of her husband about a burglary in her home. The robber had backed a truck up to the rear door and taken all the furnishings out in a most thorough manner. But the police caught him, Mrs. Pitney said, and put him in jail. There she went to visit him in his cell.
    Mrs. Pitney talked at great length to Justice Holmes about the incident.
    "I tried to find out how ever he had embarked on a career of crime," she explained. "I tried to point out the error of his ways and I hope I have done some good. I think I must have talked to him for two hours."
    "Poor man, poor man," nodded Justice Holmes sympathetically.

Pitofsky, Robert, (11f)

Plain language
> See Advertising

Plato, (281), (300)

Plimpton, Francis, (316f)

Plowden, Edmund, (170)

Poetry, (205)

Points of law
(640)
> The old saying "Show me the judge and I'll tell you the law" has a modicum of truth in it, while, on the other hand, I have known judicial personages before whom no case was certain and no case was hopeless.
> "That is your eleventh point," I once heard Holmes L.J. say to a counsel from Belfast, "and it is as bad as the other ten. Have you any more points?"
> "Well, my Lord," replied the persistent advocate, "I have one other point. I don't think much of it myself, but you never can tell what a court may think of any point."

(641)
> "Your Lordships will be glad to hear that I shall present a pure point of law uncorrupted by any merits."

Policeman, (535)
> See also Definitions

Politics
> See Constitutional law, (220)

Pollock, Frederick, (3f), (25f), (81f), (112f), (159f), (616f)

Pollock, Lord, (227)

Poor
> Good thing to be poor when young:

(643)
    ... he quoted with approval Justice Holmes' pronouncement that "it was good thing for us in our college days that we were all poor." One who has all "the luxuries of life poured into a trough for him at twenty" is hindered, and not helped.
    Poor, ambition, and very much in love, (691)

Population, principle of
    See Malthus

Posner, Richard, (386f), (660f)
    See Rodell, Fred

Posthumous praise
    See Approval, need for

Pound, Dean Roscoe, (92), (495), (508), (629d); (40f), (92f)
    See also Beale, Joseph; Law classroom

Pound, Chief Judge, (787)

Powell, Lewis
    See United States Supreme Court, (718)

Powell, Thomas Reed, (150), (219), (726)
    See Harvard Law School (393); Legal Mind (552); Opinions (618)

Precedent
    See Antitrust cases (47), Gray, Horace (382); Stare decisis (685)
(647)
    [Judge Mathew O. Tobriner] ... let me tell you the story told recently by retired Supreme Court Justice Charles E. Whittaker. It seems that in the course of argument of a case before the United States Supreme Court, a lawyer repeatedly cited as precedent the judgments of Mr. Justice Peffley. Finally the Chief Justice leaned over and said, "Counsel, the Court does not readily identify Mr. Justice Peffley. Would you please tell us who he is?"
    "Why," replied the attorney, "Mr. Justice Peffley is the Justice of the Peace of the Fifth District of Kaw Township of Jackson County, Missosuri."
    Thereupon the Chief Justice said, "Well, now, Counsel, the Court does not care to hear any more references to Mr. Justice Peffley. He is not considered to be persuasive authority here."
    Whereupon the lawyer retorted: "That is a coincidence. Only last week

140

I heard Mr. Justice Peffley make an identical statement about the judgment of this court."

(648)
      The fact that Englishmen tended to occupy the places on the Bench (in Ireland); the fact that until 1849 there was virtually no indigenous system of legal education; and, above all, the fact that there were no printed reports of the Irish decisions upon which could be founded a native system of precedent, all contributed to this result. It is said of Lord Manners, who held the great seal in the 1820's, that he once addressed counsel thus: "Are you sure, Mr. Plunket, that what you have stated is the law?" "It unquestionably was the law half an hour ago," replied the advocate pulling out his watch; "but by this time the packet boat has probably arrived, and I shall not be positive."

(649)
You ask me why
A man may speak the thing he will.
A land of settled government,
A land of just and old renown,
Where Freedom slowly broadens down
From precedent to precedent.

Prejudice
      See Jury, Learning; see also note to, (397f)

Prichard, Edward F., (8)

Prime authority
      See Holmes, Oliver Wendell, (418)

Prisoners
      See also Columbia Law School, Harvard University
(650)
      But there is some danger, perhaps, that I might say something tonight that I have said before either in America or Canada and I have debated with myself whether I ought not to begin, as a young and brilliant friend of mine began a lecture the other night in London to a most distinguished audience by saying: "Ladies and Gentlemen, I have delivered this lecture once before. It was to the prisoners in His Majesty's prison at Pentonville. I must therefore apologize if any of my hearers have heard me before."

      Do you want to take the stand?:

(651)
>Are they like the prisoner who, when asked: "Do you want to take the stand?" answered: "No, I think I had better remain neutral."

(652)
>A man was facing trial and possible imprisonment. 'I know the evidence is against me,' he told his lawyer, ' but I've got twenty thousand pounds in cash to fight this case.' 'You'll never go to prison with that amount of money,' the lawyer assured him:
>He didn't. He went there broke

(653)
>Judge to prisoner: I am afraid I must send you to penal servitude for seven years.
>Prisoner (moved) Don't let that worry you, my lord, I'm the one wot's got to do the stretch.

Pritchard, Edward F., (8)

Professors, (655f)
See also Casebooks
(654)
>P. Denison Smith taught evidence at Boston University Law School during the forties and fifties. When a point of evidence required some knowledge of substantive law, he would inquire of the class if they had reached that point in their studies. When met with no response, he would pause, and, in a stentorian voice, announce, "Then I can speak with authority."

(655)
>To Justice Stone he had once written: "You are writing ... in the first place, for the law teachers, and if you think they don't need it, you are greatly mistaken. ... Secondly, you educate students and the younger bar. Thirdly, it is more and more important to enlighten ... the other departments of the social sciences and the influence that they exert upon the young and opinion generally ..."

>>Nothing more honorable than
>>>See Frankfurter, Felix, (314)
>>Press hear to listen to...
>>>See Constitutional law, (218)
>>Some damn fool latched the door, (507)

Teachers of procedure:

(656)

I have associated with many classes of people, but I doubt whether I have ever been with any who have impressed me as having less spontaneous charm than those teachers and writers of law who specialize on procedure.

(657)

Even in academic circles scholastic enthusiasm varies. One professor's objection to lecturing on Wednesday was mordantly said to be because it spoiled both weekends for him.

(657a)

On university campuses a story is making the rounds about two citizens of Ancient Athens who met in the street.

"Have you heard the news about Socrates? He's been sentenced to death."

"What a terrible shame," said the other.

""He's such a great teacher."

"Yeah," said the first man, "but he never published!"

(657b)

You may remember the story of the head of an Oxford college. I hasten to say not my own, who was taken seriously ill to a hospital. As he recovered from his operation, still weak and faltering, the nurse handed him a large greetings telegram. She opened it and read it out. It was a telegram of greetings from his colleagues at the college: "Your colleagues send you," it read, "most good wishes for your future. This motion was passed at a meeting of the governing body this morning by a majority of 13-12 with six abstentions."

> Wake him up yourself, you put him to sleep
> See Law students, (537)

Providence
    See Judges, (450)

Proximate cause
    See Judges (452)

Public utilities course
    See Frankfurter, Felix, (316)

Publicity game
    See Arnold, Thurman, (60)

Puerto Rico
>See Court of Appeal, (229)

Puke
>See Vomit

Pusey, Merlo John, (137f), (183f), (220f), (389f), (431f), (432f), (434f), (435f), (436f), (437f), (588f), (683f)

Puzzle
>See Doctor, Hughes, Charles Evans, (431)

-q-
Question begging, (618)

Question of fact
(658)
>As Justice Holmes put it, if the case is an easy one, the judge decides it as a "question of law"; if it is a hard one, it is a "question of fact" for the jury.

Question of law
>See Question of fact

Quick, courteous, and wrong
>See Court of Appeal, (228)

-r-
Rabelais, (133)

Race
>See Coleman, William

Rationale
>See Stare decisis, (685)

Real property, (509)

Realtor and real estate dealer
(659)
>His court life was not unlit by humor. He would often convulse his associates and spectators with a merry quip and on one occasion, when counsel

was using rather indiscriminately the terms "realtor" and "real estate dealer" in arguing a case, the presiding officer, Chief Justice Taft, asked if there was any difference.

Holmes interrupted with: "A realtor gets a higher fee than a real estate man."

Recusal, (397f)

Reed, Stanley F., (619)

Rehnquist, William Hubbs (660)

Sandra Day O'Connor: One day as we gathered in our conference room to shake hands before going to the courtroom, he appeared with four gold stripes on each sleeve of his robe. We thought it must be a joke. Where did those come from, we asked. "Oh, I had the seamstress sew on one stripe for every five years I have been on the Court," he said. Just like the Lord Chancellor in Gilbert and Sullivan." And the stripes stayed. He could have added more but never did.

R. Ted Cruz: Once, when a law clerk asked him how he went about choosing law clerks, the Chief responded, "Well, I obviously wasn't looking for the best and brightest, or I wouldn't have chosen you guys."

James C. Duff: When referring to less publicized Supreme Court opinions he liked to quote Thomas Grey's Elegy Written in a Country Churchyard -

Full many a flower is born to blush unseen,
And waste its sweetness on the desert air

On his role in the Clinton impeachment trial he quoted quoted Iolanthe: "I did nothing in particular, and I did it very well."

Reid, John P., (50f)

Rentoul, (196f)

Reporters, (416)

Republican, (105), (785f)
Chances to practice in South, (785)

Restatement of Laws
See American Law Institute

Retirement
(661)

Justice Holmes had been on the Supreme Court for many years and it was after President Coolidge had been elected to fill out the term of President Harding that there was a release from one of the newspapers in Washington that Chief Justice Rugg of the Massachsetts Supreme Court would succeed him on the Bench. Justice Holmes was then 83 or 84 years of age and been on the Bench over 20 years. All during the time he was on the Bench he had worn the same robe that he had worn back when he was Chief Justice of the Massachusetts Supreme Court. A few days after this article appeared about the suggested appointment upon Justice Holmes's retirement he came out with a brand new robe (after 20 years),. And then he remained several years on the Court.

Richardson, C.J., (464)

Rickles, Don
(662)

Don Rickles: He's a great lawyer – I got a traffic ticket and he had it reduced to second-degree manslaughter.

Riggins, John, (19)

Roberts, John, (87f)
See Baseball

Robinson, Crabb, (28f), (491)
Rodell, Fred, (604)
(663)

The logical conclusion of this train of thought was reached by Fred Rodell, a Yale Law School professor who has the dual distinction of producing the most apt comment made about legal academic writing ("There are two things wrong with almost all legal writing. One is its style. The other is its content."), and of authoring Woe Unto You, Lawyers!, described by Richard Posner as "the worst book ever written by a professor at a major law school."

Rogers, Will
(665)

When Will Rogers was asked what his solution was to the traffic problem. He said that he thought all the traffic going west should go on Tuesday, Thursday and Saturday, and all the traffic going east should go on Monday, Wednesday and Friday. Sunday would be a day when everybody went, somebody then asked him, well, what about the North and South. Will Rogers then said, "there is no North and South. They are all one."

Rogers, William P., (80f)

Roosevelt, Franklin Delano, (397f)
(667)
    That very night I said [to President Roosevelt], "Would you like to give a great pleasure to a very old gentleman whom you admire?"

    He said, "Certainly."

    "Justice Holmes will have his ninety-second birthday shortly after your inauguration, on March 8, 1933. I think it would be very exciting if you called on him by way of a surprise … Suddenly the door opened and as he stumped in on the arm of Jimmy and Justice Holmes became aware that somebody was coming in, he looked sharp, leaned forward in his chair and said, "Isn't that young fellow the President of the United States?"

    He stood up, and he could hardly – well, you know he was a very old gentleman. He used to say, "The jackknife won't open." It was a wonderful scene. Then it got into the papers. He was with him for about an hour, and I said to myself, "I'll bet they're all speculating what did the President of the United States and this most revered figure in the land, this wise old, wisest of judges, what did they talk about? What great things passed between them?" We'll, somehow or other the talk got on prize fights – John L. Sullivan and Jim Corbett. Holmes was telling of the first prize fight he saw, and they got to talking about prize fights. As soon as President Roosevelt put him at his ease he quickly said, "What do you suppose I was doing just before I came here, Mr. Justice?"

    "I haven't the slightest idea."

    "I was signing an executive order calling in all the gold."

    Holmes looked a little disturbed and said, "Does that mean I must turn over my gold medal from Congress?"

Roosevelt, Theodore, (300f), (328f)

Root, Elihu, (432)

Ropes, John Codman (Ropes-Gray)
    See Law firms; also (521af)

Rosen, Jeffrey, (30f), (87f), (102f), (105f), (122f), (141f), (262f), (274f), (289f), (325f), (390f), (399f), (404f), (575f), (655f), (667f), (672af), (698f), (719f)

147

Rosenberg, Ethel and Julius, (397f)

Rossman, George, (2f), (109f), (115f), (158f), (442f), (451f), (455f), (464f), (616f), (650f), (735f), (740f), (787f)

Rovere, Richard H., (13f), (471f), (757f)

Rugg, C.J.
    See Retirement, (661)

Rule in Shelley's Case
(669)
    Professor: What is the rule in Shelley's Case?
    Student: It's the same for him as for anyone else.

Rutledge, Wiley, (617f), (658f)

-s-
Sacco-Vanzetti case
(670)
    "Did you see what I did with those anarchistic bastards the other day?" a proud Judge Thayer [the Massachusetts judge who presided at the trial of Sacco and Vanzetti] asked a friend shortly after the trial. "I guess that will hold them for a while."

Safe anywhere
    See McReynolds, James C.

Safire, William, (93f)

Salvation Army
    See United States Supreme Court, (717)

Satan
(672)
    How the edifice of justice can be supported by the efforts of liars at the bar and ex-liars on the bench is one of the paradoxes of legal logic which the man in the street has never solved. The bitter sketch of "Two Lawyers" by Daumier still expresses the accepted public view of the legal profession. So, too, does the oft-told story of Satan's refusal to mend the party wall between Heaven and Hell when it was his turn to do so, of St. Peter's fruitless protests and threats to bring suit, and of Satan's crushing comeback: "Where do you

think you will find a lawyer?"

Say's law, (547)

Scalia, Antonin, (87f)
> See also Affirmative Action

(672a)
"From watching too many episodes of The Sopranos your staff [Boston Herald] seems to have acquired the belief that any Sicilian gesture is obscene – especially when made by an Italian jurist. (I am, by the way, an American jurist)."

Schaff, Harrison Hale, (221)

Schmertz, Eric J., (647f)

Scholars
> See Casebooks

Schorer, Mark, (689f)

Schwartz, Bernard, (731f)

Scott, Austin
> See Citation, (180)

Scott, Sir Walter
> See Deliberate speed, (262)

Seasongood, Murray, (210f), (212f), (280f), (332f), (452f), (651f)

Self-made man
(673)
> Somebody boasted of being a self-made man, and Holmes said, "Well, a self-made man usually hasn't made much."

Senator, (421)

Sentencing
> See Prisoners (653)
> Defense of extreme youth of his counsel
>> See Young lawyer (786)

Sergeant, Elizabeth Shepley, (442f), (475f), (512f)

Sex
> See Novelists

Seymour, Whitney North, (699f)

Shakespeare, William, (385f)
> See also Beck, James M.

Shall and will
(675)
> Perhaps I am unjust, but he [Lewis Mumford] has rather roused my prejudice, so that I have gone back over what I have read in the vain effort to find a passage, it is there somewhere, that shows he is not at home in the differences between shall and will.

Shane, Scott
> See Baseball

Sheerman, Barry, (312f), (496f)

Sherman Antitrust Act,
> See Antitrust cases, Holmes, Oliver Wendell, (414)

Shiras, George Jr., (251)
(676)
> Mr. Justice Shiras, who at times was inclined to be a wag, was credited with saying to counsel, during the argument of the Benedict Collar Button Case in which a hump in the middle of the shank was relied on to justify the patent, that if a certain question were answered affirmatively, he might be in favor of sustaining the patent. When counsel asked what the question was, the Justice answered:
> "Will this hump prevent the collar button from rolling under the bureau when you drop it."

Sic utere tuo ut alienum non laedas
> See Client, (193)

Silberman, Lawrence H., (72f), (547f)

Simon, James, (102f), (104f), (312f), (316f), (394f), (398f), (459f), (591f),

(602f), (670f), (714f)

Simon, Lord, (379)

Sing Sing prison, (214)

Sit down, you damned fool, we are the Queen
(677)
    A well known piece of legal folklore tells of Mr. Justice Manisty on his first judicial circuit rising to honour the loyal toast and being pulled down by his senior, Mr. Baron Huddleston, with the admonition "Sit down, you damned fool; we are the Queen."

Slaughter house, (378f)

Slow, crapulous and right,
    See Court of Appeal, (228)

Smith, Al, (4)

Smith, Allen F., (629c)

Smith, F.E. (Lord Birkenhead), (451f), (455f), (679f), (680f), (681f)
(679)
    Judge (furiously): Mr. Smith, have you ever heard of a saying by Bacon, the great Bacon, that youth and discretion are ill-wedded companions?
    F.E.Smith: I have, and have you ever heard the saying of Bacon, the great Bacon, that a much-talking judge is like an ill-tuned cymbal?

    Archbishop of Canterbury:
(680)
    "Upon my soul, F.E. I shouldn't have been surprised to hear that you had been made Archbishop of Canterbury"
    "If I had," replied the Lord Chancellor, "I should have asked you to come to my installation."
    "That's damned nice of you," said Bottomley.
    "Not at all, I should have needed a crook."

    Glittering prizes:
(681)
    Then came the exquisitely insulting peroration [by F. E. Smith]: "I venture to say that the sum total of human happiness, knowledge and

achievement would have been almost unaffected if Sappho had never sung, if Joan of Arc had never fought, if Siddons had never played and if George Eliot had never written."

    I'm trying to be, and you can't help it, (679f)

Smith, T.V., (381f)

Social improvement, (495)

Social sciences, (117), (655), (734)

Socialized property, (440)

Society of Fellows (Harvard), (57f)

Socrates, (657a)

Solicitor General, (476f)
(683)
    [The Chief Justice] greeted both his son [the Solicitor General] and his son's wife with a kiss.
    "Well," he said, his whiskers parting into a broad smile, "I suppose this if the first time the Chief Justice ever kissed the Solicitor General; and certainly it is the first time the Chief Justice ever kissed the Solicitor General's wife."

Souter, David Hackett, (113)
(684)
    Justice from Nowhere

Speeches, (385)
    See also After-dinner speaker, Oratory

Spinster, (585)

Sports
    See Baseball (87, 88); for basketball, see 745; for football, see (19), (251), (398), (578); see also Mendoza line; and for all sports, see (712)

St. Peter
    See Satan

Stare decisis
(685)

[Justice Jackson] put it acidly: "The Court's reasoning adds up to this. The Commission must be sustained because of its accumulated experience in solving a problem with which it had never before been confronted."

Stark, Louis, (181)

State
    Attorney for the state
        See Heart transplant, (396)
    State judicial ladder, (228)

Stephen, Mr. Justice, (221)

Sterilization, (150)

Stevenson, Adlai, (629a)

Stewart, Potter, (105)
    See also Burger, Warren, (141)

Stone, Harlan Fiske, (30f), (91f), (151f), (176f), (180f), (308f), (399f), (516f), (530f), (596f), (643f)
(688)

    On another occasion Stone returned from conference with the air of a man bursting with a good story. "Well," he said, "the old man is still the keenest one of the lot." And then he told of a long wrangle about a case, in which certain of the Justices were asserting what seemed to Stone an untenable position. Holmes had grown drowsy, and finally sat back for his afternoon nap. As the discussion wore on, the old man suddenly opened his eyes and launched into a summary of the issues, so lucid and persuasive that it was quickly followed by a unanimous vote. "A great old man," said Stone, "he punctured their arguments like a bubble."

    Holmes liked Stone and enjoyed their occasional interchanges of wit. Stone had drafted an opinion in a conspiracy case under the Prohibition Act, involving only a buyer and seller of liquor, and had had trouble explaining why two such parties should not be held guilty of a conspiracy to make the sale. Holmes wrote him a note to the following effect: "Why don't you point out that a purchase and sale, like adultery, requires mutually consenting parties performing correlative functions?" Stone got the point, and Holmes' thought, minus the unconventional analogy, went into his opinion.

In another case, involving transfer taxes on the lending of securities to cover short sales, Holmes endorsed Stone's opinion: "I dissent. 'Loan' is not a verb." "I told him at lunch today," said Stone later, "that 'loan' is a verb except at Harvard."

Stone liked all this, but he nevertheless was suspicious of Holmes' facility and his sometimes cavalier attitude toward opinions. In one difficult case that interested Stone the opinion was assigned to Holmes (on Saturday night, as was the custom), and by Tuesday morning the printed draft had been circulated among the Court. Stone was distressed. "This is a pretty good opinion on the point that he decides," he said, "but the old man leaves out all the troublesome facts and ignores all the tough points that worried the lower courts." And every once in a while, after reading one of Holmes' opinions, Stone would say: "I wish I could make my cases sound as easy as Holmes makes his."

Stone, Irving, (471f)

Stone, Martin, (280)

(688a)
Story, Joseph
"a man of great learning, and of reputation for learning even greater than the learning itself ... fond of glittering generalities." John Chipman Gray.

Strauss, Lewis L., (409f)

Strut when he was sitting down,
(689)
Justice Holmes wrote of [Dr. Henry] Van Dyke that he was a man who could strut when he was sitting down.

Sturges, Wesley, (60)

Sullivan, Alexander M., (193f), (640f)

Sullivan, Serjeant, (247f)

Summary proceedings
See Definitions

Sutherland, Arthur E., (699f)

Sutherland, George

See Four horsemen

Swasey, Professor, (221)

Symbols
    We live by:
(690)
    "We live by symbols."
With such boring frequency am I wont to quote this phrase which Mr. Justice Holmes was fond of using that at length Mrs. Frankfurter was driven to reply, "I wish Holmes had never said that."

-t-

Tact
(691)
    Sir John Karslake, when asked what were the three things necessary for success at the Bar said the first was tact, the second tact, and the third tact. He was not far wrong. I have seen many errors made, cases lost and clients affronted by want of ordinary tact on the part of the barrister. (When Sir Edward Clarke was asked the same question he said, "To be very poor, very ambitious and very much in love." No doubt these qualifications may also have much to do with a man's success."

Taft, William Howard
(693)
    Chief Justice Taft to his class at Yale about his experiences as Chief Justice: "And I said to Holmes: 'But do you think it was right or fair to leave that fact out of consideration?'" "And," continued Taft with the mountainous chuckle, "he said, 'I'm sorry; I didn't read that far in the record.'"

(694)
    There is a story about former President Taft, after a talk with President Hoover, reporting that he had just come from a discussion of what Hoover called "legal machinery," adding, "And , you know, Hoover thinks it really is machinery."

    Advisory opinion
        See Advisory opinion
    If it is only a bag of wind, (17f)

Taxes
>	Income from a trust fund as a gift, (625)
>	Price we pay for civilization
>>	See Civilization
>
>	Satire on government:

(696)
>	Ralph Waldo Emerson: Of all the debts men are least willing to pay: the taxes. What a satire is this on government.

Taxi cab driver
>	On the Supreme Court
>>	See United States Supreme Court (721)

Tears
>	Advocate reducing himself to
>>	See Advocate

Telephone company
>	See Arnold, Thurman, (56)

Ten Commandments
(697)
>	Man is an able creature, but he has made 35,643,692 laws and hasn't yet improved on the Ten Commandments.

Testators, (751)

Thayer, Webster
>	See Sacco-Vanzetti case

Thomas, Clarence
(698)
>	"It is not a coincidence that Justice Clarence Thomas has in his chambers a sign ridiculing Douglas's opinion in the Griswold contraceptives case: 'Please don't emanate in the penumbras.'"

Thompson, Francis
>	See Deliberate speed

Thoreau, Henry David
(699)
  I must say I do remember that my wife and I were having tea with Justice Holmes one day and we got to talking about Thoreau and I'd always thought of him as a dissenter and a non-conformist, and he told me this story, which is the source of the only doubt about Thoreau I've ever had. Holmes said that a friend of his in Concord had once said, "You know, I've read everything Henry's ever written about those nuts and berries he used to eat, but I never found a word about the apple pies that he used to get at our back door."

Tobacco trusts, (414)

Tobriner, Judge Mathew O., (647)

Tobriner, Walter N., (265)

Torts, (396), (452)
  Faker goes to Lourdes for "cure," :
(700)
  Speaking of witnesses, I do want to end with this story, and I beg the forgiveness of my Androscoggin Colleagues because I have told it to them before. A trial was in progress in Dublin where a man had been hit by a tram car and he claimed terrible injury, so terrible that he was completely paralyzed. During the trial they brought him to the courtroom upon a stretcher day after day. He had sued for a hundred thousand pounds, and he made such a pathetic picture that the jury gave him the hundred thousand pounds. The lawyer for the tram company thought he was a faker and had indicated it throughout the trial, and some bitterness developed between he and the plaintiff. After the verdict was rendered and Reilly was being taken out of the courtroom on a stretcher, Mr. Kelly walked over to him and said, "Reilly, you are a faker and I know it. You are never going to enjoy the fruits of that money. I am going to follow you to the ends of the world and I will see to it that when you get up and walk that I will have you charged with perjury." Mr. Reilly looked at Kelly and said, "Mr. Kelly, that is all very fine, but let me tell you something, when they take me out of this courtroom they are going to take me down to the dock and put me on a boat and take me from there to Liverpool, and from Liverpool they will put me on ship and I will go to Calais, and Calais they will put me on a train and I will go to Lourdes, and Mr. Kelly, if you are at Lourdes you are going to see the greatest religious miracle of the 19th century."

  How high can you lift your arm? (244)

Plaintiff's side, defendant's side, and then the right side:
(701)
... there are two sides to most every question. But in this personal injury field there are three sides. There is the plaintiff's side, the defendant's side, and then the right side is usually somewhere in between. Because, after all, we defendants are apt to minimize almost as much as the plaintiffs exaggerate ...Be prepared. Don't ask for a continuance. Don't be like this lawyer that went up to the judge and says, "Judge, I want a continuance." The Judge says "You do. What is your grounds?" He says, "I want a continuance on the grounds of surprise." The Judge says, "Well, what is the surprise?" He says, "Well, Judge, two witnesses who said they wouldn't show up are here."

Toscanini, Arturo, (438f)

Traffic problem, (665)

Treatises
> Author finds his work being cited against him
>> See Citation (180)

Treby, C.J., (464f)

Trespass
> See Case

Trial court
> Could and did do justice
>> See Appellate court

Trial judge
See also Judges

> Bastard:

(703)
... the case was tried before this judge and his inimitable manner gave this attorney friend of mine a real bad time. ... and the Federal judge, apparently his conscience bothered him a little bit as the two of them descended in the elevator and he turned to the lawyer and he said, counselor, I may have been a little bit rough on you on that trial but all I can say to you is that long ago I learned in order to be a good trial judge you have to be a little bit of a bastard. My friend looked at him and he said, you're not just a good trial judge, you're a great trial judge.

Second the motion
> See Motions
> Trillin, Calvin, (744f)

Trial practice
> See Hall, Marshall (385, 385f); see, in general, many other topics such as Objections
> > Points of law
> > > See Points of law

Truman, Harry, (102f)
(707)
> The conversation went something like this: Gibson: "Mr. President, It's good to see you." Truman: "Ernest, what brings you to Washington?" Gibson: "I want to be appointed the federal judge in Vermont." Truman: "Why in hell aren't you a Democrat?" Gibson: "How in hell would I get elected in Vermont if I were a Democrat?" Without further ado, Truman picked up the phone, called the U.S. Attorney General, and said, "When you recommend an appointment for the U.S. District Judge for Vermont, I want you to recommend Ernest W. Gibson, Jr."

Trusts, (180)
> See also antitrust (414); see also Antitrust cases

Truth, (11), (46), (107), (44)1, (612), (640), (755)
> House of Truth, (35)
> See Yale Law School

Tushnet, Mark V., (141f)

Twain, Mark, (782); (57f)

Tweed, Harrison
> See Warren, Edward Henry

-u-

Underdog
> See Client

Undone vast, (495)

Unitarians, (404f)

United States Constitution
    See also Black, Hugo (103); Frankfurter, Felix, (312)
    Fool for a client
        See Blackman, Harry A., (107)
    People and the Constitution
        See God and Court, (378)

United States Government
    One club to which we all belong:

(710)

    In the words of Mr. Justice Holmes, "The United States Government is one club to which we all belong."

United States Secretary of State
    Prepared to dine for our country, (437)

United States Supreme Court
    Ability to count to five
        See Brennan, William Joseph Jr.
        Also to eight
            See Holmes, Oliver Wendell, (425)
    Beard or mustache
        See Hughes, Charles Evans, (433)

    Bench you, you are on the first team:

(712)

    The United States Supreme Court is one of the few places where when they bench you, you're on the first team.

    Chairs of Justices
        See Burger, Warren, (140)
    Chief Justice, role of
        See Law dean, (516)
    Christ, what dignity
        See Christ, what dignity

    Color line of Court:

(713)

    The talk was general, and at one stage the Governor [Hughes] said: "Butler, what was the 'color line of the Court' I heard someone refer to the other day?"

"That," was my reply, "was when Justices Gray, Brown, and White sat in a row; but as only Justice White is left there is no color in the Court now."

"Oh, no, Mr. Butler," said Mrs. Wilson, quick as a flash, "the Court is all Hughes now."

Conferences
    See Brewer, David, (126)
    Depression because of,
        See Black, Hugo, (104)

Dress code at:

(714)

Frankfurter dressed casually in an alpaca coat and slacks for his first judicial conference, but upon entering the well-appointed conference room, he was chagrined to find that all his new colleagues wore suits. At the lunchtime break Frankfurter rushed home, changed into a suit and returned for the afternoon session. He was greeted by Chief Justice Hughes, who had also made a lunchtime change of dress, and now wore his alpaca coat.

Orderly proceedings
    See Fuller, Melville Weston, (325)
Court is a puzzle
    See Hughes, Charles Evans, (431)

Craving appointment to:

(715)

I can say now without the shame that I suppose I should feel – I longed at the thing beyond all else that I craved [appointment to the Supreme Court] to get a place on it. Don't for God's sake, say I have done as well, that would miss the very point. (This is a penitential confession.) It was the importance, the power, the trappings of the God damn thing that really drew me on, and I have no excuse beyond my belief that I am not by a jugful alone in being subject to such cheap and nasty aspirations.

Damned fool told you to close that window
    See Brown, Henry Billings, (137)
Decisions are nonsense
    See McReynolds, James C., (590)
Dirtiest day's work I never did in my life
    See Grier, Robert C., (383)
Enforcing decisions
    See Marshall, John, (575)

Errors of a lower court to the errors of brethren,
    See Certiorari, (173)
Eight other men, none of whom knows any law
    See Brewer, David, (126)
Four Horsemen
    See Four horsemen
Friendship with Justice Holmes
    See Abraham's bosom
Function of
    See Court of Appeal, (228)
God save the United States, (334f)
Greatest living jurist isn't on
    See Cardozo, Benjamin Nathan, (160)

Height factor:
    See also Height

(716)

In appearance, Frankfurter did not quite live up to his own idea of what a Supreme Court Justice
ought to look like. 'Supreme Court justices should be tall and broad and have a little bit of a bay window.'

Liberal "Axis" on the Court
    See Axis
Majority opinions
    Shapeless mass of dough
        See Opinions, (618)
Tourists at
    See Marshall, Thurgood, (577)
Marshal of the Court, (334f)

Mountains out of molehills:

(717)

A young husband rushed madly into a large department store and told the saleslady he had come to purchase a brassiere for his wife. She saw his embarrassment, and to assist him she said, "Well, the three most popular models are the Malenkov, the Salvation Army, and the Supreme Court. The Malenkov model uplifts the masses, the Salvation Army model supports the fallen, and the Supreme Court model makes mountains out of mole-hills.

New appointments to the court
    See Administrative law, (8)

Nine little law firms:
(718)
Powell had said the justices work as "nine little law firms," ...

Nine scorpions trapped in a bottle:
(719)
The Supreme Court is like nine scorpions trapped in a bottle.

Persuasive authority
    See Precedent, (647)
Presumed to know
    See Blackstone's Commentary, (109)
Reading lists of members of Court
    See Ward, Lester (734)
Resigning and
    See Butler, Charles Henry (147); Columbia Law School (214);
    Day, William R. (251); Grier, Robert C. (383); (512),(512f)
    die or resign
Retirement and
    See Retirement, (661)
Robing Room, (30), (178), (383), (456)
Says x, I believe he means x
    See Naivity
Shredding latest decisions of
    See Constitutional law, (219)
Slow, rude, and right
    See Court of Appeal (228)

Talk to those damn fools than listen to them:
(720)
Certainly twice, and I think three times he [John G. Johnson] was asked to go on the Supreme Court. ... He was given to blunt talk. When his friends said to him, "Well, why don't you go on the Supreme Court?" he said, "You finally want me to tell you the true reason? I would rather talk to those damn fools than listen to them!"

Tipping by:
(721)
Justice Clark: Each morning Justice Reed would leave the Mayflower and hail a cab at about nine o'clock in the morning ... he told the driver he

would to go to the Supreme Court building. They went around the corner and the driver said, "No use going there this time of day. The big shots don't get there until twelve o'clock." ... So about two blocks farther on he said, "Do you know how many hours they stay there after they get there at twelve o'clock?" The Justice said "No," and the taxi driver said, "Four hours." The Justice said, "Well, perhaps they have to work some at home and that is just when they are sitting. I understand they write a lot of opinions." The taxi driver said, "Yes, that is true, but they don't write the opinions. You see, I carry the law clerks also and they tell me that they write the opinions." ... "Do you know how many months out of the year they sit there for four hours a day?"" Stanley said, "No." He said, "Eight months out of the year." ... "Do you know how much money they get for being there four hours a day for eight months of the year?" "No." The taxi driver said, "Thirty-five thousand dollars a year." And Stanley replied, "What in the world do they do with all that money?" The tax driver said, "I don't know, but from the size of the tips they give me, they keep it in their pockets."

(722)
Umpire of the Federal system:

{The] "umpire of the federal system"

(723)
vacancy:

"Washington adores a funeral – especially if it ushers in a vacancy," wrote Robert Jackson [on the death of C.J. Stone]

(724)
Wild horses:

The wild horses {C.J. Stone's reference to his court).

(725)
The Supreme Court's recognition of his [Leonard W. Levy] books, for instance, gave him no pleasure, he said in a 1980 interview published in Journalism History.

"Two of my books" - those on the Fifth and First Amendments – "have been cited 10 or 12 times each and not once accurately, significantly or responsibly," he said. "If the court, or the justices of the court, botches what I say in those books, how can I have contributed to any public understanding? I haven't."

(726)
In referring to some Supreme Court Justices who seek to impress upon

us in effect that it is not they that speak but the Constitution that speaks in them, TRP [Thomas Reed Powell] remarks that "Somehow this reminds me of the biographer who wrote of Gladstone that his conscience was not only his guide but also his accomplice."

(726a)
I once told Learned Hand that the Supreme Court had lost the distinction between being the referee and being the handicapper.

(727)
Lawyer addressing the U.S. Supreme Court: "I come like john the Baptist crying, "Repent, Repent!"
Oliver Wendell Holmes: "Counselor, you recall what happened to the fate of John the Baptist?"
"Yes – he lost his head to an immoral woman – but I have never believed this Court susceptible to the same influences or an immoral woman."

University presses
    See Casebooks
-v-
Vacancy on Court, (723)

Vacation time, value of
    See Brandeis, Louis, (119)

Van Devanter, Willis
    See Butler, Pierce, (151)

Van Dyke, Henry, (689)

Veeder, (550)

Verdict
    Case that got the verdict was my case
        See Attorney fees, (70)

Victoria, Queen, (217)

Virtue
(730)
    Too learned to be informed.
    Too wise to be enlightened.

Too virtuous to be improved.

Voir dire
See Definitions

Vomit
(731)
[An act violates due process] "if it makes you vomit."

Constitutional law and puking:
(732)
... Oliver Wendell Holmes' philosophically modest observation that he considered a law constitutional unless it made him want to "puke."

Vulgar herd
(733)
A German the other day quoted apropos of him their saying that in the vulgar herd there is one more than each of us suspects ...

-w-
Wall, Marvin, (476f)

Walls, Attorney General, (59)

Walsh, Ed, (689f)

Walsh, Joe, (205)

War, (409)
See also Abolition, Civil War

Ward, Lester
(734)
I shall read some sociological books – with great delight to find so much talent, civilization and good writing in American authors. Lester Ward is the leader; an original thinker of no mean degree. He has lived in Washington, but leaves to take a professorship. I called on him to express my appreciation and was delighted to have him ask what Court I belonged to and express a polite surprise that any member of our Court should read his books. The implication was obvious.

Warrant
> Consent warrant
>> See Defiinitions

Warren, Earl
> See Baseball (88); Deliberate speed (262); Eisenhower, Dwight D.

(275)
(734a)
> But when Warren and Frankfurter's relationship soured, he never again selected a clerk from Harvard, believing that a Harvard clerk might discuss the activities in his chambers with their former law professors, who in turn might relay that information to their old colleague, Frankfurter.

Warren, Edward Henry "Bull," (536); (505f), (735f), (736f)
> See also Law classroom (508)

> Conceived three times:

(735)
> More Bull Warren: ... (students) would get down on their knees and crawl under their seats and out the back door of the classroom to keep from being confronted with one of Warren's questions.
>> I remember a typical remark he made. He'd give a student a hypothetical state of facts and say, "Now on those facts the court decided so-and-so. What do you think of that?" and the student said, "Well, Mr. Warren. I can conceive of the court reaching that decision on those facts/" And then he gave him another hypothetical and said, "Well, on that the court decided so-and-so. What do you think of that decision?" And the student said, "Well, I can conceive of the court reaching that decision on those facts." Then he gave a third hypothetical and said the court ruled so-and-so on that. "What do you think of that decision?" and the student said, "Well, I can conceive of the court reaching that conclusion on those facts." And Mr. Warren said, "Well, Mr. So-and-so, you have conceived three times and haven't given birth to a single thought."

> Da, da:

(736)
> More Bull [Edward Henry] Warren: ... He once asked a student whether or not he agreed with a certain decision. "Well, I could argue that either way," the student replied. "In this course, Sir," Warren thundered back, "something more is required than mere geniality." ... he once said to a floundering student, "Sir, you are in very shallow water, but you are sinking fast." ... At any rate, on one such occasion Warren told a student he would never make a lawyer and ordered him out of the room. The student rose and mumbled something.

"What did you say? Speak up," said the Bull.

"I said you can go to Hell," the student replied.

"Come back, come back, Mr. Smith," Warren said, "I believe you will make a good lawyer after all."

(His comment to Judge Cutter '25): I am aware that 38 Harvard Law Review there is a learned note which does not agree with the view expressed by me today. I can only predict that, if the author of that note ever commits a murder, it will be a very complicated murder." ... On that occasion, Warren had explained the complicated Rule in Shelley's Case, and then called upon a student to solve a problem using the Rule. The student, paralyzed with terror, was unable to speak. The Bull then asked the student to simply repeat what he had just said. No response. Warren lowered his voice and said, "I will now repeat the Rule in Shelley's Case so slowly that you can take it down without knowing shorthand. Now. Repeat what I have just said.""Silence. "Very well,""said Warren, "We have to start somewhere. Now you will say after me: Da-Da." The student said, "Da-Da." (Note: This episode occurred in the television series, "Paper Chase.")

(737)
I [Harrison Tweed] still recall [Edward H. Warren's] instructions and his admonitions and have tried for fifty-five years to follow the advice he gave us at our first class: "Keep your minds and your bowels open."

Washington, D.C.
See Holmes, Fanny, (405)

Webster, Daniel, (335f)
See also Oral argument, (629)

Wechsler, Herbert, (307)

Weinberg, Louise, (397f)

Weightman, Justice, (124)

When did you get out?
See Columbia Law School (214)

White, Edward Douglass, (414), (713)
(740)
I remember a former Justice of the Supreme Court much given to interrogation who engaged counsel in a long colloquy of question and answer

at the very threshold of his argument. In a stage whisper audible within the bar Chief Justice White was heard to moan, "I want to hear the argument."

"So do I, damn him," growled his neighbor Justice Holmes.

White, Henry, (27)

White, Byron "Whizzer"
    Aren't you Whizzer White?:
(743)

[A] waitress looked carefully at White and asked, "Say, aren't you Whizzer White?" White took a sip of coffee, measured her slowly, and replied in a soft voice, "I was."

(744)
Adieu, Whizzer:

Well bid adieu to Whizzer White,
A running back who moved well to his right,
And thank him for the courtesy of staying
Until a Democrat could get the job of saying
Just who among our learned lawyers might
Deserve to take the place of Whizzer White.
(Apparently he thought that only fair,
Because the Democrats had put him there.)
We count his loyalty to team a boon:
The other side might well select a loon.

(745)

During argument before the Supreme Court, the gymnasium is kept closed. Some years ago, during argument before the Court, a constant thumping was heard that was most disruptive to the proceedings. A search by the Marshal revealed that one of the law clerks was dribbling a basketball and shooting basketballs at the net – in effect, holding his own court. This could not happen while Court is in session at present for the culprit was Justice Byron "Whizzer" White.

Whittaker, Charles e., (647)

Who the hell am I talking to? (627f)

Wickersham, George W., (67), (550)

Wiener, Frederick B., (533f), (587f)

Wigmore, John H., (440f)

Williams, Edward Bennett
    See Client (199)

Williams, Glanville, (616f)

Williamson, Robert B., (49f)

Wills
(746)
Now this festive occasion our spirit unbends,
Let us never forget the profession's best friends,
So we'll send the wine 'round and a nice bumper fill,
To the jolly testator who makes his own will.

(750) Entire estate was frittered away among the beneficiaries:

Only the lawyers, who have been slowly taking over the world, would lose. The story is told in London's Observer of a solicitor who was nearly given a will to challenge that, as he put it, "would have raised the law to the level of poetry." Unfortunately for the lawyer, the family members settled their dispute about the legacy out of court, and – in the unhired attorney's embittered words – "the entire estate was frittered away among the beneficiaries."

(751) Frustrating testators:

A Chancery Judge once observed: "I shudder to think that in the hereafter I shall have to meet those testators whose wishes on earth have been frustrated by my judgments." page 412

(752) Left the bulk of his fortune to his lawyer:

He left the bulk of his fortune to his lawyers. If everybody did this, a lot of time would be saved.

(753) Codicils that make lawyers rejoice:

London, Nov.3 (UPI) – As the codicil was read to the Court of Appeal

– "to remove any doubt as to the true construction of my will" – Lord Justice Justice interjected:

"All lawyers rejoice when they see those words. They know a feast is coming.

Rescues estate from enemies and keeps it himself, 260

(754)
In some instances, homemade pies are superior. Wills never

Wilson, Edmund, (117f), (424f), (449f)

Wilson, Jeremiah, (455)

Wilson, Woodrow, (397f)

Winship, Thomas, (512f), (623f)

Wister, Owen, (300f), (328f)

Witnesses, (240), (470), (520), (701)
What happens to a witness who does not tell the truth:
(755)
Darling at last turned to him sternly and said, "Tell me, in your country, what happens to a witness who does not tell the truth?" "Begor, me Lord," replied the Irishman, with a candour that disarmed all criticism, "I think his side usually wins."

(756)
A farmer, visiting a fair, and fearful of thieves, had deposited 100 pounds with the local innkeeper for safe custody, without the precaution of witnesses or a receipt. When the farmer claimed his money, the innkeeper denied having received it; and the disconsolate farmer went to Curran for advice. Curran first told him to make his peace with the innkeeper, and to say that he was sure that he must have left the money with another. He should later go with two reliable witnesses and deposit another 100 pounds with the innkeeper, and then return to Curran for further instructions. The puzzled farmer did as he was bid. He was then told to go by himself and seek the return of the 100 pounds, and again come back for further instructions. Still puzzled, the farmer did this, and returned with his money, though still without his initial 100 pounds. "Now return to the innkeeper with your two witnesses and demand your 100 pounds," said Curran; and acumen defeated dishonesty.

(756a)
A broweating counsel asked a witness during an assault case at what distance he was when the assault happened. "Just four feet five and one-alf inches," came the reply. "How come you to be so very exact?" said the angry counsel. "Because," said the witness, "I expected some fool or other to ask me and so I measured it."

(756b)
"At the end of a long but unsuccessful cross-examination of a plaintiff ... an inexperienced trial lawyer once remarked rather testily, "Well, Mr. Whittemore, you have contrived to manage your case pretty well." "Thank you, counselor," replied the witness, with a twinkle in his eye; "perhaps I might return the compliment if I were not testifying under oath."

Wives
    Of the famous
        See Holmes, Fanny

Wolfe, Humbert, (380f)

Women, (223), (405)
    See also Affirmative action, Holmes, Fanny; Pitney, Mrs. Mahlon
(757)
Justice Holmes was remarking that our ages were sixty years apart, and that he had known a man sixty years older than he was who had known General Washington. And that if we went back this way through history we could get into the room in which the Justice and I were sitting, people who would bring us back beyond recorded human history. And he talked about the costumes of these people
    You could see in a moment the colorful grouping in this room which took us from me through the Justice, back through the Cavaliers and all the costumes you can think of, to a man dressed in skins and carrying a club in his hand.
        He said, "Do you know what they would be talking about?" ...
        And I said, "What would they be talking about?"
        He said, "The one subject they had in common, women!"

    Family way all the time, (389)
    Holmes, Brandeis and their age, (424)

What does your husband do? :

(758)
Columnist Art Buchwald quipped to McCall magazine, "My biggest fear in Washington is that I'll sit down next to Sandra O'Connor at a dinner party and say, "What does your husband do?"

Women's rights:
(759)
Also Petroleum V. Nasby's summing up on the case for women's rights: "As it is now arranged, man and wife are one, and the man is the one."

Ladies' day:
(760)
It was Ladies' Day at Harvard Law School. A day that the women subjected to it never forget. Professor W. Barton Leach, who taught property, would allow female students to speak only on Ladies' Days. … Leach left the dais and went to the middle of the classroom, where he stood to interrogate them, surrounded by 140 or so male students, who hooted and laughed and sometimes stomped their feet, thinking it was marvelous fun. Actually, most of the women thought it was fun, too.

Woodbury, (229f)

Woodward, Bob, (105f), (577f), (578f)

Woollcott, Alexander, 123f, 182f, 667f

Wright, Major, (137f)

Wright, Marshal, (455)

Writing for profit
    See Casebooks

Wyzanski, Charles E., (57f), (173f), (386f), (397f)

-y-
Yale Law School, (57), (590)
(781)
Thus a Columbia professor, asked for comment on what is going on at Yale, quoted the great Justice Oliver Wendell Holmes as saying in another connection: "They think they've got the truth buy the scruff of the neck."

(782)
    A letter Mark Twain had written to Yale Law School on behalf of a black applicant. "I do not believe I would very cheerfully help a white student who would ask a benevolence of a stranger, but I do not feel so about the other color. We have ground the manhood out of them, and the shame is ours, not theirs. I would pay for it."

Young lawyer, (252f)
    Clients postponed on account of weather, (792)
    Conceit and, (525)
    Corporation lawyer, how to become, (226)
    Court is with you, (196)

    Decides to locate in Democratic South:
(785)
    You have probably all heard the story of the young lawyer from the North, who sought to locate in the South. Writing to a friend in Georgia, he inquired about the prospects for "an honest lawyer and Republican." His friend replied: "If you are an honest lawyer, you will have absolutely no competition. If you are a Republican, the game laws will protect you."

    Defense of "extreme youth of my counsel":
(786)
    … like the convict who when asked whether he had anything to say why sentence should not be passed remarked: he hoped the Court would take into consideration the extreme youth of his counsel.

    First appearance in court:
(787)
    On that basis, I give you as a final word this blunt but kindly admonition of Chief Judge Pound to a young lawyer on his first appearance in our Court: "Don't forget that you are talking to seven ordinary men like yourself."
    First great cause, least understood, (491)
    Harassed by judge
        I think I know now, (544)

    I taught you everything you know.. but,:
(788)
    Harold [Kohn] used to tell me, 'You know, young lady, I taught you everything you know. But by no means did I teach you everything that I know.'

Old bastard is with you, (457)
Oral argument not very good, (793)

Outsmarts general counsel: (789)

Hearing Josh talk about the Katy Railroad reminded me of the story of the general counsel of that organization who was quite perturbed because there was a young sprout down in that part of the country that was suing the railroad, and every time he could possibly bring up a case, he would file suit. And he had been extremely successful. So the counsel decided the next time this happened he would take the boy on, and show him how the old master handles a matter like this. He didn't have to wait long until there was a suit for a thousand dollars for a cow that was killed by the railroad. As you gentlemen all know, when animals are killed by railroads, they have unusual value. This was no exception. So the general counsel decided he was going to go down and prepare this case and really show this boy how the experts hand defense of this nature. He went down with his investigators and they searched and searched, and they couldn't find anything. He was quite bewildered. He got no information, and finally the night before trial he decided to call this boy up and see if couldn't settle it. So he called him on the phone. And the boy said, "I was just going to call you, sir." The counsel said, "Now don't interrupt me. I want to discuss this case, and if you will come over to my motel, we will discuss it." "Well, all right, sir, I will." So he came over, and to make a long story short he settled for five hundred dollars, took the release, and several times during the conversation the young fellow was going to speak, and the elder statesman said, "Now, never mind, we are going to handle it this way." So after he had given the release, delivered the check, he said to this young fellow," Now, I want you to know, young man, that you are up against the tops of our legal staff, and had you tried this case, we had no defense, and you would have got your full thousand dollars. So it just shows that when you are against the topflight men you have to watch your P's and Q's." The young fellow then said, "Well, sir, are you sure this check is good?" "Absolutely, there is nothing you can do about it now." The young man said, "Well, I have signed a release, but I just want to make sure the check is good." "Oh, yes, you have nothing to worry about on that check, this is a closed case." "Well, when you called me, I tried to tell you about this matter, and several times while I have been here I have tried to discuss the case from my point of view, and you wouldn't listen to me, and I thought now I should tell you that my client's cow came home last night.:"

You know, we have had lots of conversation about the indigent prisoner, and many before the court that should be represented by counsel, and this indigent appeared before the court, and the clerk had told him that he needed a lawyer and should have one, and he told the clerk that it was none of his blankety-blank business, he didn't need a lawyer. So when he got before the court he announced, "The Clerk has told me that I need a lawyer, Jesus Christ is my advocate." And the Judge smiled, leaned down from the bench and said, "I understand, Sir, but don't you think it would be a good idea to have local counsel?"

Peculiarities and inequities of the law, (499)

(790)
Similarity of law:

In Laconia, a young lawyer was studying in an office. He came in during the evening and read the law books. Then one of the partners used to move the bookmark back each night. This went on for some time. This young fellow was reading the law. One day the partner said to him, "What do you think of the study of the law?":? He said, "I like it very much, but there is an awful lot of similarity to it."

(791)
To Judge: Don't lose my case:

[A] freshman lawyer was trying his first case, a negligence case, in which his client, the plaintiff, was a lovely young lady. Of course, he called her as the first witness. After the young man had gotten his client's name, age, and address on the record, the court interrupted and started to ask questions. The young lawyer stood first on one foot and then on the other as the court's questioning continued. He finally sat down, and in due course the judge came to the end of his questioning and said: "Counselor, you may now continue with the witness. Proceed." The young man rose and said, "If your Honor please, I have no more questions to ask because I think the court has covered my case very thoroughly, But," he asked, "I would like to make a statement. If your Honor please, this is my first case, my first client. I have prepared my case thoroughly. I have gone back to the Year Books on the law; I have questioned all the eye witnesses to the accident with the greatest care; but if your Honor wants to try this case, it is all right with me except, for goodness' sake, don't lose it!"

(792)

On the following day, Tuesday the 5th, his life as a full-fledged lawyer began: "Read to Allen. Bought a chair of Smith - $9.50. (pd. 6th). The rush of clients postponed on account of weather."

(793)

A young barrister had been talking for about four hours to a jury who, when he had finished, felt somewhat exhausted. His opponent then arose and, looking sweetly at the judge, said:

My lord, I will follow the example of my friend who has just finished and submit the case without argument.

(794)

Corax and his pupil Tisias were reputedly the first Sophists. Like many young men with an appetite for worldly success, Tisias sought training from Corax in the hope of being able to sue his way to wealth and influence. Wishing to make sure he was not duped by his teacher, Tisias contracted to pay Corax only after he had actually won a law suit. On this condition his training commenced and soon enough was over. But Tisias became complacent. Years went by and Tisias brought no suits against anyone. Corax had been willing to wait to be paid, but not forever, so he brought a suit against Tisias to recover his fee"

Tisias: Your Honors, I stand before you today in humility of spirit and purity of motive. I ask only that you listen patiently and judge rightly in issuing your verdict.

Your Honors, I charge Corax for failing to teach me well the art of Rhetoric. The proof of this charge is here before us today. For if I should lose my case, it will surely prove that I was not taught Rhetoric very well. And this being the case I should NOT have to pay the tuition. For no one should have to pay for services that weren't rendered according to what was promised.

On the other hand, if I win the case, it shows that I had enough sense and talent to figure out the art of Rhetoric out on my own, despite the negligence of my instructor. But even this is not necessary to my case. For a ruling against Corax, is a ruling for me. And a ruling for me means I do not have to pay tuition. In either case, then, I should NOT have to pay tuition.

Corax: Your Honors, I too stand humbly before you. I too recognize, in years far more experienced than that of my adversary, your outstanding record of prudent and just decision making on behalf of those whose cause is just. We are indeed fortunate to gain a hearing before you. This, then, is my case.

I have given Tisias the very best education in rhetoric of which I am capable, on the condition that he would at some point in his career pay my tuition. This he has not done. Now, if you rule against me – that is if Tisias does in fact win his case – it serves to show that I taught him Rhetoric well, in which case he should be required to pay my tuition. If, however, Tisias does not win his case, that would show him to be a poor, or rather bad, student. (We already know he is poor.) Those who are wise will know that a teacher is not to be faulted if, in discharging his services well and faithfully, the student is simply too stupid or too lazy (or too both) to take advantage of those services, expertly rendered.

FOOTNOTES TO ANECDOTES

(1f)
[Hays, City Lawyer. Simon & Schuster, 1942, p. 231. Bander, Justice Holmes Ex Cathedra 230-231 (1991). 10 Villanova Law Review 299 (1964). See Bent, Justice Oliver Wendell Holmes 312 (1932)]

(2f)
[Chafee, Zechariah, The Disorderly Conduct or Words, in Rossman, ed. Advocacy and the King's English. Bobbs-Merrill, 1960, p. 626]

(3f)
[Howe, ed. Holmes-Pollock Letters. Harvard University Press, 2d ed. 1961, p. II:268 Bander, Justice Holmes Ex Cathedra 236 (1991). Bander, Holmespun Humor, 10 Villanova Law Review 302 (1964).See also Max Lerner, The Mind and Faith of Justice Holmes, 131.]

(4f)
[Frankfurter, Felix Frankfurter Reminisces. Reynal, 1962, p. 199. Bander, Justice Holmes Ex Cathedra 224-225 (1991).]

(5f)
[Howe, Justice Oliver Wendell Holmes, The Shaping Years 1841-1870. Harvard University Press, 1057, p. 156 . Bander, Justice Holmes Ex Cathedra 236 (1991). Bander, Holmespun Humor, 10 Villanova Law Review 307-308 (1965)]

(6f)
[Mendelson, ed. Felix Frankfurter: A Tribute. Reynal, 1964, p. 37. Bander, Justice Holmes Ex Cathedra 253-254 (1991).]

(7f)
[Galanter, Lowering the Bar. University of Wisconsin Press, 2005, p. 71; Hay, Peter. The Book of Legal Anecdotes. Facts on File, 1989, p. 3; Galanter cites many sources for this anecdote.]

(8f)
[Mendelson, Felix Frankfurter: A Tribute. Reynal, 1964, p. 98. Bander, Doing Justice: Class Action, 72 Law Library Journal 537 (1979)]

(9f)
[2 Santa Clara Law rev. 48 (1962); Bander, Doing Justice: Class Action, 72 Law Library Journal 535 (1979)]

(10f)
[McCormack, A Law Clerk's Recollections, 1946 Columbia Law Review 710 at 713-714. Bander, Justice Holmes Ex Cathedra 245-247 (1991).]

(11f)
[Robert Pitofsky, The Business Lawyer 292-293 (1973)]

(12f)
[Murphy, W.F., ed. Courts, Judges and Politics: An Introduction to the Judicial Process. Random House: 1961; 2d ed. 1971, p. 241]

(13f)
[Birkett, Law and Literature, in Rossman, ed. Advocacy and the King's English. Bobbs-Merrill, 1960, p. 779. See also Pannick, Advocates. Oxford University Press, 1992, p. 26-27 on the use of tears to sway a jury with examples by Marshall Hall and William F. Howe and others. See also Rovere, Howe & Hummel, Garrar, Straus and Giroux, 1947, p. 59-60.]

(14f)
[Anthony Lewis in reviewing Sandra Day O'Connor .. by Joan Biskupic in The New York Review of Books, April 6, 2006, p. 39]

(15f)
[Bent, Justice Oliver Wendell Holmes. Vanguard, 1932, p. 306; Bander, Justice Holmes Ex Cathedra 202 (1991). Bander, Holmespun Humor, 10 Villanova Law Review 503 (1965). See also Artemus Ward and David L. Weiden. Sorcerers' Apprentices: 100 Years of Law Clerks at the United States Supreme Court. NYU Press, 2006, p. 35]

(16f)
[44 Nebraska Law Review 403 1964. W. C. Fields had these last words in one of his movies.]

(17f)
[A Seminar on Personal Injury Litigation (1962) Seattle, Univ. of Washington. Another version appeared as Boston Globe Daily Story: Taft replied: "If it is a girl, I shall, of course name it for my lovely helpmate of many years. And if it is a boy, I shall claim the father's prerogative and name it Junior. But if, as I suspect, it is only a bag of wind, I shall name it Chauncey Depew.]

(18f)
[O'Hara, Remarks, Congressional Record, April 23, 1958, p. A3847. Bander, Justice Holmes Ex Cathedra 255 (1991).]

(19f)
[Joan Biskupic, Sandra Day O'Connor. Ecco, 2005, p. 167]

(20f)
[Hay, Peter, The Book of Legal Anecdotes. Facts on File, 1989, p. 160. See also Birkett, The Art of Advocacy in Rossman, ed. Advocacy and the King's English 924 ((1960). Mr. Birkett adds to this with: "But to hear it in the brogue, the effect was indescribabl.e." See also: Lord Carson, if he were alive, would no longer, I think, start a cross-examination of a witness as he once did: "Do you drink?" he asked. "That's my business," answered the witness. "Have you any other business?" said Carson. page. 413
[58 Law Society's Gazette (1961). See also Broad, Advocates of the Golden Age 80 (1958)]

(21f)
[Fowler, Gene, The Great Mouthpiece: A Life Story of William J. Fallon. Grosset & Dunlap, 1931, p. 238]

(25f)
[Howe, ed. Holmes-Pollock Letters. Harvard University Press, 2d ed. 1961, p. II:44 Bander, Justice Holmes Ex Cathedra 235-236 (1991). Bander, Holmespun Humor, 10 Villanova Law Review 302 (1964).]

(26)
[Butler, A Century ... Putnam, 1942, p. 182-183. Bander, Justice Holmes Ex Cathedra 215-216 (1991). Bander, Holmespun Humor, 10 Villanova Law Review 506 (1965)]

(27f)
[Biddle, Mr. Jsutice Holmes. Scribner's, 1942, p. 168 . Bander, Justice Holmes Ex Cathedra208 (1991). Bander, Holmespun Humor, 10 Villanova Law Review 504-505 (1965)]

(28f)
[Gilbert, The Oxford Book of Legal Anecdotes. Oxford University Press, 1986, p. 221 citing Robinson, Bench and Bar (1889)]

(29f)
[Freedman, National Ass'n Attorney Generals 123-124 (1963)]

(30f)
[Butler, A Century... Putnam, 1942, p. 90 . Note: Marshall always did follow the spirit of the law as well as the letter. See also 47 ABA Jl338 (1961), 1155 (1961). See also Mason, Harlan Fiske Stone 726 (1956) citing IV Beveridge, The Life of John Marshall 68 (1929). See also Rosen, The Supreme Court ... . Henry Holt, 2006, p. 34 citing Schwartz and Hogan, Joseph Story. Oceana, 1959, p. 25-27]

(35f)
[Gilbert, The Oxford Book of Legal Anecdotes. Oxford University Press, 1986, p. 123 citing Felix Frankfurter Reminisces, Phillips, ed. (1960)]

(36f)
[Bowen, Yankee from Olympus. Little, Brown, 1945, p. 394. Bander, Justice Holmes Ex Cathedra 210 (1991). See also Felix Frankfurter Reminisces 242 (1962)]

(37f)
[Peabody, ed. The Holmes-Einstein Letters. St. Martins, 1964, p. 302. Bander, Justice Holmes Ex Cathedra 257 (1991).Bander, Holmespun Humor, 10 Villanova Law Review 306 (1965)]

(38f)
[Richard Fountain, Wit of the Wig. Leslie Frewin, 1968, p. 67]

(39f)
[Gene M. Gressley, ed. Voltaire and the Cowboy: the Letters of Thurman Arnold. Colorado Associated University Press, 1977, p. 174]

(40f)
[The Path of the Law: A Lawyer's Tour of Boston . Suffolk University Law School, (1979, p. 13]. See also: Peck,David W. Decision at Law. Dodd, Mead, 1961, p. 259-260: [Edward H. "Bull" Warren: "Well, if you want to know what the law was, see Dean Pound. If you want to know what the law ought to be, see Professor Beale. But if you want to know what the law is, young man, sit down."]

(45f)
[McCormack, A Law Clerk's Recollections, 1946 Columbia Law Review 710

at 713-714. Bander, Justice Holmes Ex Cathedra 245-247 (1991).]

(46f) [Editor's comment]

(47f)
[Hay, Peter, The Book of Legal Anecdotes. Facts on File, 1989, p. 226-227. See Biddle, Justice Holmes, Natural Law, and the Supreme Court 9 (1961); see also Bander, Justice Holmes Ex Cathedra 204 (1991)]

(48f)
[38 North Dakota Law Review 640 (1962)] For extended treatment of this type of anecdote, see Galanter, Lowering the Bar. University of Wisconsin Press, 2005. And this bit of folklore from a Suffolk University Law School faculty member: "The Chief Justice of the Massachusetts Supreme Judicial Court, in a speech before the Suffolk University Law School Alumni Association, related the time that a clerk rushed into Superior Court Judge Frank Donahue's chamber to notify Judge Donahue that the Supreme Judicial Court had affirmed one of his opinions. Judge Donahue calmly looked up from his desk and answered, "I still think I was right."]

(49f)
[C.J. Robert B. Williamson, Proceedings of the Maine State Bar Association 111 (1964). See also: When I was a judge of first instance, sitting alone, I could and did do justice. But when I went to the Court of Appeal of three I found that the chances of doing justice were two to one against." Lord Denning. See The Literature of the Law… Brian Harris. Blackstone Press Limited, 1998, p. 249. Judge Magruder, a Court of Appeals Judge, and Judge Wyzanski, a Federal District Court Judge, dueled over the relative meritys of their job.]

(50f)
[Reid, Brandy in His Water, 57 Northwestern University Law Review 533 (1962). Bander, Justice Holmes Ex Cathedra 258-259 (1991). This anecdote is reported in Biddle, Mr. Justice Holmes (1942); Corwin, 27 Notre Dame Lawyer 325 (1952); Krislov, 52 Northwestern Univ. Law Review 514-515 (1957). The substance under consideration was reported as being marmalade in Brooks, New England: Indian Summer 266 (1950).]

(55f)
[The Talk of the Town, The New Yorker, March 20, 1965. Bander, Justice Holmes Ex Cathedra 261 (1991)]

(56f)
[Edward Bander was a law student at the time of this talk]

(57f)
[Thurman Arnold to William McGovern according to an interview with the editor of the letters. [Gene M. Gressley, ed. Voltaire and the Cowboy: the Letters of Thurman Arnold. Colorado Associated University Press, 1977, p. 479, 534.. This club rivals the Mark Twain Human Race Luncheon which allegedly never met for a lack of eligible candidates (see Bander, Mr. Dooley and Mr. Dunne (1981), p. 3), or the club that invited Groucho Marx to its membership only to be told he would not belong to any club that would take him as a member, or the famed Metaphysical Club which included Oliver Wendell Holmes that actually did meet, even if infrequently and fortunately left no transcript of their proceedings probably because of the one in a million people who might understand them. Groucho Marx should also be remembered for his tiff with Warner Brothers for titling his picture "Casablanca." He took issue with Warner because he was the Marx Brothers before they were the Warner Brothers. See also Martin Mayer, The Judges. St. Martin's Press, 2006, p. 116 for his take on Harvard's Society of Fellows which, according to Mr. Mayer, Judge Wyzanski, if given a choice of the Supreme Court or the Society, would prefer the latter. There is also the Union Club of Boston founded in 1863 that people lust for invitations to membership. See also (112f).]

(58f)
[Hay, Peter, Book of Legal Anecdotes. Facts on File, 1989, p. 3. Compare with "If you ... can think about a thing that is inextricably attached to something else without thinking of the thing which it is attached to, then you have a legal mind.." Galanter, Lowering the Bar. University of Wisconsin Press, 2005, p. 51. [quoted at Arnold, The Symbols of Government 102 101 (1935). See also Thurman Arnold, Fair Fights and Foul, Harcourt, Brace and World, 1951, p. 20-21. ["If you can think of a subject which is interrelated and inextricably combined with another subject, without knowing anything about or giving any consideration to the second subject, then you have a legal mind."] Compare with: "The test of a first-rate intelligence is the ability to hold two opposed ideas in the mind at the same time, and still retain the ability to function." F. Scott Fitzgerald, The Crack-up (1936), p. 69]

(59f)
[Thurman Arnold, Fair Fights and Foul. Harcourt Brace and World, 1951, p. 22]

(60f)
[Walter F. Murphy, Wild Bill ... Murphy. Random House, 2003, p. 92]

(65f)
[an old joke that I heard in the 1950s]

(66f)
[I suppose all this could come under the heading of Privy Counsel]

(67f)
[Pepper, Philadelphia Lawyer. Lippincott, 1944, p. 386. Bander, Bar Relief, 72 Law Library Journal 353 (1979). See also (93) and (93f) as to Philadelphia lawyers]

(68f)
["Talk of the Town," New Yorker, November 10, 1956, reprinted in 11 The Record (Bar Ass'n N.Y. 494)]

(69f)
[Kenison, C. J. in Concord National Bank v. Haverhill, 145 A. 2d 61, 63 (N.H. 1958). Bander, Justice Holmes Ex Cathedra 240 (1991). Bander, Holmespun Humor, 10 Villanova Law Review 303 (1964).]

(70f)
[Thurman Arnold, Fair Fights and Foul. Harcourt Brace and World, 1951, p. 265]

(71f)
[32 Mississippi Law Journal 375; see also Galanter, Lowering the Bar. University of Wisconsin Press. 2005, p. 77 citing William M. Evarts of New York as the person who created this bon mot and offering many sources but not this one.]

(72f)
[Lawrence H. Silberman, Will Lawyering Strangle Democratic Capitalism, Regulation, March/April 1978, p. 21]

(73f)
[Harding A. Orren, "Lying in Bed Thinking ... One Guinea, 19 Trial Lawyers Guide 78 (1975). See also Galanter, Lowering the Bar. University of Wisconsin Press, 2005, p. 84]

(74f)
[39 Idaho State Bar Proceedings 24 (1965)]

(75f)
[Fountain, Wit of the Wig. Leslie Frewin, 1968, p. 67]

(76f)
[Gilbert, Oxford Book of Legal Anecdotes. Oxford University Press, 1986, p. 67 citing Parker, Reminisces of Rufus Chaote (1860.]

(77f)
[See, as an example, Listen to Leaders in Law. Albert Love and James S. Childers. Holt, 1963, p. 65-66]

(78f)
[Rentoul, Gervais. Sometimes I Think. 1940, p. 67]

(80f)
[Hon. William P. Rogers, Attorney General, the Frank Irvine Lecture at the Cornell Law School. Department of Justice Release, Dec. 9, 1960.]

(81f)
[Howe, ed. Holmes-Pollock Letters. Harvard University Press, 2d ed. 1961, p. I:102. Bander, Justice Holmes Ex Cathedra 235 (1991). Bander, Holmespun Humor, 10 Villanova Law Review 302 (1964).]

(82f)
[Simon, The Antagonists: Hugo Black, Felix Frankfurter, and Civil Liberties in Modern America. Simon & Schuster, 1986, p. 115-116. Also in Gunther, Learned Hand: The Man and The Judge. Knopf. 1994, p. 564]

(83f)
[Personal experience by Edward J. Bander]

(84f)
[1963 Proceedings of the Maine State Bar Association 65]

(87f)
[41 Title News No. 1 28 (1962). N.Y. Times, Nov. 5, 2005, p. A11. Paul F. Campos, Jurismania, 1998, p. 60. For a distinction between a "bottom-up" judge, like Roberts, and a "top-down" judge, like Scalia, see Rosen, The Supreme Court ... Henry Holt ,2006, p. 220. See also Rosen on baseball analogy at p.

222]

(88f)
[no source]

(91f)
[Mason, Harlan Fiske Stone: Pillar of the Law. Viking, 1956, p. 219. Bander, Justice Holmes Ex Cathedra 251 (1991).]

(92f)
[Peck, Decision at Law. Dodd, Mead, 1961, p. 259-260]

(92af)
[From the diaries kept by Tom Lambert which were entrusted to Professor Michael Rustad, who gave me permission to thumb through them.]

(93f)
[Biddle, Mr. Justice Holmes. Scribner's, 1942, p. 145-146. Bander, Justice Holmes Ex Cathedra 207 (1991). Bander, Holmespun Humor, 10 Villanova Law Review 504 (1965). Note: A Philadelphia lawyer has been defined as a "shrewd attorney adept at the discovery and manipulation of legal technicalities." William Safire had a column on this topic in the New York Times Magazine, Oct. 13, 1996, p. 30.]

(100f)
[Peabody, ed. The Holmes-Einstein Letters. St. Martins, 1964, p. 349. Bander, Justice Holmes Ex Cathedra 257-258 (1991). Bander, Holmespun Humor, 10 Villanova Law Review 306 (1965)]

(101f)
[Univ. of Illinois College of Law. Dedicatory Proceedings 1956, p. 95; see also Galanter, Lowering the Bar. University of Wisconsin Press, 2005, p. 111 citing seven sources not this one.]

(102f)
[Gunther, Learned Hand. Knopf, 1994, p. 564. See also Simon, The Antagonists ... 116, 188 (1989). Harry Truman to Justice Black: "Hugo, I don't much care for your law, but, by golly, this bourbon is good." Rosen, The Supreme Court ... Henry Hold, 2006, p. 2 citing McCullough, Truman. Simon & Schuster, 1992, p. 901]

(103f)
[Gunther, Learned Hand: The Man and the Judge. Knopf, 1994, p. 564. Wild Bill ... Murphy 202 (2003). It was Mr. Dooley who reported that the Supreme Court reads the election returns See Bander, Mr. Dooley and Mr. Dunne. Michie, 1981, p. 201. See also Mayer, The Judges. St. Martin's Press, 2006, p. 15

(104f)
[Simon, The Antagonists ... Simon & Schuster, 1989, p. 159-160]

(105f)
[Woodward, The Brethren. Simon & Schuster, 1979, p. 80. See also Rosen, The Supreme Court ... Henry Holt, 2006, p. 160-161 citing Newman, Hugo Black. Pantheon, 1994, p. 588]

(107f)
[Justice Blackman in dissent, Faretta v. California, 422 U.S. 806, 852]

(109f)
[Lavery, The Language of the Law, in Rossman, ed. Advocacy and the King's English. Bobbs-Merrill, 1960, p. 758]

(112f)
[Howe, ed. Holmes-Pollock Letters. Harvard University Press, 2d ed. 1961, p. I:139 Bander, Justice Holmes Ex Cathedra 235 (1991). Bander, Holmespun Humor, 10 Villanova Law Review 302 (1964). Also: One Boston Brahmin to another: "He's getting very prominent lately." "Yes, but only nationally." (attributed to Robert S. Cutler in Lambert's diaries). Further observation: In Massachusetts, the law school is Harvard; the country club is in Brookline, etc. Further specification is redundant. See also (57f).]

(113f)
[Yarbrough, Tinsley E. David Hackett Souter. Oxford University Press, 2005, p. 113]

(115f)
[George Rossman, Appellate Practice and Advocacy in Rossman, ed. Advocacy and the King's English. Bobbs-Merrill, 1960, p. 253. Mason, Brandeis, A Free Man's Life. Viking, 1956, p. 580. Bander, Justice Holmes Ex Cathedra 250 (1991). Mrs. R. M. Boeckel to the author, March 9, 1944. See also Martin Mayer, The Judges. St. Martin's Press, 2006, p. 103. Also Mayer, The Lawyers. Harper & Row, 1966, p. 452 citing Mason.]

(116f)
[Liva Baker, Felix Frankfurter. Coward-McCann, 1969, p. 41]

(117f)
[Allen & Pearson, More Merry-Go-Round. Liverright, 1932, p. 110-111. Pearson & Allen, The Nine Old Men. Doubleday, 1937, p. 180. See also Bander, Justice Holmes Ex Cathedra 195-196 (1991). For a similar version, see Bent, Justice Oliver Wendell Holmes 280-281 (1932). See also Biddle, Justice Holmes 6 (1961); this collection. Wilson, Patriotic Gore 770 (1962) indicates that Holmes's only experiences with industrial life was taking out girls from the Lawrence, Massachusetts factories.]

(118f)
[New York Post, Aug. 23, 1962, p. 27:3; see also Kurland, ed. Of Law and Life… Frankfurter 38 (1965): Brandeis: "Perhaps the greatest weakness of man is his inability to say 'No.'"]

(119f)
[Biggs, Hon. John, Jr., 85th Congress, 2d Session, House. Department of State … the Judiciary 59 (1958). Bander, Justice Holms Ex Cathedra 208 (1991). In Acheson, Morning and Noon, 1965, p. 78 this is attributed to Justice Brandeis.]

(120f)
[Mason, Brandeis, A Free Man's Life. Viking, 1956, p. 514. Bander, Justice Holmes Ex Cathedra 249 (1991).]

(122f)
[Anthony Lewis in reviewing Sandra Day O'Connor .. by Joan Biskupic in The New York Review of Books, April 6, 2006, p. 40. See also Rosen, The Supreme Court … Henry Hold, 2006, p. 161]

(123f)
[Bowen, Yankee from Olympus. Little, Brown, 1945, p. 324. Bander, Justice Holmes Ex Cathedra 209-210 (1991). 10 Villanova Law Review 98 (1964). See also Woolcott, Long, Long Ago 108 (1943).]

(124f)
[Gilbert, The Oxford Book of Legal Anecdotes. Oxford University Press, 1986, p. 306 citing Ballantine, Some Experiences of a Barrister (1882). A.E. Bowker, A Lifetime with the Law. London: W.H. Allen, 1961, p. 85]

(126f)
[Butler, A Century.... Putnam, 1942, p. 188]

(127f)
[Butler, A Century ... Putnam, 1942, p. 75. Bander, Justice Holmes Ex Cathedra 213-214 (1991). Bander, Holmespun Humor, 10 Villanova Law Review 505 (1965). See also Hay, Peter, The Book of Legal Anecdotes. Facts on File, 1989, p. 137.]

(128)
[13th Annual Meeting of the American Branch of the ILA 32 (1934). Speech by Charles Warren]

(129f)
[Cooke, Journalists Who Make History, Atlantic Monthly 156 (Nov. 1959). Bander, Justice Holmes Ex Cathedra 217-218 (1991). Bander, Holmespun Humor, 10 Villanova Law Review 507 (1965)]

(130f)
[Andrews, The Lawyer in History, Literature and Humor. London: W. Andrews, 1896, p. 253]

(131f)
[Lovell, English Constitutional and Legal History. Oxford University Press, 1962, p. xi. Bander, Justice Holmes Ex Cathedra 244 (1991).]

(132f)
[Fuess, [Claude Moore] Rufus Choate, The Wizard of the Law. Archon, 1928, 1970, p. 126]

(133f)
[Gunther, Learned Hand. Knopf, 1994, p. 626]

(134f)
[1962 Ga. Bar Ass'n 234; 1913 Ga. Bar Ass'n 97]

(137f)
[Pusey, Charles Evens Hughes. Macmillan, 1951, p. I:275. See also:
  The temperature of the Court Room in the Capitol was very difficult to regulate. This difficulty was increased by the various views of the different Justices as to what its proper temperature should be. The regulation of the heat had always been under the control of the Marshal.

There is a traditional story anent this particular matter, which is generally ascribed to Justices Gray and Bradley. Justice Gray, who weighed more than 250 pounds, it is said, always wanted the thermometer kept below 70 degrees, while Justice Bradley, who was a very thin man, and of much lower weight, always wanted it kept up to nearly 80 degrees.

One day as Justice Bradley was going behind the screen back of the Bench, with hiw gown wrapped round him and apparently shivering with the cold, he pointed to an open window and said to the Marshal:

"What d___d fool opened that window?"

"That window," answered Major Wright, "was opened, Your Honor, by the order of Mr. Justice Gray."

"I thought so – I thought so. Shut it up and keep it shut," snapped the irate Justice Bradley and went to his seat on the Bench. Butler, A Century.. Putnam, 1942, p. 90-91]

(140f)
[Michael D. Davis and Hunter R. Clark, Thurgood Marshall; Warrior at the Bar; Rebel on the Bench. Carol, 1994, p. 303. Burger and Blackman were known as the Minnesota Twins at one time but their subsequent separation made it appear that they should have been called the Siamese Twins.]

(141f)
[Mark V. Tushnet, Making Constitution Law – Thurgood Marshall and the Supreme Court. Oxford University Press, 1997, p. 41; cited in Sanford Levinson's review in 75 Texas Law Review1482 (1997). "Warren Burger, who infuriated his colleagues by changing his vote in order to seize the best opinions for himself and then often losing his marorities." See Rosen, The Supreme Court .... Henry Hold, 2006, p. 193]

(142f)
[Linda Greenhouse, Becoming Justice Blackmun. Henry Holt and Co., 2005, p. 125]

(143f)
[58 Law Society's Gazette]

(144f)
[Bent, Justice Oliver Wendell Holmes. Vanguard, 1932, p. 19; Compare: "And the late Justice Holmes, when a joke by an Old Howard [Boston burlesque house] comedian outdid the Restoration drama in frankness, is reported to have muttered, "Thank God I am a man of low taste!" Editorial in the Saturday Evening Post, Sept. 26, 1959; Bander, Justice Holmes Ex Cathedra 410. See

also Hagedorn, Americans: A Book of Lives, 37]

(145f)
[Hay, Peter, The Book of Legal Anecdotes. Facts on File, 1989, p. 205. See also:
> Defendant in a County Court action: As God is my judge, I did not take the money
> Judge: He isn't. I am. You did.

Richard Fountain, Wit of the Wig. Leslie Frewin, 1968, p. 109. See also Robert Megarry, A New Miscellany-At-Law ed. by Byron A. Garner. The Law Book Exchange, 2005, p. 375 and citing to Henry Weihofen, Legal Writing Style, 1961, p. iv, and Neville Faulks, No Mitigating Circumstances, 1977, p. 52.]

(146f)
[Butler, A Century ... Putnam, 1942, p. 180-181. Bander, Justice Holmes Ex Cathedra 215 (1991). Bander, Holmespun Humor, 10 Villanova Law Review 506 (1965)]

(147f)
[King, Melville Weston Fuller. Macmillan, 1950, p. 286-287. Bander, Justice Holmes Ex Cathedra 241 (1991).]

(149f)
[McCormack, A Law Clerk's Recollections, 1946 Columbia Law Review 710 at 713. Bander, Justice Holmes Ex Cathedra 245 (1991).]

(150f)
[Hay, Peter, The Book of Legal Anecdotes. Facts on File, 1989, p. 227-228. For the same anecdote see,
{Pearson & Allen, The Nine Old Men. Doubleday, 1937, p. 117. Another version of this story is that when Holmes was reading his opinion in this case, he purposely paused after his famous "Three generations of imbeciles are enough," to give Butler, noted for his impetuous nature, an opportunity to shout, "I dissent." Then Holmes calmly proceeded to finish his reading.]

(151f)
[Mason, Harlan Fiske Stone: Pillar of the Law. Viking, 1956, p. 339]

(153f)
[Allen and Pearson, More Merry-Go-Round. Liverwright, 1932, p. 109. See also Bander, Justice Holmes Ex Cathedra 195 (1991). 10 Villanova Law Review 299 (1964). See also Lewis, A., High Drama in High Court, New York

Times Magazine, Oct. 26, 1958, pp. 10, 19-20. Also Murphy, Courts, Judges and Politics… 484(1961)]

(154f)
[Max Eastman, Enjoyment of Laughter. Halcyon House, 1936, p. 37]

(155f)
[Maryland State Bar Ass'n 1960:87]

(156f)
[no source]

(158f)
[George Rossman, Appellate Practice and Advocacy in Rossman, ed. Advocacy and the King's English. Bobbs-Merrill, 1960, p. 253. Mason, Brandeis, A Free Man's Life. Viking, 1956, p. 580. Bander, Justice Holmes Ex Cathedra 250 (1991). Mrs. R. M. Boeckel to the author, March 9, 1944.]

(159f)
[Hay, Peter, The Book of Legal Anecdotes. Facts on File, 1989, p. 32. See also: Pearson & Allen, The Nine Old Men, Doubleday, 1937, 38; and Frank, Marble Palace 110 (1958): "… with separate lavatory facilities in the office of each Justice, Holmes is perhaps apocryphally said to have observed that the abandonment of a common men's room meant that off the bench he would no longer see his brothers at all." See also 2 Holmes-Pollock 169 (1961). Also Bander, Justice Holmes Ex Cathedra 221 (1991)]. Bander, Holmespun Humor, 10 Villanova Law Review 507 (1965).

Justice Hughes, we have it on good authority, was once heard to announce to all and sundry in a much populated room of the Association of the Bar of the City of New York: "Here we are all peers."
[no authentication for this. But see Among Friends: Personal Letters of Dean Acheson. McLellan and Acheson, eds. Dodd, Mead, 1980, p. 153 for an episode between Churchill and Atlee in opposite ends of the stalls in a men's room. I suppose all this could come under the heading of Privy Counsel]

(160f)
[Gunther, Learned Hand. Knopf, 1994, p. ix]

(162f)
Gilbert, The Oxford Book of Legal Anecdotes. Oxford University Press, 1986, p. 162 citing Healy, The Old Munster Circuit (1939).]

(165)
[Jimmy Carter, May 4, 1974, Athens, Ga. New Statesman, Jan. 28, 1977, p. 112]

(166f)
[Curtis, Book review, 63 Yale Law Journal 270 (1953). Bander, Justice Holmes Ex Cathedra 218 (1991)]

(170f)
[no source]

(171f)
[Selections from the Letters and Legal Papers of Thurman Arnold. Wash., ?, 1961, p. 29-30]

(172f)
[Lord Eldon's Anecdote Book, ed. By A.L.J. Lincoln and R.L. McEwen. London: Stevens & Sons, 1960, p. 66]

(173f)
[Wyzanski, John A. Sibley Lecture, 7 Georgia Law Review 215 (1973). This anecdote comes from a Suffolk University Law School faculty member: Judge Donahue was once engaged in a conversation with an inquisitive person as they sat adjacent in an airliner. "And what is your occupation?" inquired the Judge's newly found companion. "I am a manufacturer," replied the Judge. "And what do you make?" was the next question. "I make reversible errors," was the answer.]

(174f)
[Holmes-Einstein Letters. Macmillan St. Martin's, 1964, p. 194. Bander, Holmespun Humor, 10 Villanova Law Review 305 (1964).]

(175f)
[Hovery, John Jay Chapman – An American Mind. Columbia University Press, 1959, p. 48-49. Bander, Justice Holmes Ex Cathedra 232-233 (1991).]

(176f)
[Mason, Harlan Fiske Stone: Pillar of the Law. Viking, 1956, p. 43. Bander, Justice Holmes Ex Cathedra 251 (1991)]

(177f)
[Fuess, [Claude Moore] Rufus Choate, The Wizard of the Law. Archon, 1928,

1970, p. 254. See also Wellman, Day in Court. Macmillan, 1910, p. 240 for additional anecdotes on Mr. Choate.]

(178f)
Biddle, Mr. Justice Holmes. Scribner's, 1942, p. 112. See also Bowen, Yankee from Olympus 357 (1945); King, Melville Weston Fuller 152-153 (1950); Bander, Justice Holmes Ex Cathedra 206 (1991).]

(179f)
[Biddle, Justice Holmes, Natural Law, and the Supreme Court. Macmillan, 1961, p. 8. Also Bander, Justice Holmes Ex Cathedra 204 (1991)]

(180f)
[1963 Proceedings of the Maine State Bar Association 79. Bander, Bar Relief, 72 Law Library Journal 354 (1979). Judge Botein writes that this episode with Scott happened in his courtroom and that Scott rebutted: "Would that mine enemy had written a book! I suppose it will come back to plague me throughout the trial. I'll admit that the bald statement, as quoted, appears to refute my argument. But it must be read in conjunction with other sections." Botein, Trial Judge. Simon & Schuster, 1952, p. 144. See also Mason, Harlan Fiske Stone 85 (1956): "I took the time from busy days at the bar to write occasional articles in the law journals of scientific and technical interest only to experience, in a repentant old age, the unhappy fate of hearing them, on occasion, cited to me in court in support of both sides of the same question." Columbia Alumni News, Vol. II, p. 292. Professor Milton Handler "recounts that Justice Stone complained that he 'never encountered a problem on the bench that had been the subject of any of the courses he took or taught in law school." See 66 N.Y.U. Law Rev. 1257 (1991). See also: "For a practitioner, authorship may well be a hostage to fortune: "behold, my desire is ... that mine adversary had written a book." Robert Megarry, A New Miscellany-At-Law ed. by Byron A. Garner. The Law Book Exchange, 2005, p. 92 and citing to Job 31:35. Another citation peril is grievous error as when Martin Mayer, in The Lawyer (1967, p. 167) cited an A. P. Herbert "misleading" case as a principle of law.

(181f)
[Hay, Peter, The Book of Legal Anecdotes. Facts on File, 1989, p. 226-227. See Biddle, Justice Holmes, Natural Law, and the Supreme Court 9 (1961); see also Bander, Justice Holmes Ex Cathedra 204 (1991)]

(182f)
[Leech, Reveille in Washington 1860-1865. Harper, 1941, p. 343. Goodwin, Team of Rivals. Simon and Schuster, 2005, p. 643. Bander, Justice Holmes Ex

Cathedral 242-243 (1991). See also Woollcott, Long, Long Ago, 1943, pp. 3-12. Mr. Woollcott attributes the source of this story to Harold Laski.]

(183f)
[Pusey, Charles Evans Hughes.Macmillan, 1951, p. 2: 558.Bander, Justice Holmes Ex Cathedra 257-258 (1991). Bander, Holmespun Humor, 10 Villanova Law Review 303 (1964).]

(184f)
[Brogan, American Themes. Harper, 1947, p. 173. Bander, Justice Holmes Ex Cathedra 212 (1991). Bander, Holmespun Humor, 10 Villanova Law Review 3067(1965)]

(185f)
[Freund, Mr. Holmes Had Cure for Most of Our Ills, Boston Sunday Globe, September 30, 1956, editorial page. Bander, Justice Holmes Ex Cathedra 228 (1991). Bander, Holmespun Humor, 10 Villanova Law Review 508 (1965)]

(186f)
[City Lawyer. Arthur Garfield Hays. Simon and Schuster, 1942, p.218]

(190f)
[Thurman Arnold, Fair Fights and Foul. Harcourt Brace and World, 1951, p. 265]

(191f)
[Justice Blackman in dissent, Faretta v. California, 422 U.S. 806, 852]

(192f)
[36 Journal of Patent Office Society 54]

(193f)
[Alexander M. Sullivan, The Last Serjeant. London: Macdonald, 1952, p. 48. See also:
Anthony Nicholson, Esprit de Law 55 (1973) ." Robert Megarry, A New Miscellany-At-Law ed. by Byron A. Garner. The Law Book Exchange, 2005, p. 212 also citing to Sullivan]

(194f)
[Gilbert, The Oxford Book of Legal Anecdotes. Oxford University Press, 1986, p. 122 citing Felix Frankfurter Reminisces edited by Phillips (1960)]

(195f)
[Thurman Arnold, Fair Fights and Foul. Harcourt Brace and World, 1951, p. 22]

(196f)
[Hay, Peter, The Book of Legal Anecdotes. Facts on File, 1989, p. 150. See also Gilbert, The Oxford Book of Legal Anecdotes 254 (1986) citing Rentoul, This is My Case (1944)]

(197f)
[22 Boston University Law Review 188. Bander, Doing Justice: Class Action, 72 Law Library Journal 537 (1979)]

(198f)
[Cohn, Criminal Law Seminar 305 (1961)]

(199f)
[Evan Thomas, The Man to See: Edward Bennett Williams Ultimate insider; Legendary Trial Lawyer, Simon and Schuster, 1991, p. 135-136]

(200f)
[Evan Thomas, The Man to See: Edward Bennett Williams Ultimate insider; Legendary Trial Lawyer, Simon and Schuster, 1991, p. 54]

(205f)
[1963 Proceedings of the Maine State Bar Ass'n 93]

(207f)
[Peabody, ed. The Holmes-Einstein Letters. St. Martins, 1964, p. 308. Bander, Justice Holmes Ex Cathedra 257 (1991). Bander, Holmespun Humor, 10 Villanova Law Review 306 (1965)]

(208f)
[Liva Baker, Felix Frankfurter. Coward-McCann, 1969, p. 310, See also Artemus Ward and David L. Weiden. Sorcerers' Apprentices: 100 Years of Law Clerks at the United States Supreme Court. NYU Press, 2006, p. 94]

(210f)
[Seasongood, Selections from Speeches. Knopf, 1960, p. 216]

(211f)
[10 Chitty's Law Journal 158 (1961)]

(212f)
[Seasongood, Selections from Speeches. Knopf, 1960, p. 216]

(214f)
[30 The Bar Examiner 42-44 (1961)]

(216f)
[Follansbee, Mr. Justice Holmes – a Judge with Imagination, 11 American Lawyer 10 (1903). Bander, Justice Holmes Ex Cathedra 220 (1991). Bander, Holmespun Humor, 10 Villanova Law Review 507 (1965)]

(217f)
[D.W. Brogan, American Themes. Harper, 1947, p. 213. See also Gilbert, Oxford Book of Legal Anecdotes 43 (1986) citing Cunningham, Lord Bowen (1896)]

(218f)
[observed by Edward Bander at New York University Law School]

(219f)
[I probably heard this while working at the Harvard Law School Library in the 1950s]

(220f)
[Pusey, Charles Evans Hughes. Macmillan, 1951, p. 2: 625]

(221f)
[Marsh, Daniel L. The Making of Lawyers, 22 Boston University Law Review 175, 189 (1942). Bander, Justice Holmes Ex Cathedra 247-249 (1991). Bander, Holmespun Humor, 10 Villanova Law Review 301 (1964).]

(222f)
[Frank, Courts on Trial. Princeton University Press, 1949, p. 309. Bander, Justice Holmes Ex Cathedra 221 (1991)]

(223f)
[Acheson, Morning and Noon. Houghton, 1965, p. 82. Also in Among Friends: Personal Letters of Dean Acheson. McLellan and Acheson, eds. Dodd, Mead, 1980, p. 237. Bander, Justice Holmes Ex Cathedra 267 (1991)]

(226f)
[30 The Bar Examiner 42 (1961). Bander, Doing Justice: Class Action, 72 Law Library Journal 536 (1979).]

(227f)
[Richard Fountain, Wit of the Wig. Leslie Frewin, 1968, p. 91]

(228f)
[Judge Edward T. Gignoux, Proceedings of the Maine State Bar Association 113 (1964) See also: A witty judge once said of the judicial life that the young judge spent the first third of it in fear that he might be reversed in the Court of Appeal, the middle third in the conviction that the Court of Appeal was always wrong, and the last third not caring whether it was right or wrong. Devlin, The Judge, 1979, p. 26. See Anecdotes from Bander, 73 Law Library Journal 506 (1980)]

(229f)
[Woodbury, Puerto Rico, Southernmost District of the First Circuit, 1960 Proceedings of the Maine State Bar Association 32, 33. Bander, Justice Holmes Ex Cathedra 264 (1991), Bander, Holmespun Humor, 10 Villanova Law Review 306-307 (1965)]It should be mentioned that the Third Circuit includes the Virgin Islands, and, in times past, Judge Magruder of the First Circuit and Judge Maris of the Third Circuit managed to join up to hold sessions in those islands during the winter..]

(230f)
[Richard Fountain Wit of theWig. Frewin, 1968, p. 67]

(235f)
[Margolick, At the Bar. Simon & Schuster, 1995, p. 264 quoting Eddie Hayes, a criminal lawyer. Tom Wolfe, in his introduction to Edward Hayes, Mouthpiece. Broadway Books, 2006, p. ix has Hayes saying to a prospective client: "I want you to remember two things. First, I do this for money. Second. I'm not your friend. I'm your lawyer. But I'll do more for you than your friends." For an example of the dangers of non-lawyers writing about law, see Mayer, The Lawyers. Harper & Row, 1966, p. 167 in which Mayer quotes a fictional case by an English humorist to compare American and English law. No one wold appreciate tyhis more than A.P. Herbert, whose "misleading cases" are a staple of legal humor books.]

(240f)
[[10 Chitty's Law Lournal 158 (1961)]

(241f)
[no source]

(242f)
[Gilbert, The Oxford Book of Legal Anecdotes. Oxford University Press, 1986, p. 36 citing Botein Trial Judge. Simon & Schuster, 1952, p. 104]

(243f)
[Richard Fountain, Wit of the Wig. Leslie Frewin, 1968, p. 66]

(244f)
[Hay, Peter, The Book of Legal Anecdotes. Facts on File, 1989, p. 160. See also Broad, Advocates of the Golden Age 214 (1958)]

(245f)
[11 Federation of Insurance Counsel no. 3 55(1961)]

(246f)
[From the diaries kept by Tom Lambert which were entrusted to Professor Michael Rustad, who gave me permission to thumb through them.]

(247f)
[10 Chitty's Law Journal 110 (1961). Bander, Bar Relief, 72 Law Library Journal 352 (1979). See also Sullivan, the Last Serjeant 48. See also (252)

(250f)
[Krock, In the Nation, New York Times, March 21, 1965, p. E11, col. 5. Bander, Justice Holmes Ex Cathedra 242 (1991).]

(251f)
[Bent, Justice Oliver Wendell Holmes. Vanguard, 1932, p. 270. See also Justice Holmes Ex Cathedra 201 (1991). See also Leach, Book Review, 45 Harvard Law Review 1437 (1932). It is also to be noted with poetic justice, that Justice Holmes, himself, was a block of the old chip.]

(252f)
[Anthony Nicholson, Esprit de Law 55 (1973). See also (247). This legal maxim (from the Latin maximis) is also the source of a risqué limerick:
There was a law student called Rex,

With diminutive organs of sex,
When charged with exposure,
He replied with composure,
"de minimis non curat lex."
(this version was found in http://www.absolvitor.com/humour/jokes04.html
The maxim still has vitality: see Sony Corp. of America v. Universal City Studios, 464 U.S. 417 at 451 ((1984)

(254f)
[Lyons, Leonard, in The Boston Herald, May 6, 1959. Bander, Justice Holmes Ex Cathedra 244 (1991).]

(255f)
[10 Chitty's Law Journal 86 (1961). Also, the story of a court clerk taking up a collection for a recently deceased county judge, and "requesting a donation of five dollars to bury a judge." The disgruntled lawyer reached into his pocket and gave him twenty-five dollars and said, "Here's twenty-five, bury five of them."]

(256f)
[Hand, The Spirit of Liberty. Knopf, 1960, p. 270. Bander, Justice Holmes Ex Cathedra 228 (1991). Bander, Holmespun Humor, 10 Villanova Law Review 508 (1965)] See Howe, comp. The Occasional Speeches of Justice Oliver Wendell Holmes 161 (1962): "… so, one comes to think, men may be pardoned for the defects of their qualities if they have the qualities of their defects."]

(257f)
[Bander, Doing Justice: Class Action, 72 Law Library Journal 536 (1979)]

(258f)
[Pasaic County Bar Ass'n Reporter – no date. Bander, Doing Justice: Class Action, 72 Law Library Jounral 536 (1979).]

(259f)
[Jimmy Carter, May 4, 1974, Athens, Ga. New Statesman, Jan. 28, 1977, p. 112]

(260f)
[Richard Fountain, Wit of the Wig. Leslie Frewin, 1968, p. 23]. A search of the internet attributes this comment to Lord Brougham.]

(261f)
[Richard Foutain, Wit of the Wig. Leslie Frewin, 1968, p. 110. 111, 120]

(262f)
[New York Law Journal, March 16, 1965, page 1, col. 6. Bander, Justice Holmes Ex Cathedra 26-269 (1991). Justice Black "would never join another opinion that included the phrase ..." Rosen, The Supreme Court ... Henry Holt, 2006, p. 157 citing Newman, Hugo Black. Pantheon, 1994, p. 601

(265f)
[newspaper clipping with no source]

(266f)
[32 Medico-Legal Journal 130 (1964). Bander, Bar Relief, 72 Law Library Journal 354 (1972).]

(267f)
[no source]

(270f)
[Gilbert, The Oxford Book of Legal Anecdotes. Oxford University Press, 1986, p. 110 citing Insurance Counsel Journal, No. 25. Also cited by Mayer, The Lawyers. Harper & Row, 1966, p. 230 citing Samuel W. Sears, 25 Ins. Counsel Jl 428, 429.]

(273f)
[Walter F. Murphy, Wild Bill ... . Random House, 2003, p. 300-301]

(274f)
[Walter F. Murphy, Wild Bill ... . Random House, 2003, p. 369. "... Gerald Ford, famously declared that an impeachable offense is whatever a majority of the House decides... "[in considering the impeachment of Justice Douglas] Rosen, The Supreme Court ... Henry Hold, 2006, p. 168]

(274af)
[Linda Greenhouse, Becoming Justice Blackmun. Henry Holt and Co., 2005, p. 59. See also:
Though [H.L.A Hart] he appreciated [Arthur] Goodhart's 'infinite kindness' and admired his business skills and ready wit (he is once alleged to have said in a college meeting, 'I dissent from the majority for all the reasons they have given.'

Nicola Lacey, A Life of H.L.A. Hart; The Nightmare and the Noble Dream Oxford University Press 2004, p. 171]

(275f)
[Obiter Dicta... Joseph W. Bishop, Jr. Atheneum, 1971, p. 99. See also Warren: The Man The Court The Era. John D. Weaver. Victor Gollancz, 1968, p. 18]

(280f)
[Seasongood, Selections from Speeches. Knopf, 1960, p. 220. Hay, Peter, The Book of Legal Anecdotes. Facts on File, 1989, p. 220.]

(281f)
 [Peabody, ed. Holmes-Einstein Letters. St. Martins, 1964, p. xviii. Bander, Holmespun Humor, 10 Villanova Law Review 304-305 (1964). "He [Holmes] used to tell us of Emerson telling him to hold Plato at arm's length and to say to him, "Plato, you have impressed millions. Let's see whether you can impress me." Among Friends: Personal Letters of Dean Acheson. McLellan and Acheson, eds. Dodd, Mead, 1980, p. 183]

(282f)
[Howe, ed. Holmes-Laski Letters, Harvard University Press, 1953, p. I:772. Bander, Justice Holmes Ex Cathedra 233 (1991). 10 Villanova Law Review 300 (1964).]

(283f)
[Saturday Review, May 4, 1968, p. 6]

(284f)
[attributed to W. Somerset Maugham, 10 Chitty's Law Journal 158 (1961). Bander, Doing Justice: Class Action, 72 Law Library Journal 537 (1979). see also:
 The British author Somerset Maugham cites, in A Writer Notebook, advice that a law professor gave his students:
 "If you have the facts on your side, hammer them into your jury. If you have the law on your side, hammer it into the judge."
 "An what if you have neither?" asked on of the professor's students.
 "Then hammer on the table," he replied.
Hay, Peter , The Book of Legal Anecdotes. Facts on File, 1989, p. 176. See also Galanter, Lowering the Bar. University of Wisconsin Press, 2005, p. 47 with many attributions.]

(289f)
[Gunther, Learned Hand. Knopf, 1994, p. 632. For Judge Frank's take on this see Jerome N. Frank, Some Reflections on Judge Learned Hand in Rossman, ed. Advocacy and the King's English 871 (1960). Holmes: "I hate facts." See Rosen, The Supreme Court ... Henry Hold, 2006, p. 100]

(292f)
[Hay, Peter, The Book of Legal Anecdotes. Facts on File, 1989, p. 227]

(300f)
[Boston Globe, February 22, 1960, editorial page (Globe Man's Daily Story). Bander, Justice Holmes Ex Cathedra 209 (1991). See also Wister, Roosevelt: The Story of a Friendship 133 (1930): "You see I am reading now for the Day of Judgment, so as not to dead [flunk] if I am called up on some book that every gentleman is expected to have read. ..." See also: It may be said in passing that in later life Mr. Justice Holmes was fond of uttering a dissent when reminded that he had the reputation of reading the classics in the original: Latin and Greek, as a matter of course, and French and German almost as much as a matter of course; but Italian and Spanish and even Portuguese also. With a "pony," he vowed, it was not so difficult. "But," he once added solemnly, "I always qualify that against the Day of Judgment; for I read in the original only the purple patches. ...
Bent, Justice Oliver Wendell Holmes. Vanguard, 1932, p. 35; see also Bander Justice Holmes Ex Cathedra 200 (1991)]

(305f)
[Gunther, Learned Hand. Knopf, 1994, p. 528]

(306f)
[Mason, Brandeis, A Free Man's Life. Viking, 1956, p. 578. Bander, Justice Holmes Ex Cathedra 250 (1991). See also Biddle, Mr. Justice Holmes 152 (1942)]

(307f)
[See Artemus Ward and David L. Weiden. Sorcerers' Apprentices: 100 Years of Law Clerks at the United States Supreme Court. NYU Press, 2006, p. 203]

(308f)
[Mason, Harlan Fiske Stone: Pillar of the Law. Viking, 1956, p. 339]

(309f)
[Edward J. Bander heard this at a speech given at New York University School

of Law]

(311f)
[Liva Baker, Felix Frankfurter. Coward-McCann, 1969, p. 216]

(312f)
[Liva Baker, Felix Frankfurter. Coward-McCann, 1969, p. 209. The story I read somewhere was that Frankfurter did nothing about the request but the two students were accepted at Harvard and McCarran was forever grateful.. See also Simon, The Antagonists 16 (1989). See also Kramnick and Sheerman, Harold Laski. Penguin, p. 405]

(313f)
[Among Friends: Personal Letters of Dean Acheson. McLellan and Acheson, eds. Dodd, Mead, 1980, p. 329]

(314f)
[Kurland, ed. Of Law and Life ... Frankfurter. Harvard University Press, 1965 p. 28]

(315f)
[Lewis, A. Book Review, New York Times, May 29, 1960, VIII, p. 1. See Felix Frankfurter Reminisces 78 (1962). Bander, Justice Holmes Ex Cathedra 243 (1991).]

(316f)
[Clancy, Just a Country Lawyer. Indiana University Press, 1974, p. 81. See also Ervin, Humor of a Country Lawyer. University of North Carolina Press, 1983, p. 36. Bander, Doing Justice: Class Action, 72 Law Library Journal 536-537 (1939). See also See also Simon, The Antagonists... 42 (1989): "Francis Plimpton, the future lawyer-diplomat described [Frankfurter's lecturing] the experience: 'You learn no law in Public U/That is its fascination/But Felix gives a point of view/And pleasant conversation.'"]

(320f)
[Bent, Justice Oliver Wendell Holmes. Vanguard, 1932, p. 16]

(325f)
[Frankfurter, Chief Justices I have Known, 39 Virginia Law Review 883, 888, 889 (1953). See also King, Melville Weston Fuller 290 (1950). Frankfurter, Of Law and Men (1956); Case & Comment, May-June 6 (1957); Clark, Supreme Court Conference, 19 Federal Rules Decisions 306-307 (1957); Davenport,

Voices in Court 254-255 (1958).). Also Bander, Justice Holmes Ex Cathedra 222-223 (1991). Bander, Holmespun Humor, 10 Villanova Law Review 507-508 (1965). Also Rosen, The Supreme Court ... Henry Holt, 2006, p. 73 citing Novick, Honorable Justice. Little, Brown, 1989, p. 254.]

(326f)
[King, Melville Weston Fuller. Macmillan, 1950, p. 296. Bander, Justice Holmes Ex Cathedra 241 (1991).]

(327f)
[John M. Macdonald, The Murderer and His Victim. Springfield, IL: Thomas, 1961, p. 348]

(328f)
[Holmes, 8 Advocate 185 (Nov. 1961). Bander, Justice Holmes Ex Cathedra 231 (1991). See also Brooks, New England Indian Summer 266 (1950); also Wister, Roosevelt 131 (1930).]

(329f)
[Frankfurter, Felix Frankfurter Reminisces. Reynal, 1962, p. 198. Bander, Justice Holmes Ex Cathedra 224 (1991).]

(332f)
[Seasongood, Selections from Speeches. Knopf, 1960, p. 221]

((334f)
[Gene M. Gressley, ed. Voltaire and the Cowboy: the Letters of Thurman Arnold. Colorado Associated University Press, 1977, p. 234. See also p. 427-428. See also:
"You will recall that [the Marshal of the Supreme Court] ends up his liturgy by saying "God save the United States for the Court is now sitting." Among Friends: Personal Letters of Dean Acheson. McLellan and Acheson, eds. Dodd, Mead, 1980, p. 175]

(335f)
[See Galanter, Lowering the Bar. University of Wisconsin Press,2005 p. 97 et seq. for a chapter on the devil and the law. See also Stephen Vincent Benet, The Devil and Daniel Webster for a more favorable outcome against the devil.]

(336f)
[Hurst, The Growth of American Law. Little, Brown, 1950, p. 336. Bander, Justice Holmes Ex Cathedra 238 (1991). Bander, Holmespun Humor, 10

Villanova Law Review 306 (1965)]

(337f)
[Hurst, The Growth of American Law. Little, Brown, 1950, p. 467. Bander, Justice Holmes Ex Cathedra 238 (1991). Bander, Holmespun Humor, 10 Villanova Law Review 306 (1965)]

(378f)
[Curtis, Lions Under the Throne. Houghton, 1947, p. 281. Bander, Justice Holmes Ex Cathedra 218 (1991). See also: One day a friend asked him if he had ever worked out any general philosophy to guide him in the exercise of the judicial function. "Yes," the aged jurist replied. "Long ago I decided that I was not God. When a State came in here and wanted to build a slaughter house, I looked at the Constitution and if I couldn't find anything in there that said a State couldn't build a slaughter house I said to myself, if they want to build a slaughter house, God-dammit, let them build it."
Mason, Brandeis, A Free Man's Life. Viking, 1956, p. 572. Bander, Justice Holmes Ex Cathedra 249-250 (1991). Also Raymond Clapper in the New York World-Telegram, May 22, 1936. Also: Parson & Allen, The Nine Old Men. Doubleday, 1937, p. 104]

(379f)
[58 Law Society's Gazette]

(380f)
[Humbert Wolfe – See verso of Maxwell on the Interpretation Statutes, 11th ed. 1962]

(380af)
[SeeYarbrough, Tinsley E. Judicial Enigma: The First Justice Harlan. Oxford University Press, 1995, p. 207

(381f)
[Smith, T.V. Book review, 56 Harvard Law Review 677, 679 (1942). Bander, Justice Holmes Ex Cathedra 260-261 (1991). Bander, Holmespun Humor, 10 Villanova Law Review 304 (1964). Holmes, Collected Legal Papers 159 (1920)]

(382f)
[Biddle, Mr. Justice Holmes. Scribner's, 1942, p. 103. See Bent, Justice Oliver Wendell Holmes 307 (1932); also. Bander, Justice Holmes Ex Cathedra 205 (1991). Bander, Holmespun Humor, 10 Villanova Law Review 503 (1965)]

(383f)
[Pusey, Charles Evans Hughes. Macmillan, 1951, p. 2: 681; Hughes, Supreme Court of the U.S. 76. See also Kens, Justice Stephen Field 262-263 (1997). Pearson and Allen, The Nine Old Men. Doubleday, 1937, p. 33-34. Yarbrough, Tinsley E. Judicial Enigma: The First Justice Harlan. Oxford University Press, 1995, p. 215-216

(384f)
[Beck, Justice Holmes and the Supreme Court, 1 Federal Bar Association Journal 39 (March 1932)]; Bander, Justice Holmes Ex Cathedra 198 (1991)

(385f)
[Gilbert, The Oxford Book of Legal Anecdotes. Oxford University Press, 1986, p. 139 citing Mortimer, Clinging to the Wreckage (1982). Here is the Right Hon. Sir Norman Birkett on Marshall: "I was in the chambers of Marshall Hall and I shall never forget that very great man. There were times when Marshall Hall had very great failures, and there were times when he had the most resounding triumphs. To see Marshall Hall come into the Court surrounded by a retinue of people carrying pencils and air cushions and all sorts of things was an art in itself. Marshall Hall would sit there and he was not above certain, shall I call them, small tricks. This air cushion which he had – if the cross-examination of his client was getting pretty severe he would put the air cushion under his arm and go fsh! Fsh! Fsh! So that the cross-examining counsel was very greatly disconcerted. But I have heard Marshall on some of the big cases, the defense of Fahmy at the Old Bailey, the defense of Greenwood, when Marshall Hall quoted to the jury that wonderful thing from Othello: 'Put out the light, put out the light.'" Birkett, The Art of Advocacy in Rossman, ed. Advocacy and the King's English 924 (1960). See also The Spectator, Dec. 8, 1979, at 982: The late Sir Edward Marshall Hall used to make his entrance into court preceded by a clerk with a glass of water, a pile of clean white linen, handkerchiefs and an air cushion. All the mates know that the way to ruin a fellow actor's performance is to move on his line; ;so if the prosecutor made a good point, Sir Edward would blow his nose on the handkerchiefs; if he made a better point, Sir Edward would spill the water, if he made an irresistible point the old man would blow up the air cushion very slowly, and thus capture the enthralled and undivided attention of every member of the audience or jury. The Spectator, Dec. 8, 1979, at 982. See also Ed Bander, Anecdotes from Bander, 73 Law Library Journal 507-508 (198)]

(386f)
[Gunther, Learned Hand. Knopf, 1994, p. 647. See also Charles E. Wyzanski,

Jr., Whereas – A Judge's Premises. Little, Brown, 1944, p. 82. Judge Posner, the most cited judge for his non-judicial opinions and forays into the internet "also statistically 'proves' that the adage 'Quote Learned, follow Gus' should be 'Quote Learned, follow Learned.'" See Bimonthly Review of Law Books, Jan.-Feb., 1995, p. 21 citing Posner's review of Learned Hand by Gerald Gunther in 104 Yale Law Journal 511 (1944).

(387f)
[Gunther, Learned Hand. Knopf, 1994, p. 550.

(388f)
[Martin Mayer, The Judges. St. Martin's Press, 2006, p. 406-407

(389f)
[Pusey, Charles Evans Hughes. Macmillan, 1951, p. 2:563]

(390f)
[Howe, ed. Holmes-Pollock Letters. Harvard University Press, 2d ed. 1961, p. II:7-8 Bander, Justice Holmes Ex Cathedra 235 (1991). Bander, Holmespun Humor, 10 Villanova Law Review 302 (1964). See also Yarbrough, Tinsley E. Judicial Enigma: The First Justice Harlan. Oxford University Press, 1995, p. 126-127 on the relationship between Holmes and Harlan. See also anecdote (325). See also Rosen, The Supreme Court ... Henry Holt, 2006, p. 74 citing Beth, John Marshall Harlan. Kentucky Univ. Press, 1992, p. 174. Also on Harlan: "goes to bed every night with one hand on the Constitution and the other on the Bible, and so sleeps the sweet sleep of of justice and righteousness." (according to Justice Brewer). See Rosen, p. 102 citing Beth, p. 160. Rosen, p. 103 contains additional anecdotes.]

(391f)
    Yarbrough, Tinsley E. John Marshall Harlan: Great Dissenter of the Warren Court. Oxford University Press, 1992, Preface, vii. John M. Harlan was the grandson of John Marshall Harlan and used a middle initial to distinguish himself from the elder. Rosen, The Supreme Court ... Henry Hold, 2006, p. 159.]

(392f)
[Navasky, A Matter of Opinion. Farrar, Straus & Giroux, 2005, p. 236-237]

(393f)
[Thurman Arnold, Fair Fights and Foul. Harcourt Brace and World, 1951, p. 261]

(394f)
[Simon, The Antagonists ...Simon & Schuster, 1989, p. 62. But see Victor S. Navasky, "The Yales vs. The Harvards..." New York Times Magazine, Sept. 11, 1966, p. 49: "Yale trains judges, Harvard trains lawyers; Yale doesn't teach you any law, Harvard teaches you nothing but..." as quoted in Weaver, John D. Warren: The Man The Court The Era. Victor Gollancz, 1968, p. 17. "We have to do something about the Harvard syndrome, says a Chicagoan, "you know, the attitude that there are just two very good law schools, Harvard and this one." Mayer, The Lawyers. Harper & Row, 1966, p. 84. The more generous say that Harvard is first and everyone else is tied for second. And from the University of Chicago Law School newspaper: "You can't sneeze [in Boston] without snotting seven Harvard law grads." The Phoenix, Oct. 1999, p. 16.]

(394af)
[Justice McReynolds to John Knox. See Artemus Ward and David L. Weiden. Sorcerers' Apprentices: 100 Years of Law Clerks at the United States Supreme Court. NYU Press, 2006, p. 70-71]

(395f)
[1961 Proceedings of the American Society of International Law 215; Bander, Doing Justice: Class Action, 72 Law Library Journal 536 (1979)]

(395af)
[Nicola Lacey, A Life of H.L.A. Hart; The Nightmare and the Noble Dream Oxford University Press 2004, p. 179]

(395bf)
[City Lawyer. Arthur Garfield Hays. Simon and Schuster, 1942, p. 115]

(396f)
[Langrock, Beyond the Courthouse... Paul S. Eriksson, Publisher 1999, p. 37]

(397f)
[Holmes's Failure by Louise Weinberg, 96 Michigan Law Review 691, at 721-722. It should be noted that Judge Wyzanski was about the same size as Justice Frankfurter. My better half was once sitting in a jacuzzi in a health club and struck up a conversation with an elderly gentleman, who turned out to identify himself as Judge Wyzanski. The Judge was told about a fictional biography of Ethel Rosenberg, and he replied that one of his life missions was that Judge Kaufman, who sentenced the Rosenbergs to death, would never realize his life

ambition to get on the United States Supreme Court as long as he was alive. Another anecdote about the Judge was that an attorney was very unhappy about Judge Wyzanski sitting on a Jones Act case that he was trying. He suggested that the Judge recuse himself because the attorney for the defendant has recently published a book review of Judge Wyzanski's "A Judge's Whereas," and it was so favorable that he felt it would prejudice his chances in the case. Not only did Judge Wyzanski refuse to recuse himself, but he appended the book review in the Federal Supplement. See Bander, Book Review, 15 Suffolk University Law Review 547 (1981). I cannot confirm this but there was probably a competition between Justice Frankfurter and Judge Wyzanski possibly exemplified by the Massachusetts Bonding and Insurance Co. v. U.S., 352 U.S. 128 (1956). Judge Wyzanski held that the Massachusetts Death Act was not applicable and gave judgment for the Plaintiff. The First Circuit with Judge Magruder writing the opinion reversed arguing that the Death Act set a maximum that may be recovered. The Supreme Court with Justice Douglas writing the majority opinion reversed the First Circuit, with Justice Frankfurter dissenting. This was a case of forum versus substance, and a clash more of turf than law. I should also add that Judge Wyzanski, in his book Whereas-A Judges's Premises (Little Brown, 1944 at p. 26 wrote "The Democracy of Justice Oliver Wendell Holmes" and placed him in the same pantheon as Thomas Jefferson, Abraham Lincoln, Woodrow Wilson and Franklin D. Roosevelt.]

(398f)
[Simon, The Antagonists ... Simon & Schuster, 1989, p. 30]

(399f)
[Mason, Harlan Fiske Stone: Pillar of the Law. Viking, 1956, p. 327 citing McCormack, "A Law Clerk's Recollections," Columbia Law Rev., Sept. 1946, pp. 713-714. "If people want to go to Hell, I will help them. It's my job." [Holmes to Laski] See Rosen, The Supreme Court ... Henry Holt, 2006, p. 88 citing Altschuler, Law Without Values. University of Chicago Press, 2000, p. 63

(403f)
[Howe, ed. Holmes-Laski Letters. Harvard University Press, 1953, I:390. Bander, Justice Holmes Ex Cathedra 232-233 (1991). 10 Villanova Law Review 300 (1964).]

(404f)
[contributed by Oscar Leiding. Bander, Justice Holmes Ex Cathedra 266 (1991). Mrs. Holmes "declared that they would both be Unitarians because in Boston one has to be something and Unitarian is the least you can be." Rosen,

The Supreme Court ... Henry Holt, 2006, p. 108 citing Baker, The Justice from Beacon Hill. HarperCollins, 1991, p. 77.]

(405f)
[Bowen, Yankee from Olympus. Little, Brown, 1945, p. 362. Bander, Justice Holmes Ex Cathedra 210 (1991). 10 Villanova Law Review 98 (1964). Also attributed to Edward Bennett Williams. See Evan Thomas, The Man to See: Edward Bennett Williams Ultimate Insider; Legendary Trial Lawyer. Simon and Schuster, 1991, p. 229]

(406f)
[Bowen, Yankee from Olympus. Little, Brown, 1945, p. 401. Bander, Justice Holmes Ex Cathedra 211 (1991). 10 Villanova Law Review 99 (1964).]

(407f)
[Butler, A Century ... Putnam, 1942, p. 177-178. Bander, Justice Holmes Ex Cathedra 214 (1991). Bander, Holmespun Humor, 10 Villanova Law Review 505 (1965)]

(408f)
[Bent, Justice Oliver Wendell Holmes. Vanguard, 1932, p. ix. See also 18 Virginia Law Review 922 (1932)]; also Bander, Justice Holmes Ex Cathedra 198 (1991). It may be apropos to add: "It has been neatly said that Holmes had the good fortune to survive into his own generation. Ropes Gray 1865-1940. Albert Boyden [privately printed] 1942, p. 76]

(409f)
[Contributed by Mr. Lewis L. Strauss. Bander, Justice Holmes Ex Cathedra 264-265 (1991)]

(410f)
[Hagedorn, Americans: A Book of Lives. John Day, 2946, p. 40. Bander, Justice Holmes Ex Cathedra 228 (1991)]

(411f)
[Butler, A Century ... Putnam, 1942, p. 179. Bander, Justice Holmes Ex Cathedra 214-215 (1991). Bander, Holmespun Humor, 10 Villanova Law Review 506 (1965)]

(412f)
[Biddle, Justice Holmes, Natural Law, and the Supreme Court. Macmillan, 1961, p. 12. Also Bander, Justice Holmes Ex Cathedra 204-205 (1991)]

(413f)
[Biddle, Mr. Justice Holmes. Scribner's, 1942, p. 110-111; also Bander Justice Holmes Ex Cathedra 205-206 (1991). Bander, Holmespun Humor, 10 Villanova Law Review 504 (1965)]

(414f)
[Bent, Justice Oliver Wendell Holmes. Vanguard, 1932, p. 277; Bander, Justice Holmes Ex Cathedra 301 (1991). Bander, Holmespun Humor, 10 Villanova Law Review 503 (1965)]

(415f)
[Peabody, ed. Holmes-Einstein Letters. St.Martins, 1964, p. 46. Bander, Holmespun Humor, 10 Villanova Law Review 305 (1964).]

(416f)
[Peabody, ed. The Holmes-Einstein Letters. St. Martins, 1964, p. 250. Bander, Justice Holmes Ex Cathedra 256 (1991).]

(417f)
[Peabody, ed. Holmes-Einstein Letters. St. Martins, 1964, p. 46. Bander, Holmespun Humor, 10 Villanova Law Review 305 (1964).]

(418f)
[Biddle, Justice Holmes, Natural Law, and the Supreme Court. Macmillan, 1961, p. 66-67; see also Bander, Justice Holmes Ex Cathedra 205 (1991)]

(419f)
[Biddle, Justice Holmes, Natural Law, and the Supreme Court. Macmillan, 1961, p. 5. See also Biddle, Mr. Justice Holmes 80 (1942). See also Bander, Justice Holmes Ex Cathedra 203 (1991).]

(420f)
[Bowen, Yankee from Olympus. Little, Brown, 1945, p. 414. Bander, Justice Holmes Ex Cathedra 212 (1991). 10 Villanova Law Review 99 (1964).]

(421f)
[King, Melville Weston Fuller. Macmillan, 1950, p. 280. Bander, Justice Holmes Ex Cathedra 240-241 (1991).]

(422f)
[Biggs, Hon. John, Jr., 85th Congress, 2d Session, House. Departments of State

... the Judiciary 59 (1958). Bander, Justice Holmes Ex Cathedra 208 (1991). In Acheson, Morning and Noon 78 (1965) this is attributed to Justice Brandeis.]

(423f)
[Huston, History of Court to Honor Holmes, New York Times, April 15, 1956, p. 88, col. 1. of American Law 336 (1950). Bander, Justice Holmes Ex Cathedra 238-239 (1991). See also, 119 Literary Digest, March 16, 1935, page 6: "... leaving $283, 500 to relatives, friends, servants and institutions out of an estate of $553, 752, Justice Holmes wrote into his last will: 'All the rest ... I give, devise and bequeath to the United States of America.'" Also 18 Federal Bar Journal 33 (1958) and 3 City Lawyer (N.Y.) No. 1:14 (1965).]

(424f)
[May, The Lighter Side of the Law.Michie, 1956, p. 36. Bander, Justice Holmes Ex Cathedra 252-253 (1991). Pearson & Allen. The Nine Old Men. Doubleday, 1937, p. 180. See also Fadiman, The American Treasury 783 (1955); but see letter from Laski to Holmes: "I reminded him on Fontenelle who said, you remember, to the damsel of eighteen, "Ah! Madam, would that I were eighty once more." 1 Holmes-Laski Letters 224 (1953). Holmes was eighty at the time he received this letter dated January 4, 1921. Holmes is also alleged to have said, "I wish I was ten years older." Brandeis suggested, "Don't you mean ten years younger?" and Holmes responded, "No, if I were ten years older she wouldn't bother me." This anecdote has also been placed at the corner of School and Tremont Streets in Boston, where the two, I am sure, had hot cross buns and coffee at the legendary Parker House and where the blustery winds were liable to whisk young ladies' skirts above their heads, and thus prompt the Holmes's quip. Also, Wilson, Patriotic Gore 755 (1962).]

(425f)
[no source]

(426f)
[Bowen, Yankee from Olympus. Little, Brown, 1945, p. 399. Bander, Justice Holmes Ex Cathedra 211 (1991). 10 Villanova Law Review 98 (1964).]

(430f)
[Lord Eldon's Anecdote Book, ed. By A.L.J. Lincoln and R.L. McEwen. London: Stevens & Sons, 1960, p. 159]

(431f)
[Pusey, Charles Evans Hughes, Macmillan, 1951, p. 2: 674]

(432f)
[Pusey, Charles Evans Hughes. Macmillan, 1951, p. 2: 793]

(433f)
[Leonard Lyons, New York Post, April 11, 1962, p. 55]

(434f)
[Pusey, Charles Evans Hughes. Macmillan, 1951, p. 2:666]

(435f)
[Pusey, Charles Evans Hughes. Macmillan, 1951, p. 2: 588; New York Post, April 11, 1962 (1955)]

(436f)
[Pusey, Charles Evans Hughes. Macmillan, 1931]

(437f)
[Pusey, Charles Evans Hughes. Macmillan, 1951, p. 2: 420]

(438f)
[From the diaries kept by Tom Lambert which were entrusted to Professor Michael Rustad, who gave me permission to thumb through them. Martin Mayer: "Felix Frankfurter once said that watching Hughes preside was like watching Toscanini conduct." Martin Mayer, The Judges. St. Martin's Press, 2006, p. 308]

(440f)
[Holmes, Ideals and Doubts, 10 Illinois Law Review 1 (1915). Bander, Justice Holmes Ex Cathedra 231-232 (1991). Also in Wigmore, Mr. Justice Holmes 213 (1913)]

(441f)
[Law Association of Philadelphia Centennial Collection, 1802-1902, 69 (1906). See also: Ed Bander, Anecdotes from Bander, 73 Law Library Journal 508 (1980)]

(442f)
[Bent, Justice Oliver Wendell Holmes. Vanguard, 1932, p. 16. See also "... advise that Holmes once gave to a wordy lawyer. "Counselor," he advised, "you should read French novels, they teach one to say a lot by innuendo." Congressional Record, March 25, 1959, p. A2691]. See also Sergeant, Justice Touched with Fire, Mr. Justice Holmes 202 (Frankfurter, ed 1931). See also

Eugene C. Gerhart, Improving Our Legal Writing in Rossman, ed. Advocacy and the King's English 769 (1960)]

(443f)
[New Zealand Law Journal, August 5, 1975]

(444f)
[Estes, Joe E., Speech, National Conference of State Trial Justiges, August 3-5, 1962, p. 138. Bander, Justice Holmes Ex Cathedra 220 (1991)]

(446f)
[Gerhart, America's Advocate: Robert H. Jackson. Bobbs-Merrill, 1958, p 300 It was also Jackson who said of his court: "we are not final because we are infallible, we are infallible because we are final." See Brown v. Allen, 344 U.S. 443, at p. 540 (1953).]

(448f)
[Murane, Edward E., 34 S. Dak. J. No. 4 (Supp.) (1965); see also 44 Nebraska Law Review 356; see also Galanter, Lowering the Bar. University of Wisconsin Press, 2005, p. 57 citing six sources none of them the above.]

(449f)
[Gunther, Learned Hand. Knopf, 1994, p. 592. Note: Hand was a member of the fictional Society of Jobbists created by Justice Holmes. "There is no short cut to fame or comfort and all there is is to bore into it as hard as you can. But many of our friends seem to believe they can legislate bliss.: Holmes-Laski, I:49. See also: I should say of the students what Holmes says. He belonged to the society of jobbists – that, "Do your job!" He said the fellow who tries to shoot a bird on the wing is neither an altruist nor an egotist. He wants to shoot that bird on the wing. Well, all life is a bird on the wing..
[Frankfurter, Felix Frankfurter Reminisces. Reynal, 1962, p. 29 . Bander, Justice Holmes Ex Cathedra 223 (1991). As to "jobbists" see also Book Notices 178 (1936) and Wilson, Patriotic Gore 789 (1962); also Acheson, Morning and Noon 268 (1965). "Years ago I founded an imaginary society of the jobbists, at liberty to be egotists or altruists as they liked on the usual Saturday half holiday, so long as they were neither while on their job." David H. Burton, ed. Progressive Masks: Letters of O.W.H. Jr. and Franklin Ford. University of Delaware Press, 1982, p. 130-131]

(450f)
[Hay, Peter, The Book of Legal Anecdotes. Facts on File, 1989, p. ? . See also Broad, Advocates of the Golden Age 212 (1958)]

(451f)
[See Hay, Peter, The Book of Legal Anecdotes. Facts on File, 1989, p. 147. See also Gilbert, The Oxford Book of Legal Anecdotes 279 (1986) citing The Life of F.E. Smith, First Lord Birkenhead, by his son (1959). See also Broad, Advocates of the Golden Age 212 (1958). Various versions of this exist: "I have read your case, Mr. Smith, and I am no wiser now than I was when I started." "Possibly not, my lord, but far better informed." Fountain, Wit of Wig 9. Bander, Bar Relief, 72 Law Library Journal 353 (1979). Also: "The Judge said, 'I have been listening to you now for four hours and I am bound to say I am none the wiser.' The barrister replied: 'Oh, I know that, my Lord, but I had hoped you would be better informed.' Robert H. Jackson, Advocacy Before the Supreme Court in Rossman, ed., Advocacy and the King's English 200 (1960). See also: The Judge said, "I have been listening to you for four hours and I am bound to say I am none the wiser." The barrister replied: "Oh, I know that, my Lord, but I had hoped you would be better informed."
[source unknown.] Pannick, Advocates. Oxford University Press, 1992, p. 86 gives Smith's retort as well as other examples of impertinence.] When a judge suggested that Clarence Darrow's court argument was "going into one ear and out the other" his response was: "I'm not surprised, Your Honor. Maybe it's because there's nothing to interfere with the passage, Your Honor." Kornstein, Thinking Under Fire. Dodd, Mead, 1987, p. 120]

(452f)
[Seasongood, Selections from Speeches. Knopf, 1960, p. 178]

(453f)
[116 Sol. Jl 363, May 12, 1972]

(454f)
[Hay, Peter, The Book of Legal Anecdotes. Facts on File, 1989, p. 75. Martin Mayer writes that a Runic inscription has it that "a judge is a lawyer who once knew a politician." See Martin Mayer, The Judges. St. Martin's Press, 2006, p. 197]

(455f)
[Butler, A Century... Putnam, 1942, p. 88-89. Bander, Bar Relief, 72 Law Library Journal 352 (1979). See also Cohn, Criminal Law Seminar 15 (1961). See also Lavery, The Language of the Law in Rossman, ed. Advocacy and the King's English 758; 5 N.Z.L.Jl 545 (1974); Bowker, A Lifetime with the Law 83 (1961). See also: Once he [F.E. Smith] was arguing a case before three Lord Justices in the Court of Appeal, dealing with an elementary point of

law at inordinate length. Finally the Master of the Rolls, who was presiding, intervened.

"Really, Mr. Smith," he protested, "do give this Court credit for some little intelligence."

Quick as a flash came the reply:

"That is the mistake I made in the Court below, my Lord."
A.E. Bowker, A Lifetime with the Law. London: W.H. Allen, 1961, p. 83. See also Hay, Peter, The Book of Legal Anecdotes. Facts on File, 1989, p. 152. In Sam J. Ervin Jr.'s Humor of a Country Lawyer. University of North Carolina Press, 1983, p. 145 this exchange was between Major Neal and Chief Justice William N. H. Smith.]

(456f)
[36 Conn. Bar Jl 691 (1962)]

(457f)
[no source]

(458f)
[New York Times, Jan. 5, 1966, p. 31:3]

(459f)
[Simon, The Antagonists ...Simon & Schuster, 1989, p. 130]

(460f)
[Attributed to Marshall, C.J. in May, The Lighter Side of the Law. Michie, 1957, p. 22]

(461f)
[1957 Proceedings of the Maine State Bar Association 217. See also: There is a modern version of Lord Chancellor Lyndhurst' definition of a good judge: "First, he must be honest. Second, he must possess a reasonable amount of industry. Third, he must have courage. Fourth, he must be a gentleman. And then, if he has some knowledge of law, it will help." Botein, Bernard. Trial Judge. Simon and Schuster, 1952, p. 3]

((462f)
[Butler, A Century...Putnam, 1942, p. 89. See also Daniel L. Marsh, Boston University Law Review, p. 187. President Marsh attributed this remark to Henry W. Paine responding to Associate Justice Gray of the U.S. Supreme Court. See also Mayer, The Lawyers. Harper & Row, 1966, p. 524]

(463f)
[Freedman, National Association of Attorney Generals 124 (1963). See also: "A generation or two ago a learned judge said to an eminent and energetic counsel: 'The first time I hear an argument, I appreciate it, the second time it produces an impression upon me; but after the third time that impression is effaced.' 'Is it, my Lord?' replied the learned counsel; 'then I must repeat it a fourth time, in order that I may revive the first impression.'" Henry W. Taft. Legal Miscellanies. Macmillan, 1941, p. 170 citing McCardie, The Law, the Advocate, and the Judge.]

(464f)
[Eugene C. Gerhart, ed. Lawyers Treasury. Bobbs-Merrill, 1956, p. 128. See also Birkett, Law and Literature in Rossman, Advocacy and the King's English. Bobbs-Merrill, 1960, p. 775-776. See also:
ROUGH JUSTICE. Sir – Mr. R.C. Hunter Russell and Mr. Michael Goodman have added to our amusement by their quotations in relation to the judge and the brickbat, but they might have added the following comment: The Chief Justice happened to be leaning low on his elbow when the stone was thrown, so it flew too high, and only took of his hat. Soon after, some friends congratulating him on his escape, he replied (as his fashion was to make a jest of everything), "If I had been an upright Judge. I had been slain."
The reference for this story is to be found in "Chief Justice Treby's notes to Dyer's reports, folio edition, P. 188b. (Footnote in Pepy's Diary, Vol. III. P. 246. Yours faithfully, Leonard F. Behrens. Manchester (newspaper clipping – no source)]

(465f)
[Magruder, Mr. Justice Brandeis, 55 Harv. L. Rev. 194 (1941-1942). Justice Douglas attributed this quip to Justice Holmes. See Wild Bill ... Murphy 503 (2003).]

(466f)
[John S. Copley. Also attributed to Lord Lyndhurst in Gilbert, Oxford Book of Legal Anecdotes. Oxford University Press, 1986, p. 77 citing Kenealy, ed. Memoirs of Edward Vaughan Kenealy (1898). Robert Megarry, A New Miscellany-At-Law ed. by Byron A. Garner. The Law Book Exchange, 2005, p. 94103 and citing to Martin, Life of Lord Lyndhurst, 1883, p. 286 and Memoirs of Sir John Rolt 1804-1871 (1939), p. 87]

(467f)
[Source: John T. Buckley's, An Historical Look at Appellate Divisions, New York Law Journal, March 23, 2006, p. 2]

(467af)
   [From the diaries kept by Tom Lambert which were entrusted to Professor Michael Rustad, who gave me permission to thumb through them. Attributed to PAF (Paul A Freund)]

(467bf)
   Warren: The Man The Court The Era. John D. Weaver. Victor Gollancz, 1968, p. 16]

(467cf)
   [The Judges. Martin Mayer. St. Martin's Press, 2006, 58 citing Botein, Trial Judge. Cornerstone Library, 1952; repr. 1963, p. 53]. Mr. Mayer also has this quote from Botein: "A judge first searches the facts, then searches the law, then searches his soul." (at page 52)]

(468f)
[City Lawyer. Arthur Garfield Hays. Simon and Schuster, 1942, p.40]

(470f)
[Murane, Edward E., 34 S. Dak. J. No. 4 (Supp.) (1965); see also 44 Nebraska Law Review 356; see also Galanter, Lowering the Bar. University of Wisconsin Press, 2005, p. 57 citing six sources none of them the above. Also [Robert Megarry, A New Miscellany-At-Law ed. by Byron A. Garner. The Law Book Exchange, 2005, p. 96 and citing to Morton, Law and Laughter, 1913, p. 57

(471f)
{Gilbert, Oxford Book of Legal Anecdotes. Oxford University Press, 1986, p. 101 citing Stone, Clarence Darrow for the Defense (1941). See also the Gilbert book, page 199, for Samuel Leibowitz's take on juries.See also Rovere, Howe & Hummel. Farrar, Straus and Giroux 1947, p. 63 for Howe's jury picking style.]

(472f)
 [Welburn Maycock, 48 Women Lawyers Journal no. 1 17 (1962)]

(475f)
[Mr. Justice Holmes... ed. By Felix Frankfurter. Coward-McCann, 1931, p. 206   See also Curtis, A Common Place Book 27 (1957). See also:
       In December 1902, after   Holmes had been appointed and confirmed as associate justice of the U.S. Supreme Court, the Middlesex Bar Association in his home state of Massachusetts honored him with a send-off banquet. At the

end of the festivities, one of his supporters said.

"Finally, justice will be done in Washington."

"Don't be too sure," replied Justice Holmes. "I am going there to administer the laws."

Hay, Peter, The Book of Legal Anecdotes. Facts on File, 1989, p. 226. See also:

Remember what Justice Holmes said about "justice." I don't know what you think about him, but on the whole he was to me the master craftsman certainly of our time; and he said: "I hate justice," which he didn't quite mean. What he did mean was this. I remember once I was with him; it was a Saturday when the Court was to confer. It was before we had a motor car, and we jogged along in an old coupe. When we got down to the Capitol, I wanted to provoke a response, so as he walked off, I said to him: "Well, sir, goodbye. Do justice!" He turned quite sharply and he said: "Come here. Come here." I answered: "Oh, I know, I know." He replied: "That is not my job. My job is to play the game according to the rules."

[Hand, The Spirit of Liberty. Knopf, 1960, p. 306. Bander, Justice Holmes Ex Cathedra 229-230 (1991). Bander, Holmespun Humor, 10 Villanova Law Review 508 (1965. Also Sergeant, Justice Touched With, Mr. Justice Holmes 206-207 (Frankfurter ed. 1931); Holmes, Book Notices 201 (1936); Hill, Memorial, 298 Mass. 600 (1937); Curtis, A Common Place Book 27 (1957); Wyzanski, 104 Congressional Record 7369 (daily ed. 1958); Hay, Peter, The Book of Legal Anecdotes. Facts on File, 1989, p. 226. See also:

It is said that as Justice Holmes was leaving the banquet hall after the farewell dinner tendered him by the Boston Bar, before he left for Washington to take his seat on the Bench of the Supreme Court of the United States, someone called out:

"Now justice will be administered in Washington."

To this the new justice is reported to have replied:

"Don't be too sure. I am going there to administer the law."

Butler, A Century at the Bar of the Supreme Court of the United States. Putnam, 1942, p. 50-51.. See also Galanter, Lowering the Bar. University of Wisconsin Press, 2005 p. 241-242 citing instances of this anecdote, particularly the article by Herz, "Do Justice! Variations of a Thrice-Told Tale," 82 Virginia Law Review 111-61 (1996). See also Martin Mayer, The Judges. St. Martin's Press, 2006, p. 385-386. Also Mayer, The Lawyers. Harper & Row, 1966, p. 520 citing Curtis, Law as Large as Life, p. 156-157 citing Learned Hand. This anecdote reminds one of Mrs. Frankfurter's view of "we live by symbols." ((690)

(476f)
[44 Chicago Bar Record 223 (1963). Editor's Note: Marvin Wall of the Office of the Attorney General in Washington wrote to Professor Cox, from whom the

above extract is taken, requesting the exact source of the citation. I quote from Mr. Wall's letter to Professor Cox: "After we had talked for a few minutes, I suggested that Perhaps Mr. Lehman's famous quotation was apocryphal, and merely a tradition that had passed through generations in the Solicitor General's Office. Your respolnse, as you may remember, was, "Well, don't destroy it." Mr. Wall received permission from Professor Cox to make use of this anecdote which has been passed on to this column.. See Ed Bander, Anecdotes from Bander, 73 Law Library Journal 507 (1980)]

(480f)
[Hay, Peter, The Book of Legal Anecdotes. Facts on File, 1989, p. 54.]

(482f)
[New York Times Magazine, Letter to the Editor, May 10, 1964, p. 6. Bander, Justice Holmes Ex Cathedra 254-255 (1991). See The Occasional Speeches of Justice Oliver Wendell Holmes 6 (Howe ed. 1962), the phrase "and to rejoice in it," is found after the word "life."]

(484f)
[cannot locate source]

(485f)
[Time, August 22, 1977, p. 17]

(490f)
[Peabody, ed. The Holmes-Einstein Letters. St. Martins, 1964, p. 279. Bander, Justice Holmes Ex Cathedra 256-257 (1991).]

(491f)
[Richard Fountain, Wit of the Wig. Leslie Frewin, 1968, p. 93. Editor's note: I believe that this was a quote from Alexander Pope.]

(494f)
[Howe, ed. Holmes-Pollock Letters Harvard University Press, 2d ed. 1961, p. I: xxx-xxxi Bander, Justice Holmes Ex Cathedra 234 (1991). Bander, Holmespun Humor, 10 Villanova Law Review 301-302 (1964).

For Holmes's version, see Holmes-Einstein Letters 212 (Peabody ed. 1964). See also Bowen, Yankee from Olympus 342 (1945). See also Hyde, the Life and Times of Lord Birkett 47-48 (1964). Then there was the case of the gentleman whose father was a famous composer and his son a famous philosopher. He was always referred to as either the "father of" or the "the son of."]

(495)
[Biddle, Justice Holmes, Natural Law, and the Supreme Court. Macmillan, 1961, p. 6. Also Bander, Justice Holmes Ex Cathedra 204-205 (1991)]

(496f)
[Kramnick and Sheerman. Harold Laski. Penguin, 1993, p. 397-398]

(497f)
[newspaper clipping – no source]

(498f)
[28 New Jersey Law Journal 39 (1968)]

(499f)
[42 Nebraska Law Review 421 (1964)]

(500f)
[Hay, Peter, The Book of Legal Anecdotes. Facts on File, 1989, p. 149. See also: "Lord Mansfield: If this be law, sir, I must burn all my books, I see. Serjeant Davy: Your lordship had better read them first." [Fountain, Wit of Wig 42; see also National Conference of State Trial Judges 51 (Aug. 3-5, 1962).Also Bander, Doing Justice: Class Action, 72 Law Library Journal 536 (1979). Also Wellman, Day in Court. Macmillan, 1910, p. 158]

(501f)
[Derby, Recollections of Mr. Justice Holmes, 12 New York University Law Quarterly Review 350 (1935). Bander, Justice Holmes Ex Cathedra 219 (1991)]

(502f)
[28 New Jersey [York?] Law Journal 160]

(503f)
[Walter F. Murphy, Wild Bill .... Random House, 2003, p. 412].

(505f)
[29 Detroit Lawyer 86 (1961). See Bull Warren item also. Also, Bander, Doing Justice: Class Action, 72 Law Library Journal 535 (1979)]

(506f)
[personal experience. Bander, Doing Justice: Class Action, 72 Law Library Journal 537 (1979)]

(507f)
[contributed by a witness. Bander, Doing Justice: Class Action, 72 Law Library Jounral 536 (1979)]

(508f)
[See, in general, Peck,David W. Decision at Law. Dodd, Mead, 1961, p. 259-260.]

(509f)
[Richard Peete, Anecdotes of the Jealous Mistress. Rocky Mountain Law Review, 1959, p. 21; Bander, Doing Justice: Class Action, 72 Law Library Journal 535 (1979)]

(512f)
[Winship, Justice Frankfurter, Boston Sunday Globe, November 10, 1957. Also by Winship in this article: "… a good deal of Holmes humor was founded on his skepticism. He treated death lightly." See also Sergeant, Justice Touched with Fire, Mr. Justice Holmes 209 (1931): "The secretary – a new jewel of the Harvard Law School every year – wears an exalted air. He must promise not to get engaged during the period. "But I reserve the right," says the Justice with a twinkle, "to die or resign." Bander, Justice Holmes Ex Cathedra 263 (1991). Bander, Holmespun Humor, 10 Villanova Law Review 303 (1964).]

(513f)
[Walter F. Murphy, Wild Bill … . Random House, 2003, p. 507. Note: Murphy spends much time about how Douglas terrorized his law clerks.]

(514f)
[Gunther, Learned Hand. Knopf, 1994, p. 704]

(515f)
[From the diaries kept by Tom Lambert which were entrusted to Professor Michael Rustad, who gave me permission to thumb through them.]

(516f)
[Mason, Harlan Fiske Stone: Pillar of the Law. Viking, 1956, p. 281 citing H.F.S. to F.C. Hicks, Feb. 5, 1930. The Chief Justice is "Chief Justice of the United States" not "Chief Justice of the Supreme Court." See Weaver, John D. Warren: The Man The Court the Era. Victor Gollancz, 1968, p. 194, 341. For how this change came about see Martin Mayer, The Judges. St. Martin's

Press, 2006, p. 333-334. Each member of the United States Supreme Court is designated a justice, while members of the intermediate Federal Courts are called judges, which led a probably disgruntled litigant to say that there is no justice in the Courts of Appeal and no judges on the Supreme Court.

(517f)
[Ladd, 43 Neb. L. Rev. 397 (1964); Bander, Doing Justice: Class Action, 72 Law Library Journal 535 (1979)]

(518f)
From the diaries kept by Tom Lambert which were entrusted to Professor Michael Rustad, who gave me permission to thumb through them. See Smith, F. E., for double meaning of the word "crook."]

(520f)
[Levy, Corporation Lawyer: Saint or Sinner? The New Role of the Lawyer in Modern Society. Chilton Co., 1961, p. 32]

(521f)
[Source: Can the 'Jewish Law Firm' Success Story Be Duplicated? Anthony Lin, New York Law Journal, May 10, 2006, p. 1]

(521af)
[See Ropes Gray 1865-1940. Albert Boyden, [privately printed] 1942,, p. 125; also Ropes and Gray 1865-1990. Carl M. Brauer [privately printed] 1991, p. 9. Ropes Gray, at the height of its grandeur, was known as Ropes, Gray, Best, Coolidge and Rugg. A legal wag shortened this to "We the People," and that was how many Boston lawyers referred to the firm. In 2006, there is a document firm incorporated as "We the People," which provides divorce, bankruptcy and immigration forms for laymen seeking legal solutions without a lawyer.]

(522f)
[Edward Lamb, No Lamb for Slaughter: An Autobiography, 1963, p. 25. Bander, Doing Justice: Class Action, 72 Law Library Journal 536 (1979)]

(523f)
[adapted from 14 New Zealand Law Journal 438 (1963). For the uninitiated, Benson & Hedges was a brand of cigarettes and not the name of an English Law Report]

(525f)
[contributed by Oscar Leiding. Bander, Justice Holmes Ex Cathedra 265-266

(1991)]

(527f)
[no source]

(528f)
[Botein, Trial Judge. Simon & Schuster, 1952, p. 322]

(530f)
[Dennis J. Hutchinson, The Man Who Once was Whizzer White. Free Press, 1998, p. 419. Justice White's request to law clerks. See also Mason, Harlan Fiske Stone 241 (1956) on the propriety of citing to law reviews.]

(531f)
[Nizer, My Life in Court. Doubleday, 1961, p. 285]

(532f)
[Thurman Arnold to William McGovern according to an interview with the editor of the letters. [Gene M. Gressley, ed. Voltaire and the Cowboy: the Letters of Thurman Arnold. Colorado Associated University Press, 1977, p. 234. See also p. 500]

(533f)
[Wiener, Avoidable Faults in Appellate Briefs, 41 Neb. Law Rev. 434, 446 (1962). Bander, Doing Justice: Class Action, 72 Law Library Journal 536 (1979). See also:
    Sometimes the judicial reaction to a law review citation is essentially one of amusement, as for example the remark (probably not wholly apocryphal) attributed to Mr. Justice Holmes: "I don't mind when the lads on the Law Review say I'm wrong, what I object to is when they say I'm right."
[Wiener, Effective Appellate Advocacy. Prentice-Hall, 1950, p. 130 . Bander, Justice Holmes Ex Cathedra 262 (1991). Bander, Holmespun Humor, 10 Villanova Law Review 304 (1964); and also Derby, Recollections of Mr. Justice Holmes, 12 N.Y.U. Law Q. 350 (1935).]

(534f)
[Broken Contract: A Memoir of Harvard Law School. Richard D. Kahlenberg. Hill and Wang, , 1992, p. 159]

(534af)
    [From the diaries kept by Tom Lambert which were entrusted to Professor Michael Rustad, who gave me permission to thumb through them.]

(535f)
[Bander, Doing Justice: Class Action, 72 Law Library Journal 535 (1979)]

(536f)
[Hay, Peter, The Book of Anecdotes. Facts on File, 1989, p. 65]

(537f)
[Ladd, 43 Nebr. L. Rev. 397 (1964). See also Bander, Doing Justice: Class Action, 72 Law Library Journal 535 (1979). See also Hay, Peter, The Book of Legal Anecdotes. Facts on File, 1989, p. 134 for a similar anecdote, this time with a Canadian lawyer putting a judge to sleep and the lawyer asking the clerk to wake up the judge.]

(538f)
[Broken Contract: A Memoir of Harvard Law School. Richard D. Kahlenberg. Hill and Wang, , 1992, p. 5-6. See also Sam J. Ervin Jr. Humor of a Country Lawyer. University of North Carolina Press, 1983, p. 35. Note: The notion that two out of three students flunked out of law school because law school was too hard may be pure fantasy. During the fifties, people flunked out of law school because they took the GI Bill of Rights money as an entitlement or considered it a second job. As Bull Warren said – all you needed was a cast iron bottom to get through law school in the fifties and at the turn of the century.]

(539f)
[I heard this quip from a professor at Western New England College School of Law Library during a meeting of the New England law librarians.]

(539af)
[From the diaries kept by Tom Lambert which were entrusted to Professor Michael Rustad, who gave me permission to thumb through them.]

(539bf)
[From the diaries kept by Tom Lambert which were entrusted to Professor Michael Rustad, who gave me permission to thumb through them.]

(539cf)
[From the diaries kept by Tom Lambert which were entrusted to Professor Michael Rustad, who gave me permission to thumb through them.]

(540f)
[45 Nebraska State Bar Association 392. Bander, Bar Relief, 72 Law Library

Journal 352 (1979)]

(541f)
[Liva Baker, Felix Frankfurter. Coward-McCann, 1969, p. 222 (cited from Jackson, The Struggle for Judicial Supremacy xi]

(542f)
[New York Post, Dec. 22, 1961, p. 33]

(544f)
[personal experience]

(545f)
[1963 Proceedings of the Maine State Bar Association 65]

(546f)
[Freedman, National Association of Attorney Generals 124 (1963). Bander, Bar Relief, 72 Law Library Journal 353 (1979). See also 45 Nebraska State Bar Ass'n Proc. 392 (1965)]

(547f)
[Laurence H. Silberman, Regulation, March/April 1978, p. 20]

(548f)
[cited to Richard O'Sullivan, The Spirit of the Common Law.
The Literature of the Law... Brian Harris. Blackstone Press Limited, 1998, p. 233]

(549f)
[H.D.C. Pepler, The Devil's Devices See also:
"A lawyer who's just o.k. can, maybe, lack
The eloquence of Messala or the learning
Of Cascellius, and, nevertheless, perform
Some useful functions ...' See: David Ferry, The Epistles of Horace 2001, p. 178-179 where the poem is also rendered in Latin.

(549af)
[From the diaries kept by Tom Lambert which were entrusted to Professor Michael Rustad, who gave me permission to thumb through them. Finley Peter Dunne's Mr. Dooley put it this way: "A law, Hinnissy, that might look like a wall to you or me, wud look like a thriumphal arch to th' expeeryenced eye iv a lawyer." See Mr. Dooley on the Choice of Law compiled by Edward

J. Bander. Michie, 1963 , p. 64. Professor Lambert also liked to quote Mr. Dooley's "Comfort the afflicted, afflict the comfortable." See also, in general, Mayer, The Lawyers. Harper & Row, 1966, p. 6]

(550f)
[Gunther, Learned Hand. Knopf, 1994, p. 123. "Too often, lawyers are men who turn poetry into prose and prose into jargon." John Maynard Keynes quoted in Acheson: The Secretary of State Who Created the American World. James Chace. Simon & Schuster, 1998, p. 100.]

(552f)
[Hay, Peter, Book of Legal Anecdotes. Facts on File, 1989, p. 3. Compare with "If you … can think about a thing that is inextricably attached to something else without thinking of the thing which it is attached to, then you have a legal mind.." Galanter, Lowering the Bar. University of Wisconsin Press, 2005, p. 51 [quoted at Arnold, The Symbols of Government 101 (1935). See also Thurman Arnold, Fair Fights and Foul, Harcourt, Brace and World, 1951, p. 20-21. ["If you can think of a subject which is interrelated and inextricably combined with another subject, without knowing anything about or giving any consideration to the second subject, then you have a legal mind."] Compare with: "The test of a first-rate intelligence is the ability to hold two opposed ideas in the mind at the same time, and still retain the ability to function." F. Scott Fitzgerald, The Crack-up (1936), p. 69]. See also Mayer, The Lawyers. Harper & Row, 1966, p. 86 also quoting Arnold.]

(554f)
[2 Record of the Bar of New York City 235]

(560f)
[42 North Dakota Law Review 79 (1965)]

(563f)
[Howe, ed. Holmes-Laski Letters. Harvard University Press, 1953, p. II:1019. Bander, Justice Holmes Ex Cathedra 233 (1991). Bander, Holmespun Humor, 10 Villanova Law Review 300 (1964).]

(564f)
[Richard Fountain, Wit of the Wig. Leslie Frewin, 1968, p. 80.Bander, Bar Relief, 72 Law Library Journal 352 (1979) See also Pannick, Advocates. Oxford University Press, 1992, p. 230 for the observation: 'ninety per cent of all cases win or lose themselves, and that the ultimate result would have been the same whatever counsel the parties had chosen to represent them.']

(570f)
[Bent, Justice Oliver Wendell Holmes. Vanguard, 1932, p. 17]

(575f)
[Michael D. Davis and Hunter R. Clark, Thurgood Marshall; Warrior at the Bar; Rebel on the Bench. Carol, 1994, p. 191. See also Mayer, The Lawyers. Harper & Row, 1966, p. 547. For additional, but uninspiring anecdotes about Marshall, see Rosen, The Supreme Court ... Henry Holt, 2006, p. 32-33. As to the comment by President Jackson being apocryphal, see Rosen, p. 67]

(577f)
[Woodward, The Brethren. Simon & Schuster, 1979, p. 59. See also Davis and Clark, Thurgood Marshall 8 (1992)]

(578f)
[Woodward, The Brethren. Simon & Schuster, 1979, p. 355]

(579f)
[Kornstein, Thinking Under Fire. Dodd, Mead, 1987, p. 199]

(580f)
[38 Massachusetts Law Quarterly 113 (Aug. 1953)]

(581f)
[New Zealand Law Journal, 5 Aug. 1975, p. 549. The last time I looked, this was the situation in The Court of Appeals for the First Circuit. I have seen Judge Magruder disappear over the horizon after his admonition to counsel that due process was not an issue in the case and counsel proceeded to argue the point.]

(585f)
[Acheson, Recollections of Service with the Federal Supreme Court, 18 The Alabama Lawyer 362-363 (1957)]

(586f)
[Gerhart, America's Advocate: Robert H. Jackson. Bobbs-Merrill, 1958, p. 86. See also: Pearson & Allen, The Nine Old Men. Doubleday, 1937, p. 227]

(587f)
[Wiener, Curable Faults in Oral Argument, 41 Nebraska Law Review447, 458 (1962)]

(588f)
[Kaufman, Speech, 36 Connecticut Bar Journal 694-695 (1962). Bander, Justice Holmes Ex Cathedra 239-240 (1991). 10 Villanova Law Review 300 (1964). For another and more profane version, see 2 Pusey Charles Evans Hughes 285 (1951)]

(589)
[Pearson & Allen, The Nine Old Men. Doubleday, 1937, p. 182]

(590f)
[Thurman Arnold, Fair Fights and Foul. Harcourt, Brace & World, 1951, p. 59]

(591f)
[James F. Simon, The Antagonists: Hugo Black, Felix Frankfurter and Civil Liberties in Modern America. Simon & Schuster, 1989, p. 45. Frankfurter has this more dramatically in Felix Franfurter Reminisces 102 (1962). Also Bander, Justice Holmes Ex Cathedra 223-224 (1991)]

(593f)
[Gunther, Learned Hand. Knopf, 1994, p. 565]

(594f)
[American Scholar, Spring, 1963, p. 263]

(594af)
[City Lawyer. Arthur Garfield Hays. Simon and Schuster, 1942, p.196. See also The New Mencken Letters. Carl Bode,d ed. (Dial Press 1977), p. 194-197]

(595f)
[Joseph C. Goulden, The Money Lawyers. St. Martin's Press, 2006., p. 344]

(596f)
[Mason, Harlan Fiske Stone: Pillar of the Law. Viking, 1956, p. 747 citing as told to Pearson and Allen, The Nine Old Men, 1937, p. 107. Bander, Justice Holmes Ex Cathedra 251 (1991)]

(597f)
[Martin Mayer, The Judges. St. Martin's Press, 2006, p. 211 citing Charles P. Curtis and Ferris Greenslet, eds. The Practical Cogitator. Houghton Mifflin, 1945, p. 413-414]

(600f)
[1963 Proceedings of the Maine State Bar Association 81-82]

(602f)
[Simon, The Antagonists ... Simon & Schuster, 1989, p. 158]

(604f)
[Navasky, A Matter of Opinion. Farrar, Straus & Giroux, 2005, p. 38]

(606f)
[newspaper clipping – no citation]

(608f)
[Howe, ed. Holmes-Laski Letters. Harvard University Press, 1953, p. II:1180. Bander, Justice Holmes Ex Cathedra 234 (1991). Bander, Holmespun Humor, 10 Villanova Law Review 300 (1964).]

(610f)
[Gerhart (Eugene C.), America's Advocate: Robert H. Jackson. Bobbs-Merrill, 1958, p. 45].

(611f)
[Harlan ... What Part Does the Oral Argument Play in the Conduct of an Appeal, 41 Cornell L.Q. 6, 10 (1955). Bander, Bar Relief, 72 Law Library Journal 352-353 (1979). See also: Your honor, I would like to inquire on whose behalf you are interrogating this witness. If it is in the interest of the plaintiff, who is so ably represented by my young opponent, I wish to object. If it is on behalf of my client, I desire to withdraw the question. Peete, Anecdotes of the Jealous Mistress. Rocky Mountain Law Review, 1959, p. 11.]

(612f)
[Richard Fountain, Wit of the Wig. Leslie Frewin, 1968, p. 110a]

(614f)
[Gunther, Learned Hand. Knopf, 1994, p. 336]

(615f)
[Saturday Review, Aug. 12, 1961, p. 7]

(616f)
[Glanville Williams, Language and the Law, in Rossman, ed. Advocacy and

the King's English. Bobbs-Merrill, 1960, p. 676 citing Pollock-Holmes Letters, vol. 2, p. 28]

(617f)
[Liva Baker, Felix Frankfurter. Coward-McCann, 1969, p. 219. See also Harper, Justice Rutledge and the Bright Constellation 329 (1965). Bander, Justice Holmes Ex Cathedra 268 (1991)]

(618f)
[Frankfurter, Felix Frankfurter Reminisces. Reynal, 1962, p. 296-297. Bander, Justice Holmes Ex Cathedra 226-227 (1991) As to Holmes's preserving of his opinions, see also, The Holmes-Einstein Letters 35 (Peabody ed. 1964). The Pipeline case is at 234 U.S. 548 (1914)]

(619f)
I cannot locate the source for this quote, but it would be a shame to leave it out for that reason.

(620f)
[Acheson, Morning and Noon. Houghton, 1965, p. 58. Bander, Justice Holmes Ex Cathedra 267 (1991). See also Artemus Ward and David L. Weiden. Sorcerers' Apprentices: 100 Years of Law Clerks at the United States Supreme Court. NYU Press, 2006, p. 219]

(621f)
[Beck, Justice Holmes and the Supreme Court 1 Federal Bar Association Journal 36-37 (March 1932); Bander, Justice Holmes Ex Cathedra 197 (1991)]

(622f)
[McElwain, E. The Business of the Supreme Court as Conducted by Chief Justice Hughes, 63 Harvard Law Review 5, 17 (1949). See also Martin Mayer, The Judges. St. Martin's Press, 2006, 308. See also Mayer, The Lawyers. Harper & Row, 1966, p. 524 citing Pusey, Charles Evans Hughes, vol. II, p. 664]

(623f)
[Winship article on Justice Frankfurter in the Boston Sunday Globe of Nov. 10, 1957; see also Bander Justice Holmes Ex Cathedra 262-3 (1966). Bander, Holmespun Humor, 10 Villanova Law Review 303 (1964). Bander, Bar Relief, 72 Law Library Journal 354 (1979).]

(624f)
[Gerhart, America's Advocate: Robert H. Jackson. Bobbs-Merrill, 1958, p. 193

See also Kornstein, Thinking Under Fire. Dodd, Mead, 1987, p. 174. Bander, Bar Relief, 72 Law Library Journal 353 (1979). See also 37 A.B.A.Jl 803 (1951)]

(625f)
[Biddle, Mr. Justice Holmes. Scribner's, 1942, p. 144. Bander, Justice Holmes Ex Cathedra 206-207 (1991). Bander, Holmespun Humor, 10 Villanova Law Review 504 (1965)]

(626f)
[Gunther, Learned Hand. Knopf, 1994, p. 489]

(627f)
[Told at the Middlesex Bar Association. Daniel J. O'Brien's column, Round About, Boston Globe,July 10, 1986. Note: Russell Baker told this story (I believe I heard it at an Association of American Law Library banquet): Baker was leaving a press conference at the White House, when President Johnson motioned to him to come into the Oval Office. They had talked for some time, when Johnson pressed a button and an aide came in. Johnson wrote a note, which the aide read and dropped into a waste basket. Soon the phone rang, Johnson listened and hung up. Then Johnson had to excuse himself for some reason and when he left the room, Baker reached into the waste basket to read the note. It read, "Who the hell am I talking to?"]

(628f)
[Butler, A Century...Putnam, 1942, p. 162-163]

(629f)
[Cited by James Lupo, Court Speech as Political Action..., 3 JALWD r8 at 65. and listing the Papers of Daniel Webster: Legal Papers, vol. 3, 153-154 as source. Also cited by John C. Sgeogerd & Jordan B. Cherrick, Advocacy and Emotion, 3 JALWD 154 at 165 and listing Rehnquist, Webster and the Oratorical Tradition, 1989 Yearbook of the Supreme Court Historical Society, 1, 8 as source.]

(629af)
[From the diaries kept by Tom Lambert which were entrusted to Professor Michael Rustad, who gave me permission to thumb through them.]

(629bf)
[From the diaries kept by Tom Lambert which were entrusted to Professor Michael Rustad, who gave me permission to thumb through them.]

(629cf)
[From the diaries kept by Tom Lambert which were entrusted to Professor Michael Rustad, who gave me permission to thumb through them.]

(629df)
[contributed by Professor Emeritus Alfred Maleson. See also Wellman, Day in Court. Macmillan, 1910, p. 246: "Indeed, this may be taken as a fixed rule, that the popular mind can never be vigorously addressed, deeply moved, and stirred and fixed for more than one hour in any single address" Rufus Choate.]

(630f)
[Howe, The Occasional Speeches of Justice Oliver Wendell Holmes Harvard University Press, 1962, p. 172. Bander, Justice Holmes Ex Cathedra 237 (1991).]

(631f)
[no source]

(635f)
[Pearson & Allen, The Nine Old Men. Doubleday, 1937, 181. Allen & Pearson, More Merry-Go-Round. Liverright, 1932, p. 111; Bander, Justice Holmes Ex Cathedra 196-197 (1991)]

(640f)
[Alexander M. Sullivan, The Last Sergeant. London: ;Macdonald, 1952, p. 112. See also: J. F. Grozier was not a concise thinker, and, in his arguments in Court did not always confine himself to the questions at issue, often taking up the time of the trial by his excursions into irrelevant discussion, much to the displeasure of the judges. United States District Judge Moses Hallett was especially critical.

"Counsellor, please confine your argument to the points in this case," said Judge Hallett on one occasion.

"What point, Your Honor?" asked Mr. Grozier.

"Any point," replied Judge Hallett.
Richard Peete, Anecdotes of the Jealous Mistress. Rocky Mountain Law Review, 1959, p. 57.
See also: Lord Ellenborough once rebuked and English barrister who had been arguing a case before him during the entire morning session of the court. After the lunch recess and upon the re-assembling of the court, the loquacious orator asked the judge if he "might have the pleasure of resuming his argument." His

Lordship replied quietly: "You may continue your argument, Mr. Blank, but the pleasure was gone some hours ago." Wellman, Day in Court. Macmillan, 1910, p. 246-247. "Judges know how to decide a good deal sooner than they know why." Justice Holmes as cited by Charles P. Curtis, Law as Large as Life. Simon & Schuster, 1959, p. 87 in Mayer, The Judges. St. Martin's Press, 2007, p. 102]

(641f)
[Patrick Devlin, The Judge. Oxford University Press, 1979, p. 26. See also Bander, Anecdotes from Bander, 73 Law Library Journal 506 (1980).]

(643f)
[Mason, Harlan Fiske Stone: Pillar of the Law. Viking, 1956, p. 204. Bander, Justice Holmes Ex Cathedra 251 (1991).]

(647f)
[Greenman & Schmertz, Personnel Administration and the Law, 2d ed. Bureau of National Affairs, 1972, p. 346. 346 Tobriner, An Appellate Judge's View of the Labor Arbitration Process in The Arbitrator, The NLRB and the Courts, Proceedings of the 20th Annual Meeting, National Academy of Arbitrators 37 (1967). Bander, Bar Relief, 72 Law Library Journal 353 (1979).]

(648f)
[V.T.H. Delany, Christopher Palles, ... Dublin: A. Figgis, 1960, p. 157]

(649f)
[Alfred Lord Tennyson]

(650f)
[Birkett, Law and Literature, in Rossman, ed. Advocacy and the King's English. Bobbs-Merrill, 1960, p. 776]

(651f)
[Seasongood, Selections From Speeches. Knopf, 1960, p. 210]

(652f)
[Richard Fountain, Wit of the Wig. Leslie Frewin, 1968, p. 110-111]

(653f)
[J. Tudor Rees, Reserved Judgment. London, Muller, 1959, p. 189]

(654f)
[personal experience of compiler]

(655f)
[Liva Baker, Felix Frankfurter. Coward-McCann, 1969, p. 217. "Roberts observed that the least successful Chiefs [Chief Justices] had approached their jobs as law professors rather than as leaders of a collegial Court." Interview with C.J. Roberts, July 11, 2006. Rosen, The Supreme Court ... Henry Holt, 2006, p. 222. Also at p. 224: "A justice is not like a law professor."]

(656f)
[Among Friends: Personal Letters of Dean Acheson. McLellan and Acheson, eds. Dodd, Mead, 1980, p. 178]

(657f)
[Robert Megarry, A New Miscellany-At-Law ed. by Byron A. Garner. The Law Book Exchange, 2005, p. 89]

(657af)
[From the diaries kept by Tom Lambert which were entrusted to Professor Michael Rustad, who gave me permission to thumb through them.]

(657bf)
[From the diaries kept by Tom Lambert which were entrusted to Professor Michael Rustad, who gave me permission to thumb through them.]

(658f)
[Harper, Justice Rutledge and the Bright Constellation. Bobbs-Merrill, 1965, p. 328. Bander, Justice Holmes Ex Cathedra 267 (1991)]

(659f)
[contributed by Oscar Leiding. Bander, Justice Holmes Ex Cathedra 266 (1991)]

(660f)
119 Harvard Law Review 1 at 4, 5, 16, 19 (2005). But see: "A few years ago the Chief Justice became bored with his plain black robe and added the yellow stripes, inspired by the costume worn by the Lord Chancellor in ... Iolanthe. It was in this regalia that Rehnquist presided over the trial of President Clinton by the United States Senate. The yellow stripes are a striking visual feature and drew a good deal of comment, all duly noting their comic-opera origins. The most solemn form of American trial was thus presided over by the

highest judge in the land dressed in a funny costume. Maybe (though I greatly doubt it) the Chief Justice was signaling what he thought of the proceeding." Richard A. Posner, An Affair of State: The Investigation, Impeachment, and Trial of President Clinton. Harvard University Press, , 1999, p. 168.

According to a public television program on the Supreme Court that premiered in February 2007, Justice Rehnquist's clerks dubbed him the Lone Ranger because of the 8 to 1 dissents the court registered during his early years on the court, with Rehnquist as the lone dissenter.

(661f)
[Carey, Speech, 1961 Proceedings of the Maine State Bar Association 169. Bander, Justice Holmes Ex Cathedra 216 (1991). Bander, Holmespun Humor, 10 Villanova Law Review 506-507 (1965)]

(662f)
[Joey Adams column, New York Post, Aug. 3, 1977, p. 63

(663f)
[Paul Campos, Jurismania. Oxford University Press, 1998, p. 38. Probably the most pompous statement ever made by a graduate of an ivy league school.]

(665f)
[34 Mississippi Law Journal 374]

(667f)
[Frankfurter, Felix Frankfurter Reminisces. Reynal, 1962, p. 241-247. Bander, Justice Holmes Ex Cathedra 225-226 (1991). See also Woollcott's "The Judge's Last Opinion," Long, Long Ago, Viking, 1943, p. 107-110. Also Rosen, The Supreme Court .... Henry Holt, 2006, p. 122-123 citing The Justice from Beacon Hill, HarperCollins, 1991, p. 641]

(669f)
[Bander, Doing Justice: Class Action, 72 Law Library Journal 535 (1979)]

(670f)
[Simon, The Antagonists ... Simon & Schuster, 1989, p. 55]

(672f)
[L.C. Cohen, ed. The Legal Conscience; Selected Papers [Felix S. Cohen]. Archon, 1960, 1970, p. 122. See also Galanter, Lowering the Bar..., University of Wisconsin Press, 2005, p. 97 et seq., specifically p.. 106-107]

(672af)
Rosen, The Supreme Court ... Henry Holt, 2006, p. 198 citing Scalia's letter to editor, Boston Herald, March 29, 2006.]

(673f)
[Frankfurter, Felix Frankfurter Reminisces. Reynal, 1962, p. 11. Bander, Justice Holmes Ex Cathedra 223 (1991) Bander, Holmespun Humor, 10 Villanova Law Review 308 (1965)]

(675f)
[Peabody, ed. The Holmes-Einstein Letters. St. Martins, 1964, p. 279. Bander, Justice Holmes Ex Cathedra 256-257 (1991). Bander, Holmespun Humor, 10 Villanova Law Review 305 (1964).]

(676f)
[Butler, A Century... Putnam, 1942, p. 89]

(677f)
[105 Sol. Jl 626 (1961]

(679f)
[Richard Foutain, Wit of Wig. Leslie Frewin, 1968, p. 11. Also Hay, Peter, The Book of Legal Anecdotes. Facts on File, 1989, p. 148. Also Gilbert, The Oxford Book of Legal Anecdotes 279 (1986) citing The Life of F.E. Smith, First Lord Birkenhad by his son (1959) "The Judge replied furiously, "You are extremely offensive, young man;" and F.E. added to his previous lapses by saying: "As a matter of fact we both are; the only difference between us is that I'm trying to be, and you can't help it." (279-280). See also Broad, Advocates of the Golden Age 213 (1958). See also The Literature of the Law... Brian Harris. Blackstone Press Limited, 1998, p. 263-264. According to this book Judge Willis was the butt of the sarcasm.]

(680f)
[Gilbert, The Oxford Book of Legal Anecdotes. Oxford University Press, 1986, p. 283 citing The Life of F.E. Smith, First Lord Birkenhead (1959). Note: "crook" has a double meaning. It can be the staff of the Archbishop or a slander on the person. Tom Lambert, of tort fame, was a frequent double user of this word as he explained the intricacies of tort law.]

(681f)
[Camp, The Glittering Prizes... F. E. Smith ... Macgibbon & Kee 1960, p. 61.

He also said: "The world will continue to offer glittering prizes to those who have stout hearts and sharp swords (p. 178, 216). See also Broad, Advocates of the Golden Age 264, 272 (1958)]

(683f)
[Pusey, Charles Evans Hughes. Macmillan, 1951, p. 2: 664]

(684f)
[Yarbrough, Tinsley E. David Hackett Souter. Oxford University Press, 2005, p. 126

(685f)
[Dennis J. Hutchinson, The Man Who Once was Whizzer White. Free Press, 1998, p. 218]

(688f)
[McCormack, A Law Clerk's Recollections, 1946 Columbia Law Review 710 at 713-714. Bander, Justice Holmes Ex Cathedra 245-247 (1991).]

(688af)
[Martin Mayer, The Judges. St. Martin's Press, 2006, p. 174 citing John Chipman Gray, The Nature and Sources of the Law. Beacon Press, p. 253]

(689f)
[Schorer, Sinclair Lewis. McGraw-Hill, 1961, p. 549. Bander, Justice Holmes Ex Cathedra 259-260 (1991). But see McPhaul, Deadlines and Monkeyshines 165 (1962). Dryden described Ed Walsh, White Sox spitball pitcher, as the "only man in the world who can strut sitting down."]

(690f)
[Mendelson, ed. Felix Frankfurter: A Tribute. Reynal, 1964, p. 7 . Bander, Justice Holmes Ex Cathedra 253 (1991).]

(691f)
[Gilbert, The Oxford Book of Legal Anecdotes. Oxford University Press, 1986, p. 191 citing Lord Alverstone, Recollections of Bar and Bench (1914)]

(693f)
[Karl N. Llewellyn, The Common Law Tradition: Deciding Appeals. Little, Brown, 1960, p. 21. Bander, Justice Holmes Ex Cathedra 243-244 (1991). Bander, Holmespun Humor, 10 Villanova Law Review 304 (1964)]

(694f)
[Among Friends: Personal Letters of Dean Acheson. McLellan and Acheson, eds. Dodd, Mead, 1980, p. 325. See also Ed Bander, Anecdotes from Bander, 73 Law Library Journal 506 (1980)]

(696f)
[no source]

(697f)
[Richard Fountain, Wit of the Wig. Leslie Frewin, 1968, p 109]

(698f)
[Rosen, The Supreme Court .... Henry Holt, 2006, p. 173]

(699f)
[Seymour, Comment, Government Under Law, ed. By Arthur E. Sutherland. Harvard University Press, 1956, p. 501. Bander, Justice Holmes Ex Cathedra 260 (1991). Bander, Holmespun Humor, 10 Villanova Law Review 304 (1964).]

(700f)
[1963 Proceedings of the Maine State Bar Association 122; see also Galanter, Lowering the Bar. University of Wisconsin Press, 2005 p. 129 which has many cites to this story. The Galanter one takes place in Chicago.]

(701f)
[34 S. D. Bar Jl no. 4 (supp.) 80 (1965)]

(703f)
[39 Idaho State Bar Proceedings 22-23 (1965)]

(707f)
[Langrock, Beyond the Courthouse... Paul S. Eriksson, Publisher, 1999, p. 5. See also C.E. Hughes at (436). Benjamin Franklin "urged that judge be selected by vote of the lawyers in the district, because they would choose the best of their group to get rid of the competition.." See The Judges. Martin Mayer. St. Martin's Press, 2006, p. 67]

(710f)
[Clark, Hon. Tom C., Address, 11 Federal Bar News, No. 10:315 (Oct. 1964). Bander, Justice Holmes Ex Cathedra 217 (1991). See also 18 Federal Bar Journal 33 (1958) and 3 City Lawyer (N.Y.) No. 1:14 (1965).]

(712f)
[anonymous]

(713f)
[Butler, A Century... Putnam, 1942, p. 167]

(714f)
[Simon, The Antagonists ...Simon & Schuster, 1989, p. 106]

(715f)
[Gunther, Learned Hand. Knopf, 1994, p. 569-570. See also: Margolick, At The Bar. Simon & Schuster, 1995, p. 181.]

(716f)
[Liva Baker, Felix Frankfurter, Coward-McCann, 1969, p. 214]

(717f)
[1955 Proceedings of the Maine State Bar Association 97]

(718f)
[Joan Biskupic, Sandra O'Connor. Ecco, 2005, p. 183. Martin Mayer attributes to Justice John Harlan the expression of the "Court into nine small law firms." See Martin Mayer, The Judges. St. Martin's Press, 2006, p. 307]

(719f)
[Attributed to Alexander Bickel. See Walter F. Murphy, Wild Bill ... . Random House, 2003, p. 232. 609. Attributed to Oliver Wendell Holmes in Rosen, The Supreme Court ... Henry Holt, 2006, p. 6 without attribution.]

(720f)
[Kurland, ed. Of Law and Life ... Frankfurter. Harvard University Press, 1965, p. 152. See also Among Friends: Personal Letters of Dean Acheson. McLellan and Acheson, eds. Dodd, Mead, 1980, p. 131. Thurman Arnold attributes this statement to George Wharton Pepper in Thurman Arnold, Fair Fights and Foul. Harcourt, Brace and World, 1951, p. 159.

"I would rather talk to damn fools then listen to them." Dean Acheson in turning down a nomination to the Court of Appeals of the D.C. See The Wise Men... Walter Isaacson and Evans Thomas, Simon and Schuster, 1986, p. 138. See also Mayer, The Lawyers. Harper & Row, 1966, p. 7]

(721f)
[1961 Proceedings of the Maine State Bar Association 161-162]

(722f)
[Dennis J. Hutchinson, The Man Who Once was Whizzer White. Free Press, 1998, p. 387 quoting Paul Freund.]

(723f)
[Walter F. Mutphy, Wild Bill .... Random House, 2003, p. 244].

(724f)
[Mason, Harlan Fiske Stone: Pillar of the Law. Viking, 1956, p. 580]

(725f)
[New York Times, Sept. 1, 2006, p. C11]

(726f)
[From the diaries kept by Tom Lambert which were entrusted to Professor Michael Rustad, who gave me permission to thumb through them.]

(726af)
[From the diaries kept by Tom Lambert which were entrusted to Professor Michael Rustad, who gave me permission to thumb through them.]

(727f)
[Attributed to Paul Freund. From the diaries kept by Tom Lambert which were entrusted to Professor Michael Rustad, who gave me permission to thumb through them.]

(730f)
[Current Legal Problems 1 (19860 (Lord Goff)]

(731f)
[Douglas, We the Judges. Doubleday, 1956 p. 272. See also Schwartz, Supreme Court 168 (1957). Bander, Justice Holmes Ex Cathedra 220 (1991). Bander, Holmespun Humor, 10 Villanova Law Review 307 (1965)]

(732f)
[Paul Campos, Jurismania. Oxford University Press, 1998, p. 68]

(733f)
[Howe, ed. Holmes-Pollock Letters. Harvard University Press, 2d ed. 1961,

p. I:56 Bander, Justice Holmes Ex Cathedra 235 (1991). Bander, Holmespun Humor, 10 Villanova Law Review 302 (1964).]

(734f)
[Peabody, ed. The Holmes-Einstein Letters 22 (1964). Bander, Justice Holmes Ex Cathedra 255-256 (1991). Bander, Holmespun Humor, 10 Villanova Law Review 305 (1964).]

(734af)
[See also Artemus Ward and David L. Weiden. Sorcerers' Apprentices: 100 Years of Law Clerks at the United States Supreme Court. NYU Press, 2006, p. 64]

(735f)
[Clancy, Just a Country Lawyer. (biography of Senator Sam Ervin). Indiana University Press, 1974, p. 81. See also Bander, Doing Justice: Class Action, 72 Law Library Jounral 536 (1979). See also Erwin, Humor of a Country Lawyer. University of North Carolina Press, 1983, p. 36. See also Hay, Peter, The Book of Legal Anecdotes. Facts on file, 1989, p. 66. See Eugene C. Gerhart, Improving Our Legal Writing in Rossman, ed. Advocacy and the King's English (1960) 765 for Professor Warren's critique of the literary style of judges, professors of law and editors of law reviews.]

(736f)
[Bernstein, The Inimitable Bull Warren, Harvard Law School Bulletin 36 (Spring 1979). Bander, Doing Justice: Class Action, 72 Law Library Journal 537 (1979). See also Gilbert, The Oxford Book of Legal Anecdotes 393 (1986) citing 58 Harvard Law Review 1136 (1994). Also Mayer, The Lawyers. Harper & Row, 1966, p. 71-72 citing Joseph N. Welch, 58 Harvard Law Review 1156. For a fictional treatment, see Osborne, Paper Chase. Houghton-Mifflin, 1971, p. 3]

(737f)
Listen to Leaders in Law. Albert Love and James S. Childers. Holt, 1963.

(740f)
[Davis, John W., The Argument of an Appeal, in Rossman, ed. Advocacy and the King's English. Bobbs-Merrill, 1960, p. 220. Bander, Justice Holmes Ex Cathedra 219 (1991). Bander, Holmespun Humor, 10 Villanova Law Review 307 (1965). See also: Pearson & Allen, The Nine Old Mern. Doubleday, 1937, p. 39]

(743f)
[Dennis J. Hutchinson, The Man Who Once was Whizzer White. Free Press, 1998, p. 1]

(744f)
[Dennis J. Hutchinson, The Man Who Once was Whizzer White. Free Press, 1998, p. 443 quoting Calvin Trillin, Nation, April 12, 1993]

(745f)
[Source: a former law librarian of the Supreme Court]

(746f)
[Botein, Trial Judge. Simon & Schuster, 1952, p. 151]

(750f)
[New York Times, Feb. 4, 1974, 29:6]]

(751f)
[58 Law Society's Gazette (1961

(752f)
{no source]

(753f)
[86 The Reporter (Nov.) 9]

(754f)
[Matter of Douglas, 195 Misc. (N.Y.) 661 (1949)]

(755f)
[Gilbert, The Oxford Book of Legal Anecdotes. Oxford University Press, 1986, p. 162 citing Healy, The Old Munster Circuit (1939). See also: During the early days in the Irish Courts, Carson once asked a witness what happened in his part of the country to people who told lies on oath. :"Their side usually wins, Your Honour," was the answer.]

(756f)
[Robert Megarry, A New Miscellany-At-Law ed. by Byron A. Garner. The Law Book Exchange, 2005, p. 94 and citing to Leslie Hale, John Philpot Curran (1958), p. 91 and others]

(756af)
[Wellman, Day In Court. Macmillan, 1910, p. 190]

(756bf)
[Wellman, Day In Court. Macmillan, 1910, p. 212]

(757f)
[Acheson, Recollections of Service with the Federal Supreme Court, 18 The Alabama Lawyer 355, 359-360 (1957). See also Bander, Justice Holmes Ex Cathedra 193-194 (1991). It was reported in the New York Post, Nov. 26, 1962, p. 29, that a quiz show featured this question: "Which American met, during his lifetime, both John Quincy Adams and Alger Hiss? The answer: "Oliver Wendell Holmes." See Rovere, The American Establishment 149 (1962). See also Acheson, Morning and Noon 63 (1965)]

(758f)
[Joan Biskupic, Sandra Day O'Connor. Ecco, 2005, p. 167]

(759f)
[Max Eastman, Enjoyment of Laughter. Simon & Schuster, 1936, p. 284. See also Dicken's Mr. Bumble (Oliver Twist) "if the law supposes that, the law is an ass." See Estate of Wilson v. Aiken Indus., 439 U.S. 877 (1978)]

(760f)
[Summer 2003 edition of Ms. Magazine – located on Google by requesting "Ladies' Day." Harvard Law was not the only law school to employ this form of hazing. See Bander, "A Survey of Legal Humor Books," 19 Suffolk University Law Review 1066 (1965).

((781f)
[Hull, Challenge to the Law. Providence Journal, 1949, p. 45. Bander, Justice Holmes Ex Cathedra 237 (1991).]

(782f)
[From the diaries kept by Tom Lambert which were entrusted to Professor Michael Rustad, who gave me permission to thumb through them.]

(785f)
[1962 Georgia Bar Ass'n 234. Note: As of 2000, change "Republican" to "Democrat." See also Galanter, Lowering the Bar. University of Wisconsin Press, 2005 p. 36 citing many authorities.]

245

(786f)
[Gilbert, The Oxford Book of Anecdotes. Oxford University Press, 1986, p. 19 citing Balfour-Brown, Forty Years at the Bar (1916)]

(787f)
[John T. Loughran, The Argument of an Appeal in the Court of Appeals, in Rossman, ed. Advocacy and the King's English . Bobbs-Merrill, 1960, p. 577]

(788f)
[Joseph C. Goulden, The Money Lawyers. St. Martin's Press, 2006., p. 216]

(789f)
[Murane, Edward E., 34 S. Dak. J. No. 4 (Supp.) (1965)]; see also 44 Nebraska Law Review 356; see also Galanter, Lowering the Bar. University of Wisconsin Press, 2005, p. 57 citing six sources none of them the above.]

(790f)
[30 The Bar Examiner 34 (1961)]

(791f)
[Harlan, What Part Does the Oral Argument Play in the Conduct of an Appeal, 41 Cornell L.Q. 6, 10 (1955). Bander, Bar Relief, 72 Law Library Journal 353 (1979). See also:
Another story is told of a judge who took the case out of the hands of the lawyers, and examined and cross-examined witnesses at great length and great vigor. Finally one of the lawyers could not contain himself any longer, and blurted out, "Judge, I don't mind you trying the case for me, but for God's sake, don't lose it."
Gilbert, The Oxford Book of Legal Anecdotes. Oxford University Press, 1986, p. 37 citing Botein Trial Judge . Simon & Schuster, 1952, p. 104. Also Mayer, The Lawyers. Harper & Row, 1966, p. 408]

(792f)
[Howe, Justice Oliver Wendell Holmes, The Shaping Years 1841-1870. Harvard University Press, 1957, p. 264. Bander, Justice Holmes Ex Cathedra 237 (1991). Bander, Holmespun Humor, 10 Villanova Law Review 308 (1965)]

(793f)
[Richard Fountain, Wit of the Wig. Leslie Frewin, 1968, p. 110]

(794f)
[Who won? http://americanrhetoric.com/coraz&tisias.htm. See also ." Robert

BIBLIOGRAPHY
Note: Additional sources are in footnotes.
Books – by title

Advocacy and the King's English. Rossman, ed. Bobbs-Merrill
(1960)
    Birkett, The Art of Advocacy, p. 924
    Birkett, Law and Literature, p.775-776, 776, 779
    Zachariah Chaffee, The Disorderly Conduct of Words, p. 626
    John W. Davis, The Argument of An Appeal, p. 220
    Eugene C. Gerhart, Improving Our Legal Writing, p. 765, 769
    Robert H. Jackson, Advocacy Before the Supreme Court, p. 200
    Emmet Lavery, The Language of the Law, p. 758
    John T. Loughran, The Argument of an Appeal in the Court
        of Appeals, p. 577
    Glanville Williams, Language and the Law, p. 676
Advocates. David Pannick. Oxford University Press (1992)
Advocates of the Golden Age. Broad (1958)
America's Advocate: Robert H. Jackson. Eugene C. Gerhart. Bobbs-Merrill (1958)
The American Establishment. Richard H. Rovere.. Harcourt, Brace (1962)
American Themes. Dennis Brogan. Harper (1947)
American Treasury. Clifton Fadiman. Harper (1955)
Americans: A Book of Lives. Herman Hagedorn. John Day, 1946
Among Friends: Personal Letters of Dean Acheson. McLellan and
    Acheson, eds. Dodd-Mead. (1980)
Anecdotes of a Jealous Mistress. Richard Peete. Rocky Mountain Law
    Review (1959)
The Antagonists: Hugo Black, Felix Frankfurter and Civil Liberties
    In Modern America. James F. Simon. Simon & Schuster (1989)
At the Bar. David Margolick. Simon & Schuster (1995)
Bench and Bar: Reminiscences of One of the Last of an Ancient
    Race. Serjeant Robinson , Hurst & Blackett (1889)
Beyond the Courthouse. Langrock. Paul S. Eriksson (1999)
The Book of Legal Anecdotes. Peter Hay. Facts on File (1989)
Brandeis: A Free Man's Life. Alpheus T. Mason. Viking (1956)
The Brethren. Bob Woodward. Simon & Schuster (1979)
A Century at the Bar of the Supreme Court of the United States
    Charles Henry Butler. Putnam (1942)
Charles Evans Hughes. Merlo John Pusey Macmillan. (1951)
Christopher Palles. V.T. H. Delany. A. Figgis (1960)
City Lawyer: The Autobiography of a Law Practice Arthur Garfield Hays.

Simon & Schuster (1942)
Clarence Darrow for the Defense. Irving Stone. Doubleday (1941)
Clinging to the Wreckage. John C. Mortimer. Weidenfeld & Nicolson (1982)
The Common Law Tradition: Deciding Appeals. Karl N. Llewellyn. Little, Brown (1960)
A Common Place Book Charles P. Curtis. Simon & Schuster (1957)
Corporation Lawyer: Saint or Sinner? The New Role of the Lawyer in Modern Society. Beryl H. Levy. Chilton Co. (1961)
Court, Judges and Politics. Walter F. Murphy Random House (1961)
Courts on Trial. Jerome Frank. Princeton University Press (1949)
The Crack-Up. F. Scott Fitzgerald. J. Loughlin (1936)
Criminal Law Seminar. Cohn
Current Legal Problems (1960) [Lord Goff]
Day in Court. Francis L. Wellman. Macmillan (1910)
Deadlines and Monkeyshines. John McPhaul. Prentice-Hall (1962)
Decision at Law. David W. Peck. Dodd, Mead (1961)
The Devil and Daniel Webster. Stphen Vincent Binet. Holt (1965)
Effective Appellate Advocacy. Frederick B. Wiener. Prentice-Hall (1950)
English Constitutional and Legal History. Colin R. Lovell Oxford University Press (1962)
Enjoyment of Laughter. Max Eastman. Simon & Schuster (1936)
Esprit de Law. Anthony Nicholson (1973)
Fair Fights and Foul. Thurman Arnold. Harcourt, Brace and World (1935)
Felix Frankfurter. Liva Baker. Coward-McCann (1969)
Felix Frankfurter Reminisces. Harlan B. Phillips, ed. Reynal (1960)
Felix Frankfurter: A Tribute. Mendelson, ed. Reynal (1964)
Forty Years at the Bar. J. H. Balfour-Brown. H. Jenkins Ltd. (1916)
The Glittering Prizes ... F.E. Smith. Macgibbon & Kee (1960)
Government Under Law. Arthur E. Sutherland, ed. Harvard University Press (1956) [comment by Whitney North Seymour]
Growth of American Law. James W. Hurst. Little, Brown (1950)
Harlan Fiske Stone: Pillar of the Law. Alpheus T. Mason. Viking (1956)
Harold Laski. Isaac Kramnick and Barry Sheeerman. Penguin (1993)
Holmes-Einstein Letters. James B. Peabody, ed. St. Martin's (1964)
Holmes-Laski Letters. Mark DeWolfe Howe, ed. Harvard University Press (1953)
Holmes-Pollock Letters. Mark De Wolfe Howe, ed. Harvard University Press (1961) 2 vols.
Howe & Hummel: Their True and Scandalous History. Richard H. Rovere. Farrar, Straus and Giroux (1947)

John Jay Chapman – An American Mind. Richard Hovey. Columbia
　　　University Press (1959)
Judges, The. Martin Mayer. St. Martin's Press (2006)
Jurismania. Paul Campos. Oxford University Press. (1998)
Just A Country Lawyer [Senator Sam Ervin] Clancy. Indiana University Press (1974)
Justice Holmes. Francis Biddle (1961)
Justice Holmes Ex Cathedra. Edward Bander, Edward. Michie (1991)
Justice Holmes, Natural Law, and the Supreme Court. Francis Biddle.
　　　Macmillan (1961)
Justice Oliver Wendell Holmes. Silas Bent. Vanguard (1932)
Justice Oliver Wendell Holmes: His Book Notices and Uncollected
　　　Letters. Ed. and Annotated by Harry C. Shriver. Central Book Co.
　　　(1936)
Justice Rutledge and the Bright Constellation. Fowler Harper. Bobbs-Merrill
　　　(1965)
Justice Stephen Field. Paul Kens. University Press of Kansas (1997)
Justice Touched With Fire, Mr. Justice Holmes. Elizbeth Shepley Sergeant
　　　(Frankfurter ed. 1931)
The Last Serjeant. A. M. Sullivan. London, McDonald (1952)
The Lawyer in History, Literature and Law. William Andrews (1896)
Lawyer's Treasury. Eugene C. Gerhart, ed. Bobbs-Merrill (1956)
The Lawyers. Martin Mayer. Harper & Row (1966)
Learned Hand. Gerald Gunther. Knopf (1994)
The Legal Conscience: Selected Papers [Felix S. Cohen]. L.C. Cohen.
　　　Archon (1960)
The Life of F.E. Smith, First Lord Birkenhead, by his son. (1959)
The Life of John Marshall. Albert J. Beveridge. Houghton-Mifflin (1929)
A Lifetime with the Law. A.E. Bowker. W.H. Allen (1961)
The Lighter Side of the Law. May. (1956)
Long, Long Ago. Alexander Woolcott. Viking (1943)
Lord Bowen. Cunningham. (1986)
Lord Eldon's Anecdote Book. A.L. J. Lincoln and R. L. McEwen. Stevens & Sons (1960)
Lord Justice: The Life and Times of Lord Birkett. H. Montgomery Hyde (1964)
Lowering the Bar: Lawyer Jokes and Legal Culture. Marc Galanter.
　　　University of Wisconsin Press, 2005
Making Constitutional Law – Thurgood Marshall and the Supreme Court.
　　　Mark V. Tushnet. Oxford University Press (1997)
The Man Who Once Was Whizzer White. Dennis J. Hutchinson. Free Press (1998)

Marble Palace. John Paul Frank. Knopf (1958)
A Matter of Opinion. Victor Navasky. Farrar, Straus & Giroux (2005)
Melville Weston Fuller. Willard L. King (Macmillan (1950)
Memoirs of Edward Vaughan Kenealy. Kenealy, ed. (1898)
The Mind and Faith of Justice Holmes. Max Lerner, ed. Modern Library
(1943, 1953)
The Money Lawyers. Joseph C. Goulden. St. Martin's Press (2006)
More Merry-G-Round. Robert S. Allen and Drew Pearson. Liverwright (1932)
Morning and Noon. Dean Acheson. Houghton. (1965))
Mr. Justice Holmes… ed. By Felix Frankfurter. Coward-McCann
(1931)
Mr. Justice Holmes. John Wigmore (1913)
Mr. Justice Holmes. Francis Biddle. Scribner's (1942)
The Murderer and His Victim. John M. Macdonald. Thomas (1961)
My Life in Court. Louis Nizer. Doubleday (1961)
New England: Indian Summer. Van Wyck Brooks. E.P. Dutton (1940)
The Nine Old Men. Drew Pearson & Robert S. Allen. Doubleday (1937)
No Lamb for Slaughter. Edward Lamb. Harcourt, Brace & World (1963)
Obiter Dicta… Joseph W. Bishop, Jr. Atheneum (1971)
The Occasional Speeches of Justice Oliver Wendell Holmes. Mark DeWolfe Howe.
Harvard University Press (1962)
Of Law and Life … Frankfurter. Philip B. Kurland, ed. Harvard University Press (1965)
Of Law and Men. Felix Frankfurter. Ed. by Philip Elman. Harcourt (1956)
Oliver Twist. Charles Dickens
The Old Munster Circuit. Maurice Healy. Mercier Press, Dublin (1939)
The Oxford Book of Legal Anecdotes. Michael Gilbert.
Oxford University Press (1986)
Patriotic Gore. Edmund Wilson. Oxford University Press (1962)
Personnel Administration and the Law, 2d ed.
Russell L. Greenman & Eric J. Schmerz. BNA (1972)
Philadelphia Lawyer. George Wharton Pepper. Lippincott (1944)
Recollections of Bar and Bench. Richard [Lord] Alverstone. E. Arnold, pub. (1914)
Reminiscences of Rufus Choate. Edward G. Parker. Mason Bros. (1860)
Reserved Judgment. J. Tudor Rees. Muller (1959)
Reveille in Washington: 1860-1865. Margaret Leech. Harper (1941)
Roosevelt: The Story of a Friendship. Owen Wister. Macmillan (1930)
Rufus Choate: The Wizard of the Law. Claude Moore Fuess.
Archon (1928)
Sandra Day O'Connor. Joan Biskupic. Ecco (2005)

Selection from the Letters and Legal Papers of Thurman Arnold. (1961)
Selections from Speeches. Seasongood. Knopf (1960)
Sinclair Lewis. Mark Schorer. McGraw-Hill (1961)
The Spirit of Liberty. Learned Hand. Knopf (1960)
The Struggle for Judicial Supremacy Robert H. Jackson. Vintage (1941)
Supreme Court of the United States. Charles Evans Hughes. Columbia
    University Press (1928)
The Supreme Court: The Personalities and Rivalries That Defined America. Jeffrey
    Rosen. Henry Holt (2006)
The Symbols of Government Thurman W. Arnold. Yale University
    Press (1935)
Team of Rivals: The Political Genius of Abraham Lincoln. Doris Kearns Goodwin.
    Simon & Schuster (2005)
Thinking Under Fire: Great Courtroom Lawyers and Their Impact on American History.
    Daniel J. Kornstein (1987)
This is My Case. Rentoul (1944)
Thurgood Marshall: Warrior at the Bar; Rebel on the Bench. Michael D. Davis and
    Hunter R. Clark. Carol Pub. Group (1994)
Trial Judge: The Candid Behind-the-Bench Story of Justice Bernard Botein. Simon &
    Schuster (1952)
Voices in Court. William H. Davenport. Macmillan (1958)
Voltaire and the Cowboy: The Letters of Thurman Arnold. Gene M. Gressley, ed.
    Colorado Associated University Press (1977)
We the Judges. William O. Douglas. Doubleday (1956)
Whereas – A Judge's Premises. Charles E. Wyzanski Jr. Little, Brown (1944)
Wild Bill ... Walter F. Murphy. Random House (2003)
Wit of Wig. Richard Fountain. Leslie Frewin (1968)
Yankee from Olympus. Catherine Drinker Bowen. Little, Brown (1945)

Law reviews, periodicals, proceedings, etc.
    By name of publication
Holmes, 8 Advocate 185 (Nov. 1961)
Acheson, Dean, Recollections of Service with the Federal Supreme Court,
    18 Alabama Lawyer 355, 359-360, 362-363 (1957)

37 American Bar Association Journal 803 (1951)
47 American Bar Association Journal 338 (1961)
American Branch of the ILA, 13th Annual Meeting, 32 (1934)

Follansbee, Mr. Justice Holmes – A Judge with Imagination,
11 American Lawyer 10 (1903)

American Scholar, Spring, 1963, p. 263
American Society of International Law, Proceedings, 1961, p. 215

Cooke, Alistair, Journalists Who Make History, Atlantic Monthly 156 (Nov. 1959)

30 The Bar Examiner 34, 42 (1961)

Marsh, Daniel.The Making of Lawyers,
22 Boston University Law Review 188, 189 (1942)
Pitofsky, Robert, The Business Lawyer 292-293 (1973)

Case & Comment, May-June 6 (1957)
10 Chitty's Law Journal 86, 110, 158 (1961)
3 City Lawyer (N.Y.) No. 1:14 (1965)
Columbia Alumni News, Vol. II, p. 292

McCormack, Alfred. A Law Clerk's Recollections,
1946 Columbia Law Review 710 at 713

Congressional Record, April 23, 1958, p. A3847 (Cong. O'Hara)
104 Congressional Record 7369 (Daily ed. 1958) [Judge Wyzanski]
36 Conn. Bar Journal 691 (1962)
36 Conn. Bar Journal 694-695 (1964) [speech by Judge Irving R. Kaufman]

Harlan, John Marshall, What Part Does the Oral Argument Play in the Conduct of an
Appeal, 41 Cornell Law Quarterly 6, 10 (1955)

29 Detroit Lawyer 86 (1961)

Beck, James, Justice Holmes and the Supreme Court,
1 Federal Bar Association Journal 36-37 (March 1932)

18 Federal Bar Journal 33 (1958)

Clark, Tom C., Address, 11 Federal Bar News, No. 1:315 (Oct. 1964)
Clark, Tom C., Supreme Court Conference, 19 Federal Rules Decisions 306-307 (1957)

11 Federation of Insurance Counsel no. 3-55 (1961)
1962 Georgia Bar Association 234

Wyzanski, Charles. John A. Sibley Lecture, 7 Georgia Law Review 215 (1973)
Leach, Barton, Book review, 45 Harvard Law Review 1437 (1932)
Magruder, Calvert. Mr. Justice Brandeis, 55 Harvard Law Review 194 (1941-42)
Smith, T. V. Book review, 56 Harvard Law Review 677, 679 (1942)

58 Harvard Law Review 1136 (1994)

McElwain, E. The Business of the Supreme Court as Conducted by Chief
     Justice Hughes, 63 Harvard Law Review 5, 17 (1949)
Bernstein, The Inimitable Bull Warren,
     Harvard Law School Bulletin 36 (Spring 1979)

39 Idaho State Bar Proceedings 22-24 (1965)

Holmes, Oliver Wendell, Ideals and Doubts, 10 Illinois Law Review 1 (1915)

36 Journal of Patent Office Society 54
58 Law Society Gazette (1961)
119 Literary Digest, March 16, 1935, p. 6

Maine State Bar Association Proceedings
     Judge Edward T. Gignous 113 (1964)
     1955 Maine State Bar Ass'n Proc. 97
     1957 Maine State Bar Ass'n Proc. 217
     1960 Maine State Bar Ass'n Proc. 32, 33 (Judge Woodbury)
     1961 Maine State Bar Ass'n Proc. 161-162, 169 (speech by Carey)
     1963 Maine State Bar Ass'n Proc. 65, 79, 81-82, 93, 122
     1964 Maine State Bar Ass'n Proc. 111 (C.J. Robert B. Williamson)

Hill, Memorial to Justice Holmes, 298 Mass. (1937)

1960 Maryland State Bar Association 87
32 Medico-Legal Journal 130 (1964)

Weinberg, Louise. Holmes' Failure, 98 Michigan Law Review 691, at 721-722

32 Mississippi Law Journal 375

34 Mississippi Law Journal 374

Trillin, Calvin. The Nation, April 12, 1993
Tobriner, An Appellate Judge's View of the Labor Arbitration Process in
    The Arbitrator, The NLRB and the Courts, Proceedings of the 20th
    Annual Meeting, National Academy of Arbitrators 37 (1967)
Freedman, National Ass'n Attorney Generals 123-124 (1963)

National Conference of State Trial Judges 51 (Aug. 3-5, 1962)

Estes, Joe E. Speech.
    National Conference of State Trial Judges, Aug. 3-5,1962, p. 138

Wiener, Avoidable Faults in Appellate Briefs, 41 Nebraska Law Review 434, 436 (1962)
Wiener, Curable Faults in Oral Argument, 41 Nebraska Law Review 447-448 (1962)

42 Nebraska Law Review 421 (1964)

Ladd, Mason, 43 Nebraska Law Review 397 (1964)

44 Nebraska Law Review 356, 403 (1964)
45 Nebraska State Bar Ass'n Proc. 392 (1965)
28 New Jersey Law Journal 39, 160 (1968)

Carter, Jimmy, New Statesman, Jan. 28, 1977, 112
Bander, Edward. Letter. New York Law Journal, March 16, 1965, p. 1
Matter of Douglas, 195 Misc. (N.Y.) 661 (1949)

Derby, Augustin. Recollections of Mr. Justice Holmes,
    12 New York University Law Quarterly 350 (1935)

Talk of the Town, New Yorker, Nov. 10, 1956
Talk of the Town, New Yorker, March 20, 1965

    14 New Zealand Law Journal 438 (1963)
    New Zealand Law Journal, August 5, 1975, p. 549
    38 North Dakora Law Review 640 (1962)
    42 North Dakota Law Review 79 (1965)

Krislov, 52 Northwestern University Law Review 514-515 (1957)

Reid, John, Brandy in His Water,
    57 Northwestern University Law Review 533 (1962)

Corwin, Notre Dame Lawyer 325 (1952)

    Pasaic County Bar Ass'n Reporter
    2 Record of the Bar of the City of New York 235

Laurence H. Silberman, Will Lawyering Strangle Democratic Capitalism.
    Regulation, March/april 1978, p. 20, 21

    2 Santa Clara Law Rev. 48 (1962)
    Saturday Evening Post, Sept. 26, 1959
    Saturday Review, Aug. 12, 1961, p. 7
    Saturday Review, May 4, 1968, p. 6
    105 Solicitor's Journal 626 (1961)
    116 Solicitor's Journal 363 (May 12, 1972)

Edward E. Murane, 34 S. Dakota Journal No. 4:80 (Supp.) (1965)
Bander, Edward. Book review, 15 Suffolk University Law Review 547 (1981)
Levinson, Sanford. Book review. 75 Texas Law review 1482 (1997)

    Time, August 22, 1977, p. 17
    41 Title News No. 1, 28 (1962)

Orren, Harding A., Lying in Bed Thinking .. One Guinea,
    19 Trial Lawyers Guide 78 (1975)

Faretta v. California, 422 U.S. 806, 852 (Justice Blackmun)
Estate of Wilson v. Aiken Indus., 439 U.S. 877 (1978)

    U.S. Congress, 2d Session, House. Dept of State .. the Judiciary 59

(1958)
> Hon. John Biggs Jr.

> U.S. Congressional Record, March 25, 2959, p. A2691
> U.S. Dept of Justice Release, Dec. 9, 1960
> University of Illinois College of Law. Dedicatory Proceedings 1956,
p. 95

Seminar on Personal Injury Litigation (1962) Seattle, University of Washington

Frankfurter, Felix. Chief Justices I have Known,
> 39 Virginia Law Review 883, 888, 889 (1953)

Herz, 'Do Justice! Variation of a Thrice-Told Tale,' 82 Virginia Law Review 111 (1966)
Bander, Edward J., Holmespun Humor, 10 Villanova Law Review 507 (1965)
Maycock, Welburn, 48 Women Lawyers Journal no. 117 (1962)
Curtis, Book review, 63 Yale Law Journal 270 (1953)

Newspapers

Boston Globe, February 22, 1960. Editorial page
Boston Globe, July 10, 1986
Boston Herald, May 6, 1959
Boston Sunday Globe, Sept. 30, 1956
Boston Sunday Globe, Nov. 10, 1957 (Winship article)
New York Post, Dec. 22, 1961, p. 33
New York Post, April 11, 1962, p. 55 [Leonard Lyons]
New York Post, Aug. 23, 1962, p. 27
New York Post, Nov. 26, 1962, p. 29
New York Post, Aug. 3, 1977, p. 63
Lewis Anthony. Book review. New York Review of Books, April 6, 2006, p. 39,40
Huston, History of Court to Honor Holmes, New York Times, April 15, 1956, p. 88
Lewis, Anthony. Book review, New York Times, May 29, 1960, VIII, p. 1
Arthur Krock, In the Nation, New York Times, March 21, 1965, p. E11
New York Times, Jan. 5, 1966, p. 31:3
New York Times, Feb. 4, 1974, 29:6
New York Times, Nov. 5, 2005, p. A11
Lewis, Anthony. High Drama in High Court, New York Times
> Magazine, Oct. 26, 1958, p.. 10, 19-20

Letter to the Editor, New York Times Magazine, May 10, 1964, p. 6
Clapper, Raymond, New York World-Telegram, May 22, 1936.
Hull, Challenge to the Law, Providence Journal, 1949, p. 45

QUICK INDEX TO MAJOR TOPICS (by page)

Abolition, 7
Abortion, 7
Abraham's bosom, 7. 8
Abstractions, 8
Achilles' heel, 8
Adams, Henry, 8
Ade, George, 8-9
Administrative law, 9
Adultery, 9
Advertising, 9-10
Advisory opinion, 10
Advocate, 10
Affirmative action, 10-11
Afflatus, 11
After-dinner speaker, 11
Age, 12
Alcoholic beverages, 12-14
Ambition, 15
American Law Institute, 15
Ames, James Barr, 15
Analogy, 15-16
Anecdotes, 16
Antitrust cases, 16
Appeal at once, 16
Appellate court, 16
Approval, need for, 17
Arlington National Cemetery, 17
Arnold, Thurman, 17-18
Assignees, 18
Association ... N.Y.C., 19
Attorney fees, 19-21
Attorney General, 21
Automobiles, 21
Axis, The, 21
Baker, Russell, 22
Bankers, 23
Baseball, 23
Bawdy tinge, 24
Beale, Joseph A., 24

Beck, James M., 24-25
Biography, 25
Bishop, 25-26
Black, Hugo, 26
Blackman, Harry A., 26
Blackstone's Commentary, 27
Boston University Law School, 141
Bostonians, 27
Brandeis, Louis, 28-29
Brennan, William Joseph Jr., 29
Brevity, 29-30
Brewer, David, 30
Briefs, 30-32
Brown, Henry Billings, 32
Burger, Warren, 33
Burke, Edmund, 33
Burlesque houses, 33
Burton, Harold H., 34
Butler, Charles Henry, 34
Butler, Pierce, 34-35
Candor, 35
Capital punishment, 35
Cardozo, Benjamin Nathan, 36
Carson, Edward, 36, 181
Carter, Jimmy, 37
Casanova, 37
Case, 37
Casebooks, 37
Catholic Claims, 37
Certiorari, 38
Chapman, John Jay, 38
Child, education of, 39
Choate, Rufus, 39
Christ, what dignity, 39
Christian religion, 39
Citation, 39-40
Civil War, 40
Civilization, 41
Client, 41-43

Closing argument, 43
Cohen, Morris, 44
Coleman, William, 44
Collisions at sea, 44
Collusion, 44
Columbia Law School, 45
Comma is there, 45
Conscious as we are, 45
Constitutional law, 45
Constitutional lawyer, 46
Continuance, 46-47
Contract, 47
Corporation as a client, 47
Court of Appeal, 48
Criminal law, 49
Cross-examination, 49-51
Cujos est solum, 51
Davis, John W., 51
Day, William R., 52
De minimis, 52
Deans, 52
Death and dying, 52-53
Defects of his qualities, 53
Definitions, 53-54
Deliberate speed, 54
DePugh, Chauncey, 11
Diplomatic immunity, 55
Doctor, 55
Donahue, Frank J., 56, 183, 194
Douglas, William O., 56-57
Eisenhower, Dwight D., 58
Electric chair, 58
Emerson, Ralph Waldo, 58
Enthusiasm, 59
Estate taxes, 59
Facts, 59
Fair trial, 60
Final examination, 61
Fitzgerald, F. Scott, 184, 229
Footnotes, 61
Four horsemen, 62
Frank, Jerome N., 62

Frankfurter, Felix, 62-64
Franklin, Benjamin, 241
French novels, 64
Fuller, Melville Weston, 64-65
Gallows humor, 65
Generalization, 66
Gift in contemplation, 66
God and court, 67
Goodhart, Arthur, 202
Gossip and philosophy, 68
Gray, Horace, 68
Grier, Robert C., 68
Guests that overstay, 69
Hall, Marshall, 69
Hand, Learned, 70
Harding, Warren, 71
Harlan, John Marshall, 71
Harvard Law School, 71
Harvard University, 72
Hays, Arthur Garfield, 41
Heart transplant, 73
Height, 73
Hell, 74
Holmes, Fanny, 74
Holmes, Oliver Wendell, 75-83
Horse cause, 83
Hughes, Charles Evans, 84-86
Humbug, 86
Humor, 86
Innuendo, 97
Insurance, 87
Intellect, 88
Jackson, Robert H., 88
Jesus Christ is my advocate, 88
Jobbists, 89, 216
Johnson, Lyndon, 22
Judges, 89-94
Jury, 94-95
Justice, 96
Kaufman, Irving R., 96
Kennedy, John F., 97
Knapp, Whitman, 98

Knox, Philander, 98
Labor leaders, 98
Ladies' Day, 172
Lamb, Charles, 99
Lang, Andrew, 99
Laski, Harold, 99
Law, 100-101
Law books, 101
Law classroom, 102-104
Law clerks, 104-105
Law dean, 105
Law firms, 106
Law library, 106
Law office, 107
Law partner, 107
Law professors (see Professors)
Law reviews, 107-108
Law school, 108
Law students, 108-110
Law suit, 110
Laws, 110
Lawyers, 110-114
Learning, 114
Legal mind, 115
Legislative history, 115
Levy, Leonard W., 163
Lincoln, Abraham, 116
Litigation, 116-117
Malthus, 118
Marshall, John, 119
Marshall, Thurgood, 119
Massachusetts Bar, 120
Massachusetts Sup. Jud. Court, 120
McReynolds, James C., 121-123
Megarry, Robert, 123, 192, 195, 196, 219, 220, 237, 245
Memorial addresses, 123
Mencken, H.L., 123
Mendoza line, 124
Menuhin, Yehudi, 124
Miller, Samuel, 125
Motions, 125

Murphy, Frank, 126
Naivity, 126
Noonan, Gregory, 127
North, 127
Novelists, 127
O'Connor, Sandra Day, 127
Objections, 128
Obscenity, 128
Opinions, 129-131
Oral argument, 131-134
Oratory, 135
Oyster, 136
Panaceas and sudden ruin, 136
Paternity, 136
Pitney, Mrs. Malcolm, 137
Points of law, 138
Pound, Roscoe, 135, 139
Precedent, 139
Prisoners, 140
Professors, 141-142
Question of fact, 143
Realtor, 143
Reed, Stanley, 131, 162
Rehnquist, William Hubbs, 144
Retirement, 145
Rickles, Don, 145
Riggins, John, 12
Roberts, John, 23
Rodell, Fred, 145
Rogers, Will, 145
Roosevelt, F. D., 146
Rule in Shelley's Case, 147
Sacco-Vanzetti case, 147
Satan, 147
Scalia, Antonin, 148
Scott, Austin, 39
Self-made man, 148
Shall and will, 149
Shiras, George Jr., 149
Sit down, you damned fool, 150
Smith, F.E., 150
Solicitor General, 151

Stare decisis, 152
Stevenson, Adlai, 135
Stone, Harlan Fiske, 152
Story, Joseph, 153
Strut, 153
Symbols, 154
Tact, 154
Taft, Howard William, 154
Taxes, 155
Ten Commandments, 155
Thomas, Clarence, 155
Thoreau, Henry David, 156
Torts, 156
Trial judge, 157
Trial practice, 158
Truman, Harry, 158
Twain, Mark, 173
Unite States Constitution, 159
United States Government, 159
United States Supreme Court, 159-164
Virtue, 164
Vomit, 165
Vulgar herd, 165
Ward, Lester, 165
Warren, Earl, 166
Warren, Edward Henry, 166-167
Webster, Daniel, 134
White, Edward Douglas, 167
White, Byron, 168
Williams, Edward B., 43
Wills, 169-170
Witnesses, 170-171
Women, 171-172
Yale Law School, 172
Young lawyer, 173-176

AFTERWORDS

This collection of anecdotes and wit has been a fifty year pursuit. It is not contaminated with agents, editors, MacArthur grants, Guggenheims, chairs, nepotism, reputation, windfall, graphic designers, or spin. Hard copy searching has been the main source for material although the internet has been helpful on occasion. Individuals that have provided me with material are noted in the footnotes.

I want to express my love and gratitude to Tema Nason who for the past fifteen years has made my life poetry (to borrow from Justice Holmes), to Harold Gordon, a childhood friend, who convinced me that I would make a better librarian than lawyer, and Larry Flynn, computer maven, who gratefully didn't explain to me about converting Word to PDF. I want to thank Professor Charles Kindregan, who saw to it that emeriti of Suffolk University Law School were given office space on retirement, the New England Law Librarians for giving me a lifetime achievement award in 2007, and Lida, David, Steven, Daniel, and Jeffrey, my children and grandchildren for turning out better than I had any reason to expect.

Note: Edward J. Bander is the author or compiler of:
Mr. Dooley on the Choice of Law (Michie 1963)
Mr. Dooley & Mr. Dunne (Michie 1981)
The Breath of an Unfee'd Lawyer: Shakespeare on Lawyers and the Law (Catbird 1996)
Bardell v. Pickwick (edited and abstracted by E.J. Bander) (Transnational (2004)

For input and additional material check:
http://banderblog.typepad.com

www.ingramcontent.com/pod-product-compliance
Lightning Source LLC
Chambersburg PA
CBHW070025010526
44117CB00011B/1714